C.G. JUNG
AND THE
CRISIS IN
WESTERN CIVILIZATION

The Psychology of Our Time

John A. Cahman

CHIRON PUBLICATIONS • ASHEVILLE, NORTH CAROLINA

www.ChironPublications.com

Interior and cover design by Danijela Mijailovic
Printed primarily in the United States of America.

ISBN 978-1-63051-764-9 paperback
ISBN 978-1-63051-765-6 hardcover
ISBN 978-1-63051-766-3 electronic
ISBN 978-1-63051-767-0 limited edition paperback

Library of Congress Cataloging-in-Publication Data

Names: Cahman, John A, author.
Title: C.G. Jung and the crisis in Western civilization : the psychology of our time / John A Cahman.
Description: Asheville : Chiron Publications, 2020. | Includes bibliographical references. | Summary: "The partisan split in American politics is the result of a major transformation of the West, as the psychology of the past based on hierarchy and privilege is being replaced by a psychology of equality. The status of women and minorities is at the center of this. The West's long history of inequality is gradually changing. When women's equality is considered symbolically, it represents the feminine rising to parity with the masculine, a status it has not held since prehistory. Minority groups have carried the projected shadow of the White majority for centuries; that is gradually ending. Integration of the feminine and the shadow are core concepts of C.G. Jung's psychology of individuation. The emerging equality of women and minorities indicates that our group psychology is entering a period of individuation. This is a huge change, at least as profound as pagan Rome becoming Christian or medieval Europe transitioning into the modern West. The turmoil of our time is because of the great historical change as we leave what has been the modern West. The turmoil is the widespread appearance of the same conflicts that Jung saw in his patients a century ago. The same answer still applies, the path Jung realized at the time, individuation, and it is already beginning to shape our future. In this book author John Cahman traces the history of Western Civilization as a developmental process and shows how our time marks a great turning point in that story as we leave an age of sexism, racism, and hierarchy and enter one of individuation"-- Provided by publisher.
Identifiers: LCCN 2020016244 (print) | LCCN 2020016245 (ebook) | ISBN 9781630517649 (paperback) | ISBN 9781630517656 (hardcover) | ISBN 9781630517663 (ebook)
Subjects: LCSH: Self psychology. | Shadow (Psychoanalysis) | Change (Psychology) | Individuation (Philosophy) | Civilization, Modern. | Jung, C. G. (Carl Gustav), 1875-1961--Political and social views.
Classification: LCC BF697 .C224 2020 (print) | LCC BF697 (ebook) | DDC 155--dc23
LC record available at https://lccn.loc.gov/2020016244
LC ebook record available at https://lccn.loc.gov/2020016245

Dedication

For Lillian Anne Silverstone

Acknowledgement

Thanks to my wife Lillian, who has repeatedly read, edited, and re-read this and previous versions, who has put up with me talking about it for thirty-five years. Thanks to Meghan Pinson of My Two Cents Editing for making the draft into a usable manuscript. Thanks to the staff of Chiron Publications for getting me through the publishing process.

Preface

This book is a look at change and conflict in the modern Western world through the lens of C.G. Jung's psychology. It has these central points:

The great ages of history—prehistory, the ancient world, the medieval world, and the modern Western world—follow the same developmental sequence that children follow as they grow from infancy to adulthood. History has an underlying archetypal path.

Our times mark the end of one historical age and the beginning of another, as when pagan Rome became Christian or medieval Europe became the modern West. We are leaving humanity's most materialistic age and starting anew as the archetypes structuring our world change. That change is the crisis of our time, essentially the problems Jung began to see in his consulting room a century ago.

Each age has been characterized by its own psychology, and the age we are entering will be defined by Jung's Self psychology.

Covering these points requires exploring who we are, how we develop, and the symbols of our time. It is a winding trip from peaceful hunter-gatherers of 200,000 years ago to unidentified flying objects today.

Contents

CHAPTER 1

The Times They Are A-Changin' (Bob Dylan)

The old psychology and the new psychology

The past century or so has been one of tremendous social change in Western society with great movements toward social, racial, and sexual equality. These changes have been resisted, often violently, by people invested in the status quo and by people identifying with power and position. Our politics are now divided between those who support these developments and those who oppose them. These two political positions actually represent two different psychologies, two completely contrary ways of thinking. An old way of thinking is ending and a new psychology is beginning.

Here are some of the issues of our time: Do you identify more with the idea that all people are created equal or the idea that there is a hierarchy of people with the superior ones at the top? Do you believe that women should stick to their traditional roles of raising children and maintaining a household? Should abortions be illegal or should the decision be the pregnant woman's? Do you believe some racial and ethnic groups are superior to others? Do you agree that we are all essentially equal, despite any sexist, racist, or other prejudicial ideas that may float through your mind on occasion? Or do you feel that some of us are inherently superior to the rest, deserving special privileges in relation to their peers, because of race, sex, social class, religion, or other values?

These questions highlight a significant division in the Western world, especially the United States. The problem isn't that people are on one side or the other; everyone has some feelings on both sides. The problem is that most people identify with one side and reject, and even attack, the other. I believe this division is parallel to the earth-shaking division that split Christian Rome from pagan Rome almost 2,000 years ago, when the ancient world changed into the medieval world. We are in the midst of a similar transition now as we shift from an old psychology to a new one.

Three major changes in the course of human history have led to the development of the modern Western world, and I believe that we are now in the midst of a fourth. The first was leaving a prehistoric hunter-gatherer existence to form the earliest city-states of the ancient world. The second was the pagan ancient world's transformation into medieval Catholic Europe. The third was the modern West's emergence out of the medieval world shortly after 1500. We are now in the midst of a fourth change, with a new psychology pulling us forward and an old psychology resisting.

With each of these transformations, the old myth that had structured society for centuries passed away and a new myth was born, leading to a complete restructuring of society. These changes are so significant that they are best described as changes in consciousness.

The influence of the new psychology, gradually increasing over centuries, has made it the central issue in our early twenty-first century politics. We no longer have liberal and conservative views of politics as much as two completely different views of reality. Bitter disagreements over issues, including racial and sexual roles, abortion rights, and gun control, reflect the dramatic polarization of the United States. This has been referred to as a "culture war."[1]

There is probably a basic psychological difference between liberal and conservative personalities which is intrinsic to the human condition.[2] The core issue is change. Some people are more resistant to change and hence more oriented toward keeping things as they have been in the past. Others are more open to change and hence more oriented toward how the future could be different. But traditional liberal versus conservative politics has been a matter of degree and emphasis, and that is no longer the case.

Traditional conservative politics have long been associated with lower taxes, smaller government, more states' rights, and less foreign involvement. But current conservative politics have become associated with

2

a focus on enemies and conflict, privilege and class, opposition to racial and sexual equality, increased government in military and security areas, and a drive for the West to dominate the world. The opposing psychology advocates racial and sexual equality, feels that people are equal, and is oriented toward relating to others as equals rather than ruling over them or going to war with them. These are not the traditional differences of liberal versus conservative values, but rather two different worldviews, two different mind-sets, separated by an abyss. Neither side really understands the other as each is expressing a radically different way of thinking.

The two psychologies are illustrated by American responses to the events of September 11, 2001, in New York City and Washington, D.C. Some people felt that these events meant the United States had the right to invade any country that could be even remotely associated with the perpetrators. The U.S. had the duty to punish the entire Muslim world, and the God-given right to attack as well. Even if the wrong people were punished, it would demonstrate U.S. superiority and mastery over Muslims. By this thinking, it was unequivocally clear that much, if not all, of the Muslim world hated the U.S. and wanted all-out war against the U.S. infidel. There was no reason for the attacks except for hatred of the American way of life. Any American questioning this logic was almost regarded as a traitor.

Other people pointed out that the rule of international law did not allow one country to attack another without clear evidence of an attack in progress. Otherwise, the matter should be settled by an international court. It was plain that the entire Muslim world did not attack the United States, but rather only a few individuals who had their own specific agenda, an agenda that was not very popular in the Muslim world at that time. It was also true that many Muslims had good reason to be upset with the United States due to its history of unpleasant interventions and influence in their part of the world, and perhaps it was time to consider their side of the issue. The hidden, secondary motivations of powerful groups in the U.S. was also noted, including enriching the U.S. military-industrial complex and controlling Middle-Eastern oil fields.

These two entirely different ways of seeing the world demonstrate many of the differences between the thinking of the old psychology and the new. The old psychology easily feels that God is on his or her side, the good side. The opposing side is evil. Those seen as enemies do not have legitimate complaints but operate only out of malevolence. Individuals in that group are not recognized; they are all bad. If we attack the wrong Muslim country, that is not a problem, as we are hurting some of them. We are not evil, they are, and there can be no rational reason for the other side's anger; they are irrational and they hate us for who we are. Misdeeds of the West are denied and anyone who raises the issue may be accused of criticizing their country. Any suggestions of secondary gain, such as stealing oil, are ignored. The idea that the country the United States attacked, Iraq, had nothing to do with the September 11 attack is ignored. Any suggestion that the other side may have a point, even a small one, is considered at least naive if not treasonous. Any information supportive of a contradictory standpoint is seen as a threat; hence, the media in general is held in disrepute as it may provide some facts that do not fit with the correct point of view. Education in general is held in similar contempt as it may provide facts that do not fit with the correct way of thinking. There is an exceedingly strong need to dominate and control anything or anyone remotely associated with the other side.

The new psychology, by contrast, sees two sides of the issue, and realizes that it is not treasonous to do so. This thinking does not repress facts that do not fit a black or white model. The emphasis is on the individual perpetrators as opposed to their group (all Muslims). There is also a realization of denied motivations, that is, attacking Iraq as a front for stealing its oil while generating enormous profits for military-related industries. Conflicting information and points of view are not denied, repressed, or suppressed, but considered along with mainstream ones.

Neither view is right for all time, but I believe that the history of the West, and several centuries of its wars of subjugation of people considered to be lesser beings, has been based on the old psychology, and the future belongs to the new psychology. We live in a crossover time.

Americans identifying with the old psychology have attempted to re-invigorate and re-establish a conservative Christianity oriented toward holding onto outdated and unfair social values, including homophobic, misogynist, and racist policies, and denial of scientifically based reality. Christian theologians were once the finest minds of the time; their modern counterparts proclaim that there were dinosaurs in Eden.

There is an unstated realization that Christianity is rapidly slipping from its long-held position of dominance in our society. Although Christianity has carried the core values of Western civilization for almost 2,000 years, it has moved from its position of the quiet confidence of seventy-five years ago to one of defensiveness, with fantasies of "rapture" and "end times" in place of real solutions for current difficulties. Rather than dealing with the problems we have made in our environment, the global hostilities that we have encouraged, and the other assorted problems that we have caused or contributed to, Christianity's answer is a fantasy of God ending the world. It is not an answer dealing with the problems, but a fantasy of escape that allows the problems to grow deeper. It is an attempt to hold on to the old psychology at any cost.

Meanwhile, many people have come to find it more and more difficult to "become as little children"[3] and accept what seem to be Biblical fairy tales as facts. For many people not involved in organized religions, religious values are becoming more personal and spiritual rather than group-oriented. For these people, the old group-oriented, traditional religions do not hold the emotional power and solace they once did.

Many in the Western world have moved toward psychology and away from organized religion. Problems that were once taken to a priest or preacher are now taken to a psychotherapist. And the whole field of psychology is becoming mainstream thought: what was once esoteric treatment by Dr. Freud is now practiced on television programs.

Current heated issues, such as abortion, homosexuality, military intervention, sexual equality, and race relations, reflect the sides in the underlying conflict. If you can step back and listen to an argument between the two sides without becoming swept up in it, you realize that it is an encounter between two different ways of thinking. Neither side can persuade the other because they represent two totally different worldviews.

The increasing focus on equality in the external world is parallel to an increased psychological awareness in the inner world. Psychological awareness gradually developed over the past two centuries; it accelerated in the last century and has become so commonplace that there are now psychology-themed programs on television. The average literate person is now hugely more psychologically aware than their peers of 200 and even 100 years ago. We have developed an entirely new way of looking at the world. This seemingly small change is not just the addition of new bits of knowledge, but it is another marker of a shift in consciousness in the West; it makes us see the world differently.

Our entire worldview is gradually turning on its axis toward a new direction. Internally, psychological awareness is gradually increasing. Externally, the status of women and minority people is gradually increasing as the status of white males decreases. Backlash and backsliding occur, but these changes have continued steadily through the past several generations. One sees change only in small increments in daily living, increments that easily fade into the background without notice. But when these small steps are viewed as a historical picture over a longer period of time, they reveal a major trend. Our psychology, religion, history, government, and social organization are all in the midst of a transition so huge and far-reaching that it can only be described as a change in consciousness.

In the space of a short lifespan the changes seem to be of little consequence. In one person's life in the 1800s, slavery is abolished. In a later lifetime, African-Americans gain the opportunity for education. In a mid-twentieth century lifetime education is integrated. In a still later life, an African-American man becomes president. When these small steps are taken as a whole, they show a major change in the external organization of the West and indicate an equally significant change in the psychology of the West.

It is a marvel that a mere century and a half ago, a white man could own an African-American man, and in our time an African-American man became the president of the United States. But what is even more striking is that a group psychology so based on human inequality that it allowed ownership of other human beings is changing and is relentlessly moving to a psychology that sees all people as equal.

Similar remarkable changes have occurred in the status of women. It has only been relatively recently that women could own property, vote, or achieve a higher education. Not that long ago, Western society held almost all women as being subordinate to some male, usually the father, later in life the husband, and with the husband's death, either a brother, uncle, or even a son. Male domination is gradually being eroded away, generation by generation, as society slowly moves to individual equality. Our group psychology is moving from a masculine domination of the feminine to an equality between the two.

The external structure of white male domination did not come about by chance; it reflected the underlying psychology of society. The West followed a course of white male domination for centuries, through the development of modern Europe and the spread of European civilization in the world. That period is now ending, and from a historical point of view, this change is occurring quite rapidly.

If you have ever felt the emotional pull of racial or sexual equality issues, or current conservative versus liberal politics, you have felt this conflict. These issues continue to agitate, as sides are taken and defended. The conflict is not solvable but is gradually being resolved as we slowly leave the past and move into the future. There is no solution, but rather resolution, as we develop a new orientation and a new psychology.

Human thinking changes extremely gradually over the course of time. It is hard to realize because the group's psychology changes so little from generation to generation. We tend to assume that people from generations ago thought as we do now. But that is not the case, and the gradual changes that have led from viewing African-Americans as property to African-Americans as presidential material underscores this. Even fervent abolitionists from the era of the U.S. Civil War era did not see African-American people as equals. Liberals from a generation ago could not see an African-American as president. The group's psychology is gradually shifting to viewing all people as equal, without some being held as inferior to others. These small steps amount to one huge change that is difficult to realize when we're only looking at the small section of history occurring in one lifetime.

But the realization of the accumulated impact of these small changes can be frightening. Seemingly suddenly, women and minorities appear to have too much power. Some people reject these changes; they feel that their entire world and way of life are being swept away, just as pagan Romans did 2,000 years ago as Christianity began to change their world.

Society's attitude toward homosexuality reflects this dramatic transformation. There have been two rapid, monumental changes in the status of male homosexuality in Western history, the first being with the arrival of Christianity. Before that time the sexuality of males in the ancient world was openly ambivalent. From 117 to 138 CE, Hadrian was the Roman emperor; we know him for a wall across northern England and for the Pantheon in Rome. His young male lover, Antinous, died in 130. It is striking that Antinous was worshiped as a god, coins were made with his likeness, and games were being held in his honor even after the death of Hadrian,[4] and yet only 260 years later, after the rise of Christianity, male prostitutes were executed by burning.[5]

The second such change in thinking about homosexuality is more recent. The last executions in the West for what were probably homosexual acts were in 1785 in the United States and 1835 in Britain. Approximately two centuries later (oddly similar to the 260 years just noted), homosexual marriage has been legalized. Now it seems obvious that the anti-homosexual laws should have been revoked long ago, but that is only our view in our time. When viewed historically, these two great legal changes represent huge psychological changes that have occurred in the blink of an eye.

The changes in external organization of society correspond with changes in the internal psychology of society. We are leaving a society of hierarchy and position and entering one based on equality, exactly as we are leaving a hierarchy-oriented psychology and entering an equality-oriented psychology in the inner world.

The United States was founded on the old psychology of aristocracy, racism, and sexism, but with ideals of a new psychology of equality of all. The ideals of 1776 and the realities of 1776 were two entirely different worldviews, two entirely different psychologies. They represent the last millennium and the new one. Despite ideals of equality, the reality of 1776 was slavery, a well-established class structure, and strong sexual stereotypes. Through gradual change, through minor crises, such as the social unrest and sexual revolution of the 1960s, and through major crises, such as the American Civil War and World War II, the old structure and the old psychology have been, and continue to be, gradually eroded as a new psychology develops. Typically for the United States, a national crisis pushes three steps into the new psychology, then the old way of thinking gradually pulls two steps back. As this occurs over the years, both the group social structure and the group psychology gradually change.

Psychological awareness

The awareness necessary to understand our psychological orientation has only developed over the past century. During that time we have developed psychological insight and knowledge that was not present 150 years ago. This represents an entirely new way of thinking and a new way of viewing the world. We take it for granted that such thinking has always been available, but in actuality it is quite new.

Our current understanding of human psychology is primarily the product of Pierre Janet, Sigmund Freud, Alfred Adler, and Carl (C.G.) Jung, all European physicians who began their explorations in the mid- to late 1800s.[6] Aside from their specific findings, they began an expansion of our consciousness by introducing us to psychological awareness, an entirely new way of seeing the world. This development of consciousness is a critical part of the current changes. Janet, Freud, Adler, and Jung went just ahead of us on the developmental path; we are right behind them. As the West has become more psychologically minded over the past century, we have integrated many of the core ideas of Janet, Freud, and Adler; for example, most people are aware of the unconscious mind and its motivations. We are now at the beginning of integrating Jung's ideas.

I think that Jung's psychology has become more and more relevant with the passage of time. That is because the seemingly remote problems Jung found in some of his patients in his time have become the obvious problems central to Western society's struggles in our time. The core problem is the myth that was the guiding principle for Western consciousness has lost its position and has not yet been replaced.

We are now significantly more psychologically minded than people of 100 years ago. In fact, the average literate person is much more psychologically minded than either Jung or Freud were early in their careers. It is only a slight exaggeration to say that what used to be the arcane process of analysis is now conducted on television, and what's more, the audience understands it. Psychological terms such as sadism and masochism are just over a century old, yet they are now understood by most Western people. What is common knowledge for us was pioneering work for Adler, Janet, Freud, and Jung; the new terrain and the paths through it have become much clearer with the passage of time and with our increasing awareness.

Jung's ideas in particular are a foreshadowing of our time. He focused on problems that only began to appear in a few people decades ago. Jung's concepts such as "conflict of opposites" or the "shadow problem" might make little sense until you realize that they accurately describe much of what is occurring in our politics. The current difference in values in the United States is perhaps the greatest it has been since the U.S. Civil War, but this time the conflict is not over a specific issue as much as a difference of psychological orientations. It is an excellent illustration of the conflicts that Jung sensed decades ago, which are now widely active in Western consciousness.

Both the old and the new psychologies are present in each of us, and people tend to take one side and identify with it. The denied side becomes a part of the shadow, a part of the "dark side" which is "found" in the opposing group. Each side accuses the other, so that both sides serve as the shadow, that is, the repressed side, of the other. Understanding the shadow is critical to understanding our time, and it gets its own chapter later. At this point, just consider the shadow to be a major aspect of the unconscious mind.

Jung wrote of integrating the feminine and the shadow to achieve individual psychological growth, and that is exactly what we have been doing, both as a society and as individuals, over the past century. The external integration of women and minorities into positions of equality in mainstream society is the external parallel to Jung's suggested pathway for internal growth, and we are well on our way down that path, the path of our development. Minority people have carried shadow values projected onto them by the majority, and they have been forced to live out those roles, while women have been restricted to traditional female roles; this is slowly ending. It is important to remember that Janet, Adler, Freud, and Jung did not pull their core ideas out of thin air; rather, they intuited basic truths of human nature and development. They just did it the hard way, alone and before anyone else. Now we have them to follow.

Another of Jung's concepts is inflation,[7] essentially thinking that you are more (or less) important than your fellow human beings, rather than just being another person in the world. This was not a major concern at the time, but it has become one. We have a society with swarms of famous "special" people, and even more people who obsess about the famous. The West is dominated by people who feel that they are somehow special and better than their fellow human beings; it is an epidemic of our time. Those whom fate has given power and position feel that they are "special" enough to take advantage of their fellow human beings by taking their jobs, their voting rights, their savings, their resources, or even their lives. It is an attempt to return to the old class structure and privilege when that world is rapidly fading into history.

The great change of our time

Our psychology, our society, our politics, and our religious views are changing as a part of a developmental process that is intrinsic to human consciousness. That process has established the characteristics of each of the great ages of history. Our path has been fixed for the past 500 years, and now it is turning a corner as we leave one age and begin another. As a result, our society and each person in it are torn between the old and the new.

When people feel these changes, some identify with the old ways and struggle to resist change; others identify with the new and struggle to make change. In truth, both sides are in each of us. We are in the midst of a great change in consciousness.

CHAPTER II

A Case History of the Western World

The West's history as a case history

The psychology of our time is the end product of all the psychology and history of our forebears. It is the latest result of our progress through history. Thus human history can be viewed as a case history, similar to a patient's case history. The patient is the human race, or more specifically, the Western world and its ancestors. A case history reveals how an individual has been influenced by ideas; some ideas are ignored, some are repressed, and some come to dominate the person's thinking and influence behavior. It is the same for the group's history, but with individuals promoting ideas that influence events, rather than the ideas themselves. Some of those individuals are ignored, some are repressed (executed), and some influence the course of history. Just as an idea must be strong enough to cause behavior to manifest in an individual, enough people must hold an idea for it to become manifest in a society.

By history, I mean all of recorded history plus prehistory, the entire course of existence of anatomically modern humans leading to the modern West. This is our developmental history, our case history. It is a history of development from an entirely instinctual life beginning at least 200,000 years ago when the first modern humans appeared, through progressive periods of civilization, to our time in history. This case history is the basis for understanding our current situation and what the future might hold.

This great stream of Western history breaks down into four major periods: the prehistoric world, the ancient world, the medieval world, and the modern West. These divisions are somewhat arbitrary and nebulous, but no more so than dividing a lifetime into infancy, childhood, adolescence, young adulthood, middle age, and old age. The major periods of history differ sufficiently that each may be considered as a separate world. In a psychological context, they may be considered as four stages of development in the case history of the Western world.

When world history is taken as a case study, one sees the same developmental stages that are observed in children growing into adulthood. There is a close parallel between the psychology of child developmental stages and the great historical ages. This means that history follows a basic developmental pattern, as opposed to being only a series of random events over time. At a fundamental level, there is an order to history, just as there is an order to the development of a child. Understanding this order helps explain the psychology of our time.

Jung repeatedly referred to the impact of historical thinking on modern thought. He described the mind as "an extremely historical structure."[8] He thought it probable that individual psychological development repeated human development, noting the similarities between mythological thinking, dreams, and children's thinking.[9] Jung noted that the development of a child repeats the development of civilization, with earlier layers still active in the mental processes of adults.[10] He felt that human minds "have been made by the history of mankind"[11] and the "historical ways in which our mind has developed" should be taken into account in dream interpretation.[12] Developmental psychology connects child development, historical development, and their residuals in modern adults.

Developmental psychology

Until the early twentieth century it was held that children thought exactly like adults, only lacking knowledge, experience, and discipline. They were seen as empty containers waiting to be filled with information and experiences. Development was held to be a process of acquiring more information and experience, that is, filling the container.

This changed with Jean Piaget, a Swiss psychologist who discovered that a sequence of developmental stages takes place as a child matures from infancy to adulthood. Piaget found that each stage is marked by a different intellectual approach to the world; the stages he defined were later expanded to include moral and psychological aspects. The basic idea is that a child in the West passes through four stages in the process of becoming an adult.

Keep in mind that these stages are so subtle that they were not noticed until the early twentieth century. Likewise, the differences between the ancient world and the medieval world are subtle. But when those subtle differences are multiplied by millions of people living over centuries, they set a tone for an age, just as developmental levels set the tone for behavior in specific age ranges of children's lives.

What concerns us here is not child development itself, but the fact that the psychological characteristics of these four stages are parallel to the psychology, thinking, religion, and worldviews of the corresponding historical periods, that is, the prehistoric world, the ancient world, the medieval world, and the modern West. Understanding individual development helps us understand historical development, and vice versa. Once that underlying pattern is realized, then history becomes, at a basic level, predictable.

I am confining this argument almost entirely to the West's developmental history to avoid the danger of misjudging other cultures in our world today. There has been a trend to describe countries in the Middle East as "medieval" but exactly what "medieval" means in this context is not entirely clear and it may reflect subtle disparagement. There is a great danger of judging other living cultures and assessing them incorrectly based on our own values and prejudices. Discovering what medieval means to the West is best done by reviewing our own medieval past.

About a century ago, an effort was made to show that non-Western, tribal people used patterns of thinking and logic different from those of Western people.[13] The movement failed for two reasons. The first was that two world wars and their aftermath spread Western culture and thought over the globe, so that much of the old thinking and logic of tribal people was lost, replaced by Western logic. Because of this, later studies failed to show the stark differences that had been observed earlier.

The second reason was the general development of thought in our time, toward seeing all people as equals. Although the reporting of the thinking of tribal people was not derogatory of them, it was taken to be by many critics. They argued that the logic of tribal people was not different from that of Westerners, and Westerners had been prejudicial and disparaging in making their observations. Rather, tribal people were solving problems in their world just as well as, if not better than, Western people solved problems in the Western world.[14]

To avoid these pitfalls, I have chosen to explore the problem almost entirely through historical comparisons. But it is important to keep in mind that while there may be differences in thinking between groups, that does not make the two unequal. The historical approach makes this easier, as there are fewer prejudices about historical periods than about other cultures in our world today. And Western culture and thinking have virtually enveloped the globe so that clear comparisons between existing groups are almost impossible.

The change in our psychology

The problem of viewing the psychology of another time or another group is that of a fish living in water observing a bird in the air. Just like the fish, we are completely immersed in our view of the world, making it difficult to understand that ours is one possible world while the bird's is another. There are two parts to the problem. One is realizing that we (the fish) have our own reality orientation (the water) and it is not the same as the bird's, and two, that after allowing for our way of thinking, what we can determine about the bird's world? That is, we in the West have a psychology and it is an error to assume that everyone in every culture for all time has thought the same way we do now. Understanding that we have a particular way of thinking comes first, and holding that aside, what can we learn about other cultures, specifically those of our ancestors?

Understanding who we are is further complicated by the fact that our psychology is changing. We are living in the end period of what has been the modern West. If you consider the history of the modern Western world, beginning with Columbus, Luther, Copernicus, Henry VIII, and their compatriots, you find a history in which the authoritarian white male exploded out of what was a relatively rustic northern Europe and proceeded to conquer the globe. Before 1500, northern Europe was somewhat of a backwater of civilization; although it was a center of culture and power, there was no indication that it would rise to the heights it did.[15] By the early twentieth century, European culture dominated the world, and it was literally true that the sun never set on the British Empire. The dominant symbol of that era was the conquering white male. Now that symbol is in retreat, making last-ditch attempts to turn back the clock and regain control.

Recent decades have seen a huge rise in the status of women and the minority people who had once been subservient to white males. We have seen an explosion of psychological knowledge, as opposed to church dogma, for examining the inner world. Despite lapses, there has been an ongoing march toward equality of all people. These new developments are not a part of the old Western tradition. They represent steps in a profound change of consciousness for the West and the formation of a new tradition.

Until relatively recently, women were not considered intellectually capable of making the decisions necessary for voting; now it is unquestioned. Women, as symbols of the feminine, have risen in status, reflecting a similar rise in the status of the feminine and its values, with a corresponding lowering of the status of the masculine and its values. This has come at a time in history when we are moving closer to the ideal that all people are created equal, with a greatly diminishing importance of seeing some people as better, and other people as inferior, to oneself.

Despite what the news media may suggest, we are far less violent than in our past. Steven Pinker, in *The Better Angels of Our Nature*,[16] makes it clear that the rate of human violence has been declining for centuries. It is especially clear that the West has gradually become substantially less violent during the past 500 years. He provides evidence that the murder rate in the West has declined precipitously since 1500. Even considering the killings of two world wars, the violence rate has declined, and it has declined even more steeply since World War II. The West has changed from a medieval world with frequent brutal executions as a public spectacle, to nations with relatively few, if any, executions, and none as public spectacle.

These are not minor adjustments, but represent major changes in both our inner psychology and our outer society. Our view of the case history of the West must allow for the fact that we have our particular view of reality, while at the same time our view of reality is changing. This gives us three views: the past, the changing present, and hints of the future we can gather from understanding current development. Each of these can then be contrasted with the medieval world or the ancient world. The only science I have found capable of dealing with this is developmental psychology, and I will use it as a well-researched yardstick to measure our developmental history.

The medieval world we developed out of was so different from the modern West that it may be considered as having a different consciousness. By consciousness, I mean the entire package of thinking, religion, psychology, and social organization. It is the entire way a person or a society organizes its world and thinking. It includes the way they view, relate to, and structure both the inner and outer worlds.

I have referred to both the consciousness of the West and the psychology of the West. They are almost the same, but I use consciousness as a more global concept, including, but not limited to, psychology, social order, and religion. Psychology is more specific and describes the mental processes created by consciousness. Consciousness includes everything about how the person or the group views, reacts to, and structures their world.

I am unable to say exactly what consciousness is, other than to define it as how we view, relate to, and organize the world, both the outer world and our inner one. Perhaps consciousness is only one's awareness of the world. Consciousness determines how people see their world and how they shape their reality, how they see and understand other people and themselves. In recent years we have learned that animals have some degree of consciousness. Animals have been shown to use tools, plan ahead, work in groups, even to have an awareness of themselves. But the consciousness of animals does not develop. It remains eternally fixed at the same level. Human consciousness develops.

Developmental psychology has shown that individual development occurs in stages; I will show that it is parallel to historical development. During each stage, gradual change occurs, and toward the end of the stage the rate of change accelerates. Thinking begins to expand in new directions as a stage ends, preparing the way for the next, and by this process, proceeds from stage to stage. These stages appear to be intrinsic to human consciousness. Maybe consciousness development is the only real difference between humans and animals; but that is no small difference.

The new psychology

One example I have used of a change in consciousness is the impact of the early medical psychologists, Freud, Janet, Adler, and Jung, on Western thought. Our world has expanded because of their efforts. Our worldview now incorporates the concept of both unconscious and conscious motivation. Our view of the world has enlarged; we know our world and ourselves better. This is not a simple increase in knowledge but a change in how we think, a change in orientation toward reality, a change in our consciousness. It is a step in a greater change occurring as we move from our previous orientation into a new one.

Group consciousness, our shared consciousness, is broadened by individuals who pioneer new frontiers and bring those ideas into the mainstream. When new ideas are first introduced, more conservative elements resist them. It is the role of the conservative part of each of us, and the more conservative people in our society, to steer us clear of weirder ideas that may arise. The more liberal tendency is to accept the new, and between the conservative and liberal approaches, we shape our group consciousness, that which the group holds as reality. In the tension between conservative and liberal, a debate ensues on a group level, and some ideas are incorporated into the group's conscious orientation, and others are rejected. A good illustration is the gradual construction of Christian dogma during the European medieval era.

The concept of the unconscious mind is a relatively new one, from the middle 1800s, but it is now well integrated into our thinking. I also suspect that, since its discovery, a significant portion of the unconscious itself has become more accessible to the conscious mind. When reading Freud's or Jung's descriptions of their patients, I have often felt that the individuals were much less aware of their personal unconscious motivations than modern people; this is probably because they had only just learned that they had an unconscious, much less what was in it. Modern Western people are more aware, or at least potentially aware, of their own unconscious motivations than any earlier people in history, including people of only a century ago. The upper layers of the unconscious have become relatively accessible to conscious thinking. More than a little of psychotherapy involves dealing with what the patient is already dimly aware of; that was not the case a century ago when the revelations were more shocking.

Even though the upper layers of the unconscious mind are somewhat accessible, at least at times, the unconscious is not a direct consciousness. Unconscious awareness is a twilight consciousness, like a dream state or a fugue state. Have you ever mislaid an item, say your glasses or a pen, and when you finally found it, you cannot recall having put the item where it was? You placed it there unconsciously. I've heard of people making a trip, perhaps driving home from a store, and not being able to recall the drive; they made the trip unconsciously. In these instances, unconscious does not mean asleep or in a coma, but a lack of focused consciousness.

In a class I once attended, a student under hypnosis was given a posthypnotic suggestion by the instructor that he would retie his shoelaces when a specific word was spoken; he was then released from the trance. Another student "unconsciously" said the key word before the instructor did and the first student retied his shoelaces. No one in the class consciously noticed this until the instructor said the key word with no response from the student who had been hypnotized. We then realized, bit-by-bit, what had occurred. When we discussed the shoelaces being retied we were each aware that it had happened but we were not conscious of it until we discussed the events that occurred; they then became conscious. "Oh, yes, he did retie his shoelaces earlier. You are right!" The vague unconscious awareness was there in each of us, but it was not brought into the light of consciousness until discussed.

While the work of Janet, Adler, and Freud have been fairly well integrated into modern thought, society is now coming up against the problems that Jung wrestled with. First among these is the idea of the shadow,[17] the "dark side" in each of us.

The shadow can be viewed as a part of one's unconscious, one's "dark side." The shadow is the parts of a person's personality that they would rather not have, or pretend not to have. It is composed of naughty ideas, inferior traits, inadequacies, personality weaknesses, and so forth, plus material that has never made it into conscious thought. Remember the naughty behaviors you had as a child, which were left behind as you grew up—they are in the shadow. Its content can range from hostile thoughts toward others, jealousy, and resentment, to denied sexual feelings or felonious impulses, to inadequately developed personality aspects. Most of us are on the minor end of the scale, with the routine jealousy, envy, petty nastiness, minor inadequacies, and so on, but it can extend to the corrupt, sordid, and murderous. It includes the sort of material that is humiliating and an insult to one's self-esteem, so that it is usually kept repressed, that is, unconscious. Tell me about a person you dislike or who irritates you and I will tell you about your shadow.

Realizing one's shadow, much less attempting to integrate it, is a moral challenge. It takes a moral effort for the ego to recognize and accept the denied qualities it has managed to repress and project to others. It goes against the ego's view of itself to accept such unacceptable properties. Parallels in the external world are the moral arguments made by American abolitionists against slavery and by civil rights leaders against segregation; it was morally difficult for the majority to grasp the horrors inflicted on minorities and much easier to pretend those horrors did not exist. In a similar way, it is easier to pretend that one's own personal shadow values do not exist. It is embarrassing to realize that you have the same negative characteristic that you criticized someone else for having.

It is always easier to overlook one's own faults and find them in one's supervisor, coworker, neighbor, spouse or any other person, and see them as mean, nasty, stupid, evil, and so on. It is the same in the external world, where it is easier to see one's own group, political party, or country as correct and the other as wrong.

Throughout my time in the military (a mercifully short career) I repeatedly met some extraordinary bullies. If there was a bully around, I managed to make his acquaintance, and he managed to make my life miserable. At a later point, after I had grown up some, I realized that this represented a part of me, that is, a part of my shadow. How else did I manage to find these people on such a regular basis?

The shadow has positive value, however, and integrating the shadow is a part of current consciousness development. For me, you don't get through graduate school without pushing yourself; you have to bully yourself to keep at that stuff. Shadow qualities in themselves are not necessarily "bad," but they certainly may manifest in a negative way.

Realizing that you have shadow qualities is really just another way of saying that you have some psychological insight and some awareness of your unconscious mind. If a person has a degree of psychological insight, that person realizes their less than perfect qualities, that is, they have some realization of their own shadow. It is only insight and awareness that allow you to deal with your shadow. I can never eradicate bully qualities from my personality, but I can become more conscious of them. I can catch myself when the issue arises, and attempt to deal with it. I can feel myself becoming upset when I hear about someone being bullied, for example, or if I feel like bullying someone else. If I catch myself and realize what is happening, that is, become conscious of the process, the upset resolves. That way, I don't get carried away with fantasies of attacking the offending party, that is, fantasies of bullying the bully, and I don't become a threat of being a bully to someone else.

If I were to attack a bully, then I would be the bully, and the shadow would have "won" and dominated me and my thinking. Likewise, if I allow myself to be bullied, the shadow wins again, and dominates. Neither is acceptable; I must find a middle path between the two. Only then am I consciously dealing with the issue. And that takes consciousness beyond what was commonplace in 1900, when Jung was just starting to figure this stuff out.

Shadow integration takes work. But so has every other step in the development of human consciousness.

As the twentieth century progressed, individual insight and individual shadow awareness developed as a byproduct of the growth of psychology in general. With the growth of psychological awareness, many people have begun to have more insight into themselves than was ever possible in our past. Hand-in-hand with awareness of the internal shadow came the development of awareness of the group external shadow, the shadow of the majority projected onto minority groups. Prior to World War II, extraordinary racism was commonplace and widely accepted. Western thought was rife with anti-Semitism; even the Jung institute in Switzerland had a Jewish quota.[18] African-Americans were held in a dreadfully inferior place in American society. One of the unique things about the twentieth century is how both internal and external shadow awareness and shadow integration began in Western society and gradually developed over the course of the century.

In the twentieth century the archetype of the shadow, that is, the basic psychological concept of the shadow, began its rise from the depths of the unconscious into the West's internal and external worlds. In the internal world, knowledge of the unconscious and its motivations forced its way into Western psychology. In the external world, African-American people, who carry much of the shadow for mainstream white society, marched into society and began to integrate.

There is a dynamic relationship between the conscious mind and the unconscious mind in each person's inner world, and changing one affects the other. That same relationship exists in the external world between the group majority and the minority individuals who carry the shadow for the group. Inner world (psychological) dynamics affect the outer world; if inner world dynamics change for enough people, the outer world dynamics change as well. It is not only a matter of the relationship between majority and minority people in the outer world, nor is it only a matter of one's realization of one's own shadow, one's personal minority. It is a whole that includes both, a gestalt, in which our entire world—both inner and outer—changes; it is a change in consciousness. The same symbols dominate in both the inner world and the group's psychology, and as the symbols change, the world changes.

It is not by accident that racial integration began during the time that internal psychological integration of shadow values was beginning. Likewise, chance has not caused the increased equality of women to occur at the same time that males have become more aware of their own feminine and feeling values, and women more aware of their masculine and thinking values. The internal world and the external world develop concurrently, as they both reflect the same psychology.

Psychological insight and shadow awareness are major aspects of the new consciousness that is beginning to develop in our time. Some people have embraced this, and some people have resisted it. These two groups have come to see the other as their own shadow, and hence we have two different psychologies facing one another. This is not liberal versus conservative; there are liberal and conservative aspects of each of these orientations. It is two different orientations of consciousness.

As John Donne put it, "No man is an island, entire of itself; every man is a piece of the continent, a part of the main." Both sides of the conflict are in each member of society. What happens is that some of us identify with one side and some with the other, a conflict of opposites in each person and in our society. Some see the increasing shadow presence as a threat, and some welcome it as an increase in their psychological awareness. Some see the increasing strength of the feminine as a threat, and some welcome it. Each side usually fails to realize that the other side is its own shadow, and that there are aspects of both in each of us.

CHAPTER III

Shadow Psychology

The dark side

A person's shadow is their "dark side," their "dirty laundry," the thoughts, wishes, emotions and actions that they would like to keep hidden from the world and perhaps even from themselves. It includes impulses and behaviors that were repressed as we left childhood, inferior traits, inadequacies, weaknesses, socially unacceptable tendencies, hidden emotional wounds, and other unacceptable qualities. It is made up of material repressed from consciousness, as well as material which has never been conscious. The shadow is part of, but not all of, the unconscious.

Shadow psychology has been central to the West and Christianity. Being a "good person," a church member, and a good citizen meant that naughty and evil shadow values were repressed from conscious thinking. Those values were typically projected onto outsiders, criminals, and nonbelievers. It is only with the development of psychological awareness that this has begun to change.

The "good person" whose shadow is unconscious still has short-comings—lust, anger, greed—but they are denied and only "seen" in people carrying their shadow. Projecting one's own bad side onto others does not make it go away. An example is the angry person who sees others as being angry, and does not realize his own anger and perhaps even how his anger provokes the anger of others. The anger may be there and observable by others, or it may be truly repressed into the unconscious, so that only the effects of the anger are visible. Or a person may have strongly repressed their sexual drive, and only sees it in other people. A slave owner could beat his slaves because of their violence, and rationalize his own violence in doing so as something necessary and correct. Again, tell me about the people you dislike or can't get along with, and I'll tell you about your shadow.

Shadow psychology was not a significant issue in the ancient world; it only began in earnest with Christianity. An ancient Greek could worship Ares or Aphrodite, or any other god or goddess, with no sense of sin. If you were lustful, you worshiped Aphrodite or Venus. If you were a hothead, your god was Ares or Mars. People felt remorse and shame but there was no concept like the idea of sin that we have; they had little of the sense of shadow that we do. Shame was associated with loss of honor, not sin. Each god and goddess had their realms of authority and their rules, and trouble followed if the rules were violated, but it did not cause a sense of guilt. The god could be placated with an offering, and life went on. There was no need to deny one's unacceptable characteristics and project them onto others.

For most of the ancient world, it was Christianity that introduced the principle that certain ideas were not acceptable and should be repressed from one's conscious mind by the believer. Unacceptable ideas such as lust, anger, greed, doubt, pride, and so forth were to be completely dismissed from one's thinking, that is, suppressed into the unconscious. Thus the shadow was created.

In the ancient world, sex and lust were not seen as "bad," but rather as part of the realm of Aphrodite, Venus, or a parallel goddess. Lust as sin came with Christianity, and the ancient goddesses were transformed into Mary Magdalene, a supposed repentant prostitute, and Mary the virgin mother of Christ.

Genitalia were frequently and freely portrayed in the art of the ancient world. This disappeared with Christianity and the medieval mind-set. Similar illustrations still provoke moral outrage among some people today. It is only since the beginning of the Christian era that sex and the body, especially the lower half of the human torso, fell into disrepute.

The medieval mind-set that came with Christianity created a great split in the Western personality, a separation of the conscious mind from the instincts and impulses which had characterized the ancient world, and created the shadow in doing so. The shadow contained all the material repressed with the coming of the new mentality, including the primitive impulses not compatible with the new medieval civilization. The Christian scriptures repeatedly refer to the separation motif, the separation of the saved from the damned, heaven from hell, and the sheep from the goats. The central figure, Jesus, was separated from his shadow, Satan, and separation served as a basic principle for the 2,000 years of psychology to follow.

Separation of the conscious mind from its shadow by repression has been very effective in promoting development. Through the past 2,000 years, Western people have constructed an extremely good ability to control their impulses and appetites that could never have been realized in the Ancient World. Lust and sexual impulses were brought under strict control, as well as anger, although to a lesser degree.

But unacceptable material repressed into the unconscious doesn't just sit there. The human mind doesn't work that way. Whatever is repressed into the basement (the unconscious) is found in the street (the outer world). The shadow materials are projected onto others as images are projected onto a screen, instead of being realized as a part of one's identity.

Shadow development

For the most part, shadow psychology began when the medieval world began, and increased as time passed, and we are only now beginning to integrate the shadow into conscious thinking with the new psychology. The absence of the shadow in the ancient world, its appearance in the medieval world, its development in the modern West, and its resolution in the new psychology demonstrate a dynamic relationship between consciousness and the shadow. Like consciousness, the shadow has a developmental arc of its own.

Individual shadow development parallels historical development. As children age they initially form a repressed shadow and later show that they can control their shadow in projection. At first older children repress their impulses and that material becomes their shadow, completely cut off from conscious thinking. They do not do naughty behavior, although they might tell you that the kids in the next block do that sort of thing. On becoming young adults, they may attempt to prove themselves by conquering or controlling the projected shadow; they might beat up the school bad guy, for instance. Complete separation from shadow material in one stage is followed by controlling the projected shadow in the next.

Historically, treatment of people carrying the shadow followed the same steps: Medieval people completely separated minority people into walled ghettos, while the modern west accepted Africans in large numbers, even into their homes, but as controlled slaves.

In our time, many Western adults past midlife have developed insight and shadow awareness. They have a strong enough sense of themselves that they can accept and integrate their shadow values without threat of their minds being harmed. For example, I might realize that I have short-comings, less than desirable qualities, and naughty thoughts without being overwhelmed by such thoughts, or thinking that I am a disgusting sinner for having such ideas. I can allow such ideas into my thinking without acting them out or succumbing to guilt for having them.

That is, for a portion of the developmental process it is necessary for the shadow to be completely suppressed from the conscious mind. Later it is addressed in projection, as people carrying the projections are controlled. Then, as an older adult develops psychological insight, integration of the shadow becomes a goal in a step toward psychological wholeness.

Shadow psychology is usually only considered as a part of individual psychology, but groups have shadows as well. The same considerations that apply to the individual also apply to the group. The psychological dynamics and symbols are the same.

About five hundred years ago, the Western world was beginning to emerge from the medieval world. The Renaissance was in full bloom, inspired by a rediscovery of classical learning and art. Columbus had just discovered the New World. Luther would soon initiate the Protestant Reformation. These actions were all based on a new way of thinking characterized by increasing independence and individualism, as well as a reliance on personal reason as opposed to medieval faith. But this stance of independent individual reasoning was weak, as it was new in the world and was not fully weaned from medieval faith and belief. Because of this, the Renaissance and the Reformation were both almost destroyed by reactionary medieval forces. The new consciousness needed to achieve, overcome, and defeat its medieval enemies in order to build strength and confidence in itself. The psychological term for this is "building ego strength." Defeating any shadow manifestation in the external world facilitates inner world ego-building. By defeating a reactionary medieval establishment, the new thinking established and strengthened its position in the world. This need to conquer and achieve would lead to the establishment of the modern West; it would lead to defeating enemies as well as defeating ignorance and disease.

A young adult's ego is in a similar position to Europe as the medieval world ended. He or she must confront their projected shadow to develop and strengthen their ego. The need to overcome life's obstacles, to prove oneself, to demonstrate conquest and control of the shadow is exactly parallel to the early years of the modern Western world. It was in those early years of the West when heroic discovery, heroic conquest of other people, and heroic confrontation by the new and independent Protestants against the medieval church were so pronounced. A modern young adult has the same needs.

Each success that the developing ego achieves adds to its strength and feeling of capability. Confidence, identity, and self-esteem are all built up, leading to a strong sense of personal identity and ability. A medieval person would reject this as vanity; medieval artists typically left their work unsigned and anonymous. But for a young adult of our time, and for the West of five centuries ago, personal success is an essential part of development.

For our time, in a more mature society with mature adults, further ego aggrandizement and increased shadow control are no longer useful. Many adults past midlife have reached a time when their sense of individuality is sufficiently developed that the shadow may now be reconciled with and accepted by the conscious mind. This is a major part of the work of achieving "wholeness" which Jung speaks of. It is not an appropriate task for a young adult, just as it would not have been appropriate for Western society 500 years ago. But it is becoming desirable to some modern adults who have reached the maturity of midlife.

The parallels between individual development and historical development, and their changes over time, underline the importance of the developmental model of the mind, as opposed to a static model. As an individual goes through life and their personality develops, the tasks demanded by the mind change. The same holds true with the passage of the group through historical eras. Developing the shadow is important earlier in development, and reconciling it is important in a later stage of development, both for the individual and for the group. There is no static, true-for-all-time psychology for the individual or for historical groups, as the psychology of both changes over time. It follows that there is no specific eternal philosophy or religion, good for all time; the only thing permanent is change.

Shadow relationship

Unacknowledged shadow values are typically projected. If my group is not the "bad guys," then someone else is. European history is built on repressed greed and disbelief projected onto Jewish people, who were barred from almost every position except merchant and moneylender. When they lent money and expected the money to be returned, they were seen as greedy. The borrowers denied their own greed and projected it onto the Jewish lenders, who became subject to forfeiture of their property, citizenship, and lives as a result. Judaism itself implied a disbelief in the ideas of a man returning from the dead and a human being as a god. Such disbelief was threatening to individuals with a psychology built on the idea of the hero Jesus who was said to have returned from the dead and ascended to heaven. When Jewish people did not accept the idea that someone could be dead and somehow return to life, they were punished by people who had repressed their own doubts on the subject.

When Europeans ventured out into the world beginning in 1492, their maltreatment of native people by conquest, slavery, and outright murder was based on the projection of their own shadow values onto these people. For a white person, the shadow can easily take the form of a person with dark skin, resulting in the West's history of maltreatment of aboriginal people, a pattern already established by the maltreatment of the lower classes and Jewish people. Native Americans and Africans then began to carry much of the shadow for white European conquerors.

Thus we have the ugly, brutal side of Western history: I am a Godly person, these Negroes in Africa are not, let us take them to the plantations in America to save their souls, and by the way, use them for labor. I do not doubt that someone died and came back from the dead, but Jewish people do, so punish them for their non-belief. Lower-class whites steal because they are wicked, not because they are starving (caused by ruling-class greed), so we will hang them or send them to exile. I am special, ordained by God to inherit the American continent, so it is right to kill off the savage and ungodly Indians; I am not being savage in killing them. The socialists, Communists and trade unionists are trying to take control, so I must take control of them by any means possible. Obviously these are egregious examples, but you get the point.

Each of us has a shadow, as does the group. It was in observing the behavior of the United States that I realized that the shadow problem is emerging from repression in the unconscious and now preoccupies the country. The group shadow of the United States is easiest to demonstrate by its effect, primarily fear. This fear has accelerated during my lifetime. It is seen both in racism and international affairs. Fear stalks the United States, and politicians play on it.

Racially based fear continues to be a major issue in the United States. After Hurricane Katrina struck New Orleans in 2005, the press reported that mobs of people, implied to be poor inner-city African-Americans, were running amuck, shooting at rescue helicopters, raping, and killing.[19] These rumors were initially reported as factual news, and it was not until later that it was determined that there was no substance to them. Such racial threats are easily and frequently manipulated by cynical politicians: evoked as the specter of a dangerous, threatening African-American man, Mr. Willie Horton was used to help a presidential contender win his position in 1988.[20]

An analysis of campaign advertisement images from the 2008 presidential campaign showed that the darkest images of Barack Obama appeared in the most negative, most stereotypically consistent political advertisements, especially in those linking Obama to crime. These images were more frequent in advertisements used closer to election day.[21]

From the late 1940s until the late 1980s, the Soviets were repeatedly presented as an imminent threat that the United States must work day and night to keep up with. It was certainly odd when the enemy that had been continually touted as being extremely dangerous suddenly fell apart in 1989. We continue to be sold even more threats from what are really outdated and non-threatening forces, marketed as soon-to-be major threats to our well-being.

I breathed a sigh of relief with the fall of the Berlin Wall and the east-west split it symbolized. It was as if the separation of us from the shadow that had characterized the West was crashing down as well. But it did not provide resolution for many Americans; another enemy was needed. A replacement had to be found for the failed Soviet Union, and the Muslim world was provoked into filling the role. This behavior demonstrates that the psychology of many Americans requires an enemy, and not just any enemy but a vicious and potent threat. Many Americans need someone to hate and fear.

This same drama has played out on an individual level. When and where I was raised, it was not unusual to have a rifle in the house. For most of my youth there was one behind our kitchen door. My schoolmates went rabbit and squirrel hunting and I did target shooting. That was then, and those were single shot, small caliber weapons. Now individuals own machine guns, large caliber weapons, armor piercing ammunition, body armor, and huge ammunition magazines. Something has changed. Why would anyone want that sort of armament unless they were really afraid?

Why is there a need to feel threatened, both as a group and as individuals? What is there to be afraid of?

The fear is fear of our own shadow, because our group psychology is changing so that the shadow is no longer as well repressed as it once was, and this affects both our inner and outer worlds. In the inner world, our conscious minds are more aware of the shadow. This repeats in the outer world where minority people, who have served as symbols of the shadow, are not as repressed and controlled as they were. The shadow is no longer strongly suppressed in either the group or the individual. The next stage of development requires reconciling with the shadow, but for many people their conscious orientation is not ready or willing to do so. For these people, the shadow is a greater threat than ever, requiring greater and greater measures of control and confrontation. It feels closer at hand and more threatening. This is a problem for many Westerners; they want to keep their shadow values—and the minority people who symbolize those values—repressed and unacknowledged.

At our stage of development, continuing to deny, repress, and project the shadow is a dangerous game; the shadow is pushing its way into the world. One way or another, the ego will make contact with its shadow. On the one hand, a great deal of integration has occurred, both in the inner and outer worlds. On the other hand, there certainly is much further to go, and many people continue to see shadow traits only in projection.

In other words, one of the basic problems of our time is whether a person is able to realize at least some of their own evil and shortcomings in themselves, or if they only see them in projection in others. Is there some realization of the shadow, or does it remain in projection? Is there personal psychological awareness?

Twentieth-century psychological development brought shadow material, including insight into unconscious sexual and aggressive motivation and similar repressed material, into public awareness. Repressed material is now nearer to conscious awareness. We are more conscious of the totality that we are, including our dark side. Yet that material can be threatening if the ego does not feel strong enough to handle it; it was repressed for a reason.

For the past 2,000 years, the shadow—our bad and weak side—has been repressed and projected onto the devil, minority groups, and whatever enemy one happened to be at war with. This all worked pretty well until about the time of World War I, when both sides realized they were praying to the same God for help in murdering the other side. Shadow projection has been intrinsic to the West's Christian religious orientation, the glue that has held our society together. Many millions have died convinced that God was on their side.

The hero and his shadow

The psychology of overcoming the shadow has been present in our stories for almost 2,000 years, from Jesus to Lancelot and Galahad, to Roy Rogers, Gene Autry, and John Wayne. It has been the hero's role to overcome the "bad" side, the shadow. The hero's conquest of his evil adversary is symbolic of one's conscious mind overcoming and controlling one's own shadow. It is the good guy versus bad guy shootout in the movie "High Noon."[22] This combination of symbols has dominated 2,000 years of history; it is starting to change in our time. The hero's role has been to overcome the "bad" so that the hero would be seen as not having a shadow. The "bad guys," from Satan to "bad guys in black hats," were suppressed and sent either to hell or jail. The West later added another step, that the hero gets the girl after completing his shadow conquest; that last step was only added about 900 years ago when ideas of courtly love and courtly behavior began to be circulated by troubadours.

Television has presented many thousands of hours of murder mystery dramas, in which the bad guy is caught and taken out of society, that is, the shadow is repressed. These programs are rituals just as the Aztec prisoner sacrifice was a ritual. They serve their purpose for us just as the Aztec's removal of the functioning heart of a prisoner and offering it to their Sun God served them. Like us, the Aztecs did their ritual to achieve the psychological reassurance they needed. Our ritual offers the reassurance that the shadow, no matter how wicked, remains repressed.

Crime fiction, including detective stories, is a relatively recent form of literature. Its roots are in the middle 1800s, but it really took off with the Sherlock Holmes stories in the late 1800s, followed by numerous other detectives and crime solvers. The huge demand for these stories, first in print and later in movies and television, underscores the very recent, historically speaking, awareness of the need to capture and control a near and threatening shadow. It reflects a growing awareness in society's consciousness that control of the shadow is slipping, and a desire to regain that control. These stories, in which the detective almost always captures the criminal, serve to assuage fears of the shadow. But they also mean that the days of absolute control over the shadow are over for Western people.

It is not a coincidence that Sherlock Holmes appeared at about the same time as Freud, Janet, Adler, and Jung began their work.

Because the old psychology isn't so dominant any more, the individual shadow slips out more easily. We see the shadows of people who were not supposed to have them with increasing frequency. We now know that John Kennedy was an adulterer and Richard Nixon was a "crook." Sports figures are routinely shown to have significant shortcomings, from predatory sexual behavior to drug use. Philandering clergymen and molesting priests are commonplace. The shadow just isn't staying repressed like it used to be.

The change in the status of the shadow is reflected in new stories that have become very popular with the public. Traditional stories in the Western world have been about a hero struggling against and finally conquering his shadow. A typical hero for the modern West, like Roy Rogers, rounded up the bad guys. It had always been clear who was on the good side, and who was on the bad side, but in recent years, the dividing line has blurred more and more. And lately there has been a very different take on the story.

In "The Lord of the Rings," the only way Frodo Baggins succeeds is with the help of his shadow, Gollum. In the original "Star Wars" trilogy, Luke Skywalker is only able to defeat the evil Emperor with the help of his shadow, Darth Vader. These are not traditional Western heroes; they represent a different orientation to the problem of the shadow. Roy Rogers did not have the help of the bad guys to reach his goal.

These new stories are evidence of the evolving role of the shadow that is occurring in our time. They not only suggest that our shadows aren't being repressed as they once were, but also that our conscious minds are much more aware of them, to the point of forming a connection, even an alliance. Shadow reconciliation is a part of the new psychology; to some people it is intriguing, and to others it is frightening. Some people feel that their conscious mind is strong enough to deal with their own shadow material, and some do not.

This is where the question of whether or not you truly feel that all people are created equal comes in. If you do, then you cannot project your shadow onto them, and you must realize your shadow is a part of yourself as you develop psychological awareness. If you do not, you can continue to project your shadow onto people you consider below you in the system and avoid the issue—for a time.

Coming to terms with and relating to one's own shadow is a new and difficult process, one that is just beginning in Western society. Neither our psychology nor our religion can keep it locked in the basement any longer. The rules and rituals for this process have yet to be established. Although a new psychology is beginning to form, it has yet to create a clear and widely-accepted ethic to deal with the shadow problem.

For 2,000 years, we have dealt with evil by projecting it and denying it. Offending thoughts were suppressed into the unconscious mind, and offending people were segregated from the majority, into ghettos or penitentiaries (to be penitent and reform), or removed completely by execution. The church and the courts dealt with evil for the group, and each individual repressed his or her own evil with the help of their religion. That time is ending, and each individual is, hopefully, mature enough to assume that burden and deal with their personal evil.

The process of shadow integration in the internal world is precisely parallel to racial integration in the external world. It appears that they are progressing at about the same rate, hand in hand, through many painful steps. I am repeatedly reminded of how far we have to go in this process, yet I am just as often amazed by just how far we have come. These huge changes in our internal psychology and our external social structure, and resistance to them, define much of who we are in our time.

This is not a simple process. Just when progress with African-American integration suggested that the West was making some headway in dealing with its shadow problem, anti-Muslim sentiment popped up. Jung saw the shadow as being associated with the "trickster" motif,[23] meaning that the minute you thought you had your shadow explained, figured out, and nailed down, it would change its form and appear in some new guise. The shadow is not exact and specific, but vague and undefined by its nature of being a part of the unconscious mind. It is also continuously changing in reaction to the orientation of one's conscious view. The Batman movie "The Dark Knight" (2008)[24] illustrated the extreme difficulty of the ego (Batman) winning control over his shadow (the Joker), as well as the potential for resorting to evil in an attempt at shadow control. The only reason Batman was finally successful was that the movie had to end, and we know that it will only be a short time until the Joker is back in action again; he's Batman's own dark side.

Typically the shadow is composed of greed, clumsiness, hostility, stupidity, less acceptable sexual impulses, and so on. These things are problematic, to be sure, but they are not usually terrible. However, a mind functioning in the old psychology sees them as terrible and as threatening, and this is made worse by a feeling that society's control over shadow people is slipping in general. This leads to fantasies of much larger than life enemies: African-American people are shooting down helicopters. Huge numbers of women are having irresponsible abortions. Teenagers are constantly having promiscuous sex. Terrorists threaten from every direction and from every possible place. Hordes of vicious minority people are about to swarm out of the cities and attack the American heartland. The only recourse seems to be owning a big gun, dropping a bigger bomb, increasing surveillance, and making more draconian laws. No hint of shadow threat can be ignored, and no effort to bring the shadow under control can be spared.

On the other hand, for many other people the shadow is not such a big deal. It is possible to be aware of personal shortcomings, that is, shadow values, without being overwhelmed by feelings of inferiority. I know I have a dark side, naughty thoughts, a bully aspect, and any number of less than desirable attributes, but I have made some degree of peace with them. I can only say that since I have become more aware of my internal bully aspect, I have encountered far less of it in the external world. On the other hand,

I know it is a part of me that will be with me throughout my life. It is pushing me to write these pages.

While it is clear that much shadow material is more embarrassing than harmful, that is not always the case. There are some people in prisons who have committed crimes so heinous that they can never be integrated back into society under any circumstances. Likewise, I assume that there are people with vicious, murderous impulses which must remain in repression for their entire lifetime. There are reasons the shadow has been held in repression, and integrating it is not to be taken lightly. Yet shadow integration will remain a major theme of the era we are entering.

People who are more accepting of the shadow see those who do not as dangerous and as provoking conflict. They also tend to project their own unrealized shadow rejection on the other group, rather than seeing it in themselves. "I'm not racist, those other people are; I only hate people who are racist." And people who are less accepting of the shadow look at the other group as foolish and weak. The shadow is, after all, a very tricky thing. Just ask Batman.

The shadow is coming into Western conscious awareness. Some of us do not like it and see it as more threatening than ever. Some of us are more accepting. And of course, each is a part of the shadow of the other.

CHAPTER IV

Symbols of Our Time

Western religion

I was raised with a Christianity that considered heaven as a factual thing, almost as you might think of another room in your house: it is where you go after you die. This was not a hope, a possibility, or a theory, but a fact of life. No one thought of challenging it any more than they would have challenged the fact that gravity pulls down and not up. My school classmates and I were well aware of the theory of evolution, the enormous age of the earth, dinosaurs, and so on, but it didn't conflict with the underlying faith. It didn't matter if the creation took exactly seven days or not. Faith then was secure and unworried. That is not the Christianity of today.

The current situation is best described by the title of a 2016 book summarizing recent public opinion poll data: *The End of White Christian America*.[25] Another author suggests options for Christians in a "post-Christian" America.[26] Church and religious affiliation have been, and continue to be, decreasing. This decrease is accelerating with the passage of time and with each new generation.

Modern Christianity is a very nervous thing. On the one hand, it claims to have exclusive access to a pleasant afterlife. It has produced any number of books telling itself that it is right and has nothing to worry about. On the other hand, even with assurances the anxiety continues and is growing. I really don't believe it has been this worried since the Inquisition, a reaction to the forces that resulted in the Protestant Reformation. Christianity is worried again, so worried that it feels the need for believers to be "born again." For someone from the old days like me, that is positively strange, and one wonders how long it will be until the need arises—as the anxiety increases—to be born three times. When Harry Potter is seen as a threat, you know someone is scared and walking on thin ice.

Faith was once strong enough that scientific ideas such as evolution could be held side-by-side with biblical teachings without conflict. Science said this and the scriptures said that, but one did not necessarily disprove the other. Faith was sufficient that the two could coexist without conflict. That is no longer the case. Weak faith demands absolute adherence. Psychologically speaking, anything strongly defended is inherently weak. That is the state of Christianity today.

The weakening of Christianity has provoked three principal reactions. One is a childish holding on to the most simplistic of Christian teachings, and rejecting anything that even hints of conflict with those teachings. The opposite is a cynical rejection of all religious values, based on observations that religion has been an instrument of social control and has actually done a great deal of evil. The third is a movement away from specific group doctrines to personal spirituality.

There are those who cling to a naive, childlike belief system, determined to believe at any cost, who believe the Grand Canyon was formed by Noah's flood and that they will be transported to a heavenly mansion at any minute when the "rapture" occurs. The cynic may appreciate the consolation of religion but can't stomach the intellectual sacrifice that current religions demand. The believer is willing to sacrifice the intellect to maintain the consolation. The two positions reflect a religion that is no longer viable and cannot present a mature religious position to a modern person.

Both the cynic and the believer are locked in the same mind-set: they share an underlying psychology. The believer in atheism is much more psychologically akin to the believer in childlike Christianity than either would like to admit. The opposite of childlike belief—wholesale acceptance of myths of return of the dead, miracles and magic—is the cynical rejection of all religious values deemed to be hollow. The cynic throws out the baby with the bathwater, while the fundamental believer clings to the bathwater.

While religion, including the belief that there is no deity, is a long-standing part of human history, what someone believes is a manifestation of their group's psychology and their individual psychology. We human beings have had some sort of religious orientation for tens of thousands of years, and probably much longer. It has been a central part of our lives and our cultures in some form or other for millennium upon millennium. Religion was ancient long before the time of the Exodus or the time of Christ. It was ancient before the first great civilizations. But the modern person is so immersed in shopworn Western religious stories that the true, eternal nature of religion is overlooked.

The essence of religion is timeless, and is as much a part of us as our noses. It may be felt in a sense of awe of life and the world. It underlies our orientation toward death, both our own death and the deaths of those we love, and what may or may not happen after death. It may give an explanation of how we got here. It may give hope and help us cope with fear. It can give dignity and hope in the face of suffering and appalling experiences. The thoughts and feelings you have when you consider those eternal questions form the backbone of your religion. That is the true core, and everything else, including all the dogma, writings, creeds, opinions, myths, stories, rituals, and so on, are just the icing on the cake, and it is all terribly subjective, despite what particular religions claim.

Each great age of humanity has had a basic religious view of the world as a manifestation of the consciousness of the age. It has answered the belief question according to the psychology underlying the age; Christianity has filled this role for almost 2,000 years. It has succeeded in the West because it has most accurately reflected the psychology underlying Western thought. Its icons have reflected the dominant symbols of the age, and that age is now ending.

The psychology of Christianity

Christianity was initially built on the principle of separation into a black and white dichotomy. It separated the saved from the damned, the holy from the profane, male from female, sheep from goats, the believer from the nonbeliever, and the thief on the right (of the crucified Christ) from the one on the left. The underlying psychology is one of separating, specifically, separating oneself from, or repressing, the "dark side" or shadow. Just as sinners are separated and damned to hell in the outer world, sinful thoughts are separated and suppressed into the unconscious in the inner world. The ideal has been to banish all "evil" ideas from one's mind; such ideas were works of the devil and hence evil.

Christianity's first job was to bring control to the ancient world. It wasn't Christian to be angry, lustful, or any of a number of other sins. Sex was seen as something done only—if you had to do it—in marriage, to procreate. Saint Paul recommended that "a man not touch a woman," but if one had to, then get married.[27] Justin Martyr recommended marriage only to produce children; otherwise one should abstain from intercourse.[28] Christians weren't to become angry; they were to "suffer fools gladly"[29] as Saint Paul put it. Everything unacceptable was suppressed and formed the shadow.

The ancient world was an extremely licentious place. For example, sexual control was only achieved by careful segregation and control of females. Even today there are societies that feel that a female must be kept covered, often from head to foot. Other people demand that parts of women's genitals must be excised or sewn up to provide control of their sexuality. The need to control females means that control of the impulses is less than complete, so that male loss of control and regression to impulsive behavior are ongoing threats. By contrast, Western women wear bikinis to the beach and men are able to maintain control. Westerners have this control because we have developed a great deal of ego strength over the past few hundred years.

Christianity helped Western people learn, over the past twenty centuries, to control their anger, sexuality, and assorted impulses and vices. From the point of view of a developmental process it has been successful.

Now we don't need to practice that degree of control any longer because we have learned to do it automatically. We have developed a sufficiently strong psychology that most of us can deal with our impulses without the need for traditional religious structure; in other words, we are now mature enough to reconcile with our shadow.

As our psychology changes and shadow repression diminishes in Western society, the ability to declare a personal problem evil and suppress it is not as possible as it once was. We don't hear of people praying for removal of a "thorn in the flesh"[30] as Saint Paul complained, but rather they go to a therapist to learn to deal with the problematic part of themselves. If a serious problem arises, they look for a competent counselor as opposed to a priest or a preacher. That is the meaning underlying the title of Friedrich Nietzsche's *Beyond Good and Evil*;[31] other than mass murderers, the conventional, black-and-white ideas of good and evil are useless in dealing with the problems of most people in today's world. We can no longer declare a problem evil and attempt to pray it away. We are moving beyond black-and-white, good versus evil answers to anything.

What was an ideal to strive for 2,000 years ago is now built into our psychology through the development we have achieved. Traditional religious ideals provided a path for the development of our psychology. Our problem is that we have come to the end of that path as we reached those goals and we are now reorienting toward new ideals. The West is out-growing Christianity, at least as it currently exists.

The problem with the psychology that Christianity is based on is that the undesirable qualities that were suppressed, such as sexuality and anger, are fundamental parts of the human mind. If they are denied in one's conscious mind, then they will become part of the shadow and appear in projection. This splits the personality into the conscious and unconscious minds.

For both the group and the individual, the shadow was projected to the lower classes, to aboriginal people, and to enemies. As shadow carriers, these people were destroyed, enslaved, punished, or otherwise treated poorly because they were seen as a living embodiment of everything denied and repressed. They became the rejected qualities embodied and walking about on two legs. The best example is racism, wherein one's own undesirable traits are projected onto another racial group. The old psychology depended on shadow projection, and Christianity provided the religious justification.

When the invading and colonizing whites from Europe began expansion over the globe, the culture of native people was disregarded and they were seen as ignorant, savage, and sexual. When we look back at that period in time, we can see that those accusations fit the accusers at least as accurately as they fit the victims. The West did succeed, and its methods and beliefs were adopted, because its technology was superior. But those methods and beliefs relied heavily on projection of the shadow onto the non-whites. Dark-skinned native people then bore the burden of being living symbols for the darkness of the Western shadow. This thinking is illustrated in *The Book of Mormon* (1830) by Joseph Smith; the people who behaved badly became black because of their sins,[32] and later became white again once they straightened up.[33]

Our psychology and the shadow

In each stage of human history, the psychology of the inner world reflects that of the outer world and its politics. The structure of the individual mind is reflected in the structure of society, and internal debate and division in the individual reflects the same debate and division in group politics. This is because each stage is dominated by its own set of symbols, and those symbols serve as the basic organizing principles for the entirety of life, both internally by psychology and externally in politics, government, and religion.

As ideas of the new psychology have entered Western society, the old psychology has resisted them. The ideas of Darwin, Marx, Nietzsche, and the early psychologists were tolerated but not wholly accepted. As of late, Darwin's theory of evolution has been denied and Marx's labor has been "outsourced." Modern psychiatry has developed medications to "treat" troubling psychological problems (and I am not referring to medications for the significantly mentally ill). Despite American movement toward equality for African-Americans, they remain in second-class status, and if that is insufficient, we now have Muslims, the West's new Negroes, to hate and kill as one feels the need.

We are gradually outgrowing the shadow psychology that has been shaped by the past 2,000 years of Western tradition. Every day it is changing more and more rapidly. Some people sense that change, and fearfully grasp for the past, particularly past thinking and beliefs, and attempt to deny and reject the change. Evangelical and fundamentalist religions have made blatant attempts to deny "shades of gray" and make the world return to black and white once again. Those who would turn back the clock are particularly vigorous in their attempts.

The group psychology is torn between those who identify more with the new psychology and those who identify more with the old. The old psychology is bent on maintaining the power and control of the status quo, and wants more than ever to keep all shadow values under control and domination, at any cost. Of course, that very pressure to conform to group norms pushes individuals, in time, toward finding individuality.

Jung noted that integrating the opposites—the shadow and anima or animus—can only be accomplished in the individual.[34] That is because everyone's internal world is, more or less, different; this is not a group process. But the new psychology fosters that integration, just as the old psychology encouraged ego development. External world racial integration has been accompanied by internal world psychological awareness and shadow integration. By experiencing integration and acceptance of others in the external world, internal acceptance is furthered.

Dealing with the shadow is a tricky affair. Denied thoughts and facts must be brought to light without prejudice. It is so very, very easy to find one's shadow problems in other people rather than in oneself. It is extremely easy to project one's own shadow on to the other person or group, and judge them according to your shortcomings. It is so easy to see our own sins in another person. If you aggressively accuse others of aggression, what happens to your own shadow aggression qualities? They are projected onto the other person, and they remain in projection, unresolved. After the other person is confronted, one's own shadow values slyly reappear in another guise, projected in a different form.

Consciousness change

Consciousness appears ambivalent about developing from one stage to the next, as if it is conflicted about change, clinging to the past while peering into the future. Jung noted that many people are afraid of higher consciousness, as it represents greater responsibility and danger.[35] People typically handle the conflict by identifying with the old or the new and attacking the other. As the modern West dawned about 500 years ago, Henry VIII, king of England from 1509 to 1547, identified somewhat with the new psychology of the time, the modern Western psychology of the nation-state. Sir Thomas More identified with the old, the medieval world of belief led by the Catholic church. Henry dealt with their differences by having Thomas beheaded. Religious values were the overt cause of their disagreement, but the underlying cause was a clash of psychologies as one developmental stage ended and another began.

A society ends a period of developmental history when sufficient psychological strength has been developed in most of its members. For example, the medieval world ended because enough people could handle a greater degree of freedom of thought. Enough people of the time had developed sufficient psychological strength and moral character from centuries of church-imposed rules to allow increased personal freedom. The conflict between Henry VIII and Sir Thomas More illustrates this.

Henry decided that the church, that is, religious values, should come second to the nation-state. He identified to a modest degree with the new psychology of the time, one of increased individual freedom, particularly freedom based on reason as opposed to faith. This was directly opposed to the church-imposed "should" rules that had dominated centuries of the medieval world. Specifically, Henry wanted a divorce that the church would not grant, so that he could father an heir and successor. Thomas felt that a divorce was unacceptable, and that one should stay in the medieval rules of "should" and "should not" as outlined by church doctrine. For him, faith was master, and individual will and reason were dangerous and to be kept under strict control.

The new and the old psychologies were probably active in both Henry and Thomas, but each took one side of the conflict and projected the other side to the other person. Neither had the maturity to realize that they both had the problem, and Henry took care of it by repressing the other side, that is by executing Thomas. He was not capable of seeing the other side of the conflict in himself; he could only see it in projection. It is with our new psychology that we have come to realize that both sides of every conflict are in every person involved. When you project something, some aspect of your shadow, onto another person, it is part of you, not of him or her. Understanding that is a new way of thinking, and it conflicts with the old psychology, which was built on complete denial of the shadow.

The new psychology in 1500 was stronger in Henry than in Thomas. Henry had more "ego strength" than Thomas. Henry felt confident of his new thinking based on reason, but Thomas mistrusted independent individual reason and saw it as a danger to faith. The new psychology was weaker in Thomas, and he was not developmentally strong enough to put his medieval values aside and enter the new age, the modern West. Henry could not tolerate his own medieval fears, so he repressed it by executing Thomas, the symbol of his doubt and the possibility that the medieval Catholic dogma might be right.

Henry's thinking was liberal for its time in that it was a new psychology breaking away from the old. Thomas' thinking was conservative, holding on to old values. In the outer world, Henry's thinking would lead to the primacy of the nation-state over the church. In the inner world, Henry's thinking would lead to the psychology of the West and its dominance over medieval faith- and belief-centered psychology.

Luther and Henry VIII broke away from the medieval church and helped usher in the reliance on individual reason that has been the hallmark of the modern West. Similarly, 1500 years before Henry and Luther, Christianity brought faith and moral control to the licentious ancient world. These are the conflicts of change that occur in moving from one developmental stage to another.

In times of change, people dominated by the old psychology see change as a threat, and they respond by shoring up their belief systems and worldviews. They attempt to force their values on those who no longer hold with the old psychology because they fear that these changes could destroy their society. Ancient Roman authorities did not tolerate early Christians and occasionally executed them. Thomas More disapproved of Henry's divorce, and would have stopped it if he could. Currently, the old psychology is attempting to control the feminine by preventing equal rights and criminalizing abortions, control sex by preventing birth control and abortions, control the shadow by stifling minority people, and so on. These people see their world unraveling and falling into chaos because their psychology is no longer in complete control of their world. They see their religion as being under siege as the group's values move away from the religious traditions and beliefs of the past centuries.

Change in the underlying psychology causes change in religion, which causes change in the group's perception of God. Two thousand years ago, the ancient Romans and Greeks were beginning to see their gods and goddesses as an immoral lot, and they became increasingly open to a more moral, more disciplined image of the deity. Saint Paul's version of Judaism, Christianity, filled the need, and the result was the medieval Christian church. That same questioning and discontent regarding religious values is again being felt in our time. Change is in the air. Our consciousness is changing, and with that comes change in everything that makes up our world and who we are.

I have heard it remarked that people who do not uphold traditional religious values are "godless." One can imagine a Roman citizen of 2,000 years ago complaining about "godless" Christians because they refused to worship the emperor and the gods of the city. Such behavior was regarded as treasonous because it indicated a lack of allegiance to the emperor and the city-state, and dangerous because failure to worship the gods could mean disaster for a city. I imagine it was distasteful for an upper-class Roman to accept the new politically correct Christian view that salvation from sin was democratic as all believers were equal before God; the poor had been non-persons in Rome. Today, it seems to be equally difficult for many people to accept the politically correct idea that Americans are all created equal, much less the idea that they are all equal citizens. Christianity is now in essentially the same position that the old Roman pagan religions were about 2,000 years ago, when the pagan gods and goddesses were being replaced by Christianity. That is not to say that God has changed. Our image of God has changed repeatedly over the centuries as we have changed, and we are now changing again.

Like the pagan Romans, people holding conservative religious views feel their world is being upended and ruined as their religion gradually loses its grip on society. They cannot see that a new order is being established on the ruins of their loss. They feel that their teachings and their holy stories are true for all time and all people, ignoring the fact that this attitude has been held before, and we now call those old religious views myths. There is no teaching, religion, or philosophy that is true for all people for all time. Human nature and human behavior change extensively as development proceeds over time, and major changes in that process always make for difficult transitional eras.

None of this means that Christianity has failed. In fact, the opposite is true and it has succeeded extraordinarily well. Christianity civilized the Western world and developed the Western mind. But psychologically it has done all that can be done, at least in its present form.

Rather than leading into the future, much of current Christianity is attempting to return to the past. The recent popularity of the religious idea of "rapture" underscores this. There was no widespread acceptance of the rapture in Christianity until relatively recently. I never heard of it in my very Christian upbringing. There is no substantial basis for it in either the Christian or Hebrew scriptures. One has to stretch the text to arrive at such an idea.[36] The rapture gets importance because it fills a psychological need of our time, due to an unstated realization that Christianity is losing its long-held dominance in the West.[37]

In a similar fashion, in the 1600s the church preached against the idea that the earth rotates around the sun. That idea was the first of many new ideas which would form the modern West. The church argued against it, citing a battle of Joshua.[38] According to the text, God caused the sun and moon to stand still until the battle was over; therefore, the sun had to rotate around the earth. A verse from Psalms stating the world was "established that it shall not be moved"[39] was also considered proof the earth did not rotate.

Religious values are products of the culture's underlying psychology; when the psychology changes the religion changes. Christianity will either change greatly as it did during the Reformation, or it will continue to diminish.

CHAPTER V

The Research Evidence

Introduction to development

My impression is that people generally assume that our ancestors thought like we do today. After all, it was only about 100 years ago that Piaget figured out that children don't think like adults. But if you accept the idea that humans gradually evolved over millions of years, with our ancestors arriving about 200,000 years ago, then you have to consider some form of psychological change over time.

There can only be a psychological explanation for the change from the earliest primitive conscious awareness of the first modern humans, which must have been that of an intelligent animal, to the thinking of modern people; evolution occurs too slowly to account for this. Even if you believe that people were created in the Garden of Eden only a few thousand years ago, you still must explain the differences between the ancient, medieval, and modern worlds.

The only satisfactory explanation for this change is human development. I feel that the development of prehistoric primitive conscious awareness into modern thinking has taken the same path through stages that the development of infant thinking takes in becoming adult thinking. Our consciousness, including how we view reality, how we think, and how we structure society, is the end product of these stages, the same for the group and the individual. Once nature engineers a method of dealing with a problem, it tends to reuse it.

The path of development that children take from infancy to adulthood has been studied extensively and is well documented in the field of developmental psychology. The results of a great deal of research have established objective characteristics for the specific stages of child development.

This chapter is a basic survey of the developmental stages, not an in-depth coverage of child development. Only the three most important writers in the field will be considered: Jean Piaget, Lawrence Kohlberg, and Jane Loevinger.

Modern developmental researchers have shown that human development occurs in four basic stages, with the fourth being adulthood. Individual writers have suggested sub-stages, but there is general agreement on the four major stages. These stages occur in the same order worldwide. Some individuals and cultures may develop further or faster than others, but all follow the same basic path. Development in the individual is an interaction between the individual and the group; no one progresses much beyond the group level, as group interaction is required for progress.

Throughout a given stage, development proceeds according to the structure of that stage, and continues along the same lines until the stage is complete. Once a stage is complete, the child's psychology develops along the lines of a new stage. This process continues, stage by stage, until the child reaches the developmental level of society as a whole. With each stage comes a better grasp of reality, a more capable intellect, more individuality, and a richer personality.

The original work in development was specifically with intellectual development, but that was later expanded into moral development and then personality development, all of which follow the same developmental path.

There are suggestions of stages past the four basic stages. However, these have never been as clearly delineated as the first four, and they seem to be more ideals of behavior, such as being self-actualized, as opposed to clearly defined stages marked by thinking and behavior unique to that particular stage. These stages are not consistent from author to author, and I suspect that they reflect the authors' ideals and speculations rather than their research. Because of this, they are not covered here.

Beginning in this chapter and continuing in the next six chapters, I will show the parallels between the four basic stages of child development and the four great periods of civilization: the prehistoric world, the ancient world, the medieval world, and the modern West.

Jean Piaget - intellectual development

Jean Piaget was concerned primarily with intellectual development[40] as opposed to development of personality factors. About a century ago, Piaget was the first to observe that children in particular age groups tend to come up with the same wrong answers to certain intellectual problems. This implied that all children in that age range were thinking the same way, a way different than older or younger children. That finding led to his discovery of the stages of intellectual development.

Piaget refers to the first stage, usually from birth to age two, as the sensorimotor stage. The child's world is focused on sensory input from the environment and motor control acting on the environment. The child in this stage is quite egocentric. It is during this period that symbolic thought and language appear. Thinking is marked by animism, that is, objects seem to have a life and will of their own.

Piaget's second stage is the preoperational period, typically from age two to seven. Early in this stage a child sees dolls as having their own life, and thus the child's tea party, with each of the dolls being served tea and cookies. This tendency (animism) to view inanimate objects as living gradually diminishes later in the stage.

What is so striking about the image of a child having a tea party with dolls is that in the earlier civilizations of the ancient world, it was not unusual for priests to clothe, wash, and feed the statues that they regarded as being their gods.[41,42] If a battle was won, the city's gods would be thanked; if lost, the gods would be blamed, and men might go so far to overturn their alters or throw stones at their temples.[43]

When the Inca had to deal with a resistant province, they might flog the captured statue of a god or ruler from that province, to force the province to capitulate; some provinces gave up and cooperated because they felt distraught over the maltreatment of their deity.[44]

Historians have reported ancients feeding, bathing, dressing, and flogging the statues of their gods, but it has been a strict reporting of the facts with the psychological implications ignored. The blatant strangeness of this behavior is more or less dismissed by the tacit assumption that ancient people were a bit silly when they washed the hands of their statues before feeding them and changing their clothes, but really they were the same as we are today. But historians do not look at behavior as psychologists do.

A psychologist cannot dismiss such odd behavior. In the ancient world, these "graven images" carried much more psychological weight than they do with us. Notably, the ancient Hebrews needed to prohibit such images relatively early, and this was continued by Islam. There are numerous references in the earlier Hebrew scriptures to the problem of graven images, beginning in Exodus.[45] Serious bans were imposed, designed to deal with what were felt to be serious problems. The need to vigorously prohibit something, like our laws against drug abuse or speeding, indicates that it was a common crime of the times, and hence that people were very apt to do it. The frequent and pronounced emphasis on banning graven images reinforces the significance of the issue.

But if you closely consider the "graven images" problem, it becomes evident that it represents an entirely different psychology than ours. It is a psychology dominated by animism.

Adults in the West are immersed in images, graven and otherwise. A new car, striking architecture, or a clever electronic device may be attractive for a while, although its allure fades. You could argue that Western adults are simply immune to images, due to repeated exposure. But even at its worst, when someone is absolutely in love with a new car, it never becomes such a threat that we need to have laws to control it. No one wants to pray to it. In contrast, the Hebrew scriptures ascribe to graven images as much seductive power as we now attribute to drugs for an addict.

So where do graven images still have their impact with us? There are two places. One is in children, ages two to seven, as Piaget observed.

The other is in the child part of each of us, and that is the part that is enamored by the graven images of the world. This is well illustrated by one of my all-time favorite comic strips, "Calvin and Hobbes." In these cartoons, Bill Watterson shows the thinking of both children and adults. Calvin, a five year old, sees his toy tiger doll, Hobbes, as living and "animated" while the adults see Hobbes only as an inanimate toy.[46] By seeing Hobbes as a living tiger, Calvin and his friend Susie demonstrate the thinking of a two- to seven-year-old child. But more importantly, we as adults each realize the Calvin or Susie inside, the child within. A part of each of us identifies with the child in the cartoon. That is the charm of the series, the realization of our own inner child orientation separate from the adult part of our personalities.

Historians looking back can only dimly grasp the life and authority the ancients ascribed to their graven images, that is, their gods. The more imposing the statue, or object (as possibly a meteorite) the greater its power. This is not a feeling that we can completely understand with our present thinking. We can try to step outside of our worldview and enter that of the ancient world, but it is an almost impossible task. We can get a hint of it by observing children and reading "Calvin and Hobbes."

A serious difficulty arises when we deny any difference between our psychology and that of other civilizations. If a modern person were suddenly thrust back 3,000 years, he or she would not behave like ancients. A modern person would look at a statue of a deity and say, well, it's beautiful, but so what? The ancients were captivated in a way we cannot understand. They saw those statues much more like Calvin sees Hobbes, rather than how we see a well-wrought piece of art. There were reasons that the ancients would even sacrifice their own children to these objects, reasons we can only vaguely understand. While we don't quite understand, Calvin does; he knows full well that Hobbes is a living tiger.

"Calvin and Hobbes" brings up another developmental rule of thumb. Earlier stages are no longer the dominant part of our personality, but they do remain with us. The child of the past remains active in the inner world and continues to influence our personality.

Piaget observed that animism diminishes later in stage two, and likewise, the belief that a statue of a god actually was the god diminished later in the ancient world. It became clear that the statues were representations of the gods, rather than the gods themselves.

Piaget referred to his second stage as preoperational. That is, the child is unable to perform certain operations, including "conservation." The most famous of these illustrations involves pouring a quantity of liquid between two glasses, one short and wide, the other tall and thin. A child in the preoperational stage will insist that there is more liquid in the tall glass than in the short one, despite watching the same fluid poured from one container to the other. Piaget said that these children are unable to understand the idea that the same fluid is in both glasses, making the containers inherently equal; we can see this, but the child in the pre-operational stage cannot.

Superficially, there is no evidence of significant intellectual limitations in the ancient world. For example, we know that ancient engineers were quite clever. We still don't really know how the Egyptians built the pyramids. The Egyptians were able to shape very hard stone extremely well; we could do as well with modern machinery, but it is not clear how they were able to do so with the bronze tools available at the time. There are huge stones in various ancient sites, some of which we would have a hard time moving today, yet the ancients quarried, dressed, and placed them quite accurately. They were able to dig aqueduct tunnels by beginning at each end and meeting in the middle with good accuracy; we would have to use lasers to direct the digging.

While there is no evidence that earlier people were intellectually inferior to us, there are indications that the psychology of the times would only allow a certain degree of intellectual grasp. The medieval Arab world, the height of civilization of the time, gave us chemistry and algebra, but was unable to match those brilliant discoveries afterward. In a similar manner, there were no significant scientific findings in southern Europe for hundreds of years after Galileo, and I do not believe it was solely due to repression of thinking caused by the Church's treatment of Galileo. Rather, the medieval thinking of the Arabic world and of Catholic southern Europe was spent, having given the world their greatest gifts. It took a new psychology, with symbols embodied by independent thinking of northern Europe, to carry on intellectual development.

While the Romans had all the components for a steam engine, they never made one. There was a toy steam engine known to the ancient Greeks, the aeolipile, but it was never developed to do work. The Romans knew of the aeolipile and had the necessary parts to make a steam engine, including pistons and valves (used in water pumps), but never used them to make an engine.[47,48] The idea of putting a machine to work would not enter the human imagination until the modern West. The Greeks were the intellectuals of the ancient world, but their knowledge is, for us, extremely basic. It is notable that the Greeks were able to invent geometry, but not algebra or calculus. It is not that they were intellectually incapable of algebra or calculus, but they did not have the psychological need for algebra or calculus. They defined basic concepts, such as truth and beauty, but they did not do much with the ideas they developed. There was no conception of extending knowledge by making and testing hypotheses, as with the scientific method, so the knowledge of the time was not based on facts.

For an adult, the developmental stage does not determine intelligence. There are people in the West in different stages, and there is no evidence that any one group has more raw intelligence than the other. Rather, a person's developmental psychology encourages the application of intelligence along certain lines. The Greeks and Romans had no need for machines; they thought no further than having slaves do the necessary tasks. The Western ego derives pleasure from conquering problems and overcoming limitations; our drive to make machines to remake our world has stemmed from this. The Western need to conquer and control has produced antibiotics, a method to destroy bacteria. By contrast, one could imagine science of the new psychology developing some way to live with the bacteria, as opposed to destroying them. Development does not entirely determine adult intelligence, but it helps determine how the intelligence is applied.

Piaget's third stage is that of concrete operations, ages seven to 11 or 12. A child in this stage understands conservation, that is, it is the same amount of fluid that pours between the short wide glass into the tall thin one. But he is unable to give a generalized reason why that is the case; his thinking is concrete. A child in this stage can classify by size or similarities, but is unable to explain the meaning behind the classifications. The child is unable to abstract from the facts and tell you what the facts mean. It is reasoning based on concrete facts and not on the abstract rules behind those facts. Similarly, medieval scholarship was dominated by a concrete, dogmatic approach with little original thought. Writings of the ancient world, as those of Aristotle, were taught, with little interest in investigating what the ancients proclaimed. Serious thought was given to such considerations as to whether a mouse eating a communion wafer might actually be eating Christ's flesh. There was virtually no abstract, generalized understanding of the physical world.

As the medieval world ended, a new way of thinking began to develop, allowing people to see the world as it was and not through preconceived medieval notions. Copernicus and Galileo asserted that the earth orbited the sun, although the thinking of the time held the earth to be the fixed center of the universe. Kepler found that planets moved in ellipses, based on his measurements, and not in perfect circles as had been believed. Investigators in physics, astronomy, medicine, chemistry, botany, and other fields found rational, mechanical rules to explain reality, replacing medieval explanations of spirits and humors. Newly developed abstract rational principles began to allow a greater understanding of the physical world than had ever been possible in the past. It was not just that thinking was freed from the concrete limitations of medieval thought, but that a new method of thinking developed beyond those limitations. This thinking could grasp cause and effect relationships and understand the rules behind them. Ideas of relationships could be tested and revised to fit the results. With this, modern thinking was born. Piaget referred to this thinking as formal operations.

Piaget's fourth and last stage of formal operations is a move away from the concrete thinking of the previous stage. A good summary of this stage of the intellect is that the child is essentially able to apply the scientific method, that is, make observations, form generalizations, test the generalizations, and arrive at logical and correct conclusions. For Piaget, an individual in this stage has reached maximum development for our society. Once a person has reached stage four, further intellectual development is only a matter of adding more knowledge.

In his survey of Western history,[49] historian Jacques Barzun reported a handful of basic themes which have characterized the past five centuries of the West. Chief among these are abstraction and analysis, themes he repeatedly uses to describe Western intellectual and scientific developments. It is no accident that the ability to abstract and analyze is essentially the definition of Piaget's stage four thinking. Our rational thinking had no significant presence prior to 1500 C.E. It grew out of the medieval world and shaped the West, and now it dominates the world.

While there are precedents over many centuries, the scientific method only became a hallmark of rationally thinking people in the modern West. It was not part of thought in the ancient world when the Greeks had numerous ideas but rarely experimented to verify them. Medieval thought was dominated by theological concepts that prevented a true assessment of the physical world. It was the uncompromising, pragmatic Western mind that allowed the unfettered blossoming of the intellect using the scientific method.

Lawrence Kohlberg – moral development

Piaget's primary concern was intellectual development, but Lawrence Kohlberg, an American psychologist, focused on moral development.[50,51] Kohlberg found that morality develops through a series of stages similar to those of the intellect, and comes with or follows intellectual development. That is, you have to have sufficient intellectual development to reason morally, but not all people who are sufficiently intellectually developed have learned the appropriate moral principles.

A typical question Kohlberg used in assessing a child's moral development was whether it is right to steal a medicine to save the life of a dying spouse if one could not afford to buy it. Answers include, "just let her (the hypothetical spouse) die and get another one;" that stealing is always wrong; that anything that could be done to save the spouse should be done; and so on. When asked about having to spend time in jail, one child might say that it "wouldn't bother you much to serve a little jail term" but another might report that it would bring great dishonor to them and their family. Like Piaget, the answers Kohlberg received led him to describe a series of stages of moral thinking.

Kohlberg found the morality of children in stage one to be a literal obedience to rules and authority, and avoidance of breaking rules to avoid physical punishment. Doing the right thing means avoiding punishment and conflict with authority. Having a right is confused with being right, and being right implies having power or authority to control others. Punishment automatically follows a bad act, so if you get away with it, it was not a bad act. Moral behavior at this stage is mostly the simple fear of punishment, as opposed to guilt or remorse.

We know little about the psychology of the prehistoric world, but I strongly suspect that it was of a stage one nature. There was probably little, if any, sense of "right" based on fairness or even revenge. If I stole your stone ax it was good, but if you stole mine it was bad. The occurrence of bad events meant that someone had done bad behavior; therefore any misfortune could indicate wrong behavior and create taboos. If someone were struck by lightning while approaching a particular spot, it would be many generations before anyone else would go near there.

Children functioning at stage one morality are unable to pass Piaget's test of logical reciprocity or reversibility, that is, the child does not understand that he is his brother's brother, or that a person facing him has his right hand opposite his own left hand. A stage one child sees bad events as being any event followed by punishment; there is no sense of justice being an equal exchange between two people. If punishment occurs then the behavior must have been bad.

It is of note that, according to the story of Adam and Eve in Genesis, they did not know good and evil until after they ate fruit from the tree of knowledge of good and evil. At that point they were thrown out of the Garden of Eden. Or you could say that they left stage one morality and began stage two.

It is with stage two that the idea of right, morality, and justice become seen as an equal interchange between two parties, such as an equal exchange of favors or of blows. A stage two child might say, "Be good to God and he'll be good to you." These statements summarize much of the law of the ancient world. Hebrew morality was based on a reciprocal agreement, a "covenant," between the Hebrews and God, essentially a promise of worship in return for protection. Socrates described Greek religion as a "business transaction" between man and the Gods; there was no sense of sin, repentance, atonement, purification, or fear of judgment.[52] Much of the worship of various deities in the ancient world involved bargains or deals: here's a nice burnt ox for you, now please let us win this battle. The "eye for an eye" Hebrew morality was probably based on the earlier Babylonian code of Hammurabi with similar laws. This is justice as an equal exchange, "eye for an eye," stage two morality.

Values for stage two children are strongly influenced by social status, so that a higher status person is valued more than a person of lesser status; Hammurabi's code contains similar gradations of punishment that depended on the status of the victim. The fine would be less if you stepped on a slave's toe, as opposed to the toe of someone from a noble family.

In looking back at the ancient world, these cultural events, the code of Hammurabi and the covenant of the Hebrews, are two of the primary markers of the culture of the ancient world. Other law codes followed Hammurabi's, and the covenant between the Hebrews and God was repeated, in a less codified form, throughout the ancient world. All of these were marked by the "fair deal" between people and a god, or between people. It is exactly the hallmark of stage two morality of modern children wherein fairness is an equal exchange. Punishment is seen as a sensible exchange for the offending behavior.

Conscience and morality for the stage two child are strictly matters of fear of punishment and paying the price for transgression, but there is no sense of guilt or remorse. There is no sense of shame. This is demonstrated in a comparison of the Hebrew and Christian scriptures. There is little shame in the former but a great deal in the latter.

A good illustration is the story of David, Bathsheba, and her husband Uriah the Hittite, taken from the Hebrew scriptures.[53] David had sex with Bathsheba, Uriah's wife, and impregnated her. He then had Uriah sent into "the hottest battle" to get rid of him, and sure enough, Uriah was killed. David then added Bathsheba to his harem of wives, and she had his son. But David's misbehavior was pointed out by the prophet Nathan. Nathan told David that his actions had displeased God, and that his son by Bathsheba would die. When the child did become ill, David fasted and "lay all night upon the earth." But once it became clear that the child was dead, David recovered and continued about his business. David never showed shame or guilt. Rather, he paid the price after being caught, and continued as before. There is no indication of continuing remorse, or change in future behavior.

It is also interesting that the record does not reveal any complaints from Bathsheba.

Contrast David with Judas Iscariot, who, according to Matthew, "hanged himself"[54] because of the guilt he felt for betraying Jesus. The same author indicates that Peter denied Jesus three times before the cock crowed, and because of this he "wept bitterly;"[55] Mark adds "And when he thought thereon, he wept."[56] This is a different morality, that of stage three, a morality of guilt and sin, regardless of whether one is caught or not. (I think that the turning point from stage two to stage three morality was the Babylonian captivity of the Hebrews; but Christianity carried this much further.)

David's behavior is exactly parallel to that of Calvin of "Calvin and Hobbes": you do as you will, and if you get caught, you pay the price and feel that it was worth it,[57] and you try not to get caught next time. There is a list of rules that you should not violate, such as the Ten Commandments for David, or don't throw snowballs at Susie for Calvin. You know you'll be punished if you break the rules, and occasionally you do if the temptation is great enough, and if you're caught you accept a fair price for the behavior. There is no sense of internalized guilt, no conscience, no shame. Kohlberg notes a pragmatic assessment of punishment by the stage two child. I would be willing to bet that David felt that his punishment was worth having sex with Bathsheba, just as Calvin would say that his punishment was worth throwing the snowball at Susie; then they would both change the conversation to a new subject, with their transgressions forgotten. David would be eyeing someone else's wife, and Calvin would be thinking about hitting Susie with another snowball. Meanwhile, Judas and Peter would be feeling guilt for years afterward; I could see them both on antidepressant medication and facing years of psychotherapy.

There certainly are modern adults in the West who function as David and Peter; we usually refer to the former as sociopathic, and the latter as neurotic. Every modern person has an ego, but it has a dominant inner child in the first case, and a dominant superego in the second. The ego is there, but it does not have the mastery that the average person's ego does. The former is charming, amoral, and cleverly avoids the wrath of the gods, while the latter has internalized that wrath and carries it around in his chest. Therapy, if possible at all, focuses on increasing ego strength.

As I noted, the Babylonian captivity seems to have had a strong psychological influence on the ancient Hebrews. They developed a more internalized sense of right and wrong, with corresponding morality, as opposed to simply following the Mosaic law to the letter. Judaism after the Babylonian captivity was more solidly monotheistic, actually quite aligned with medieval Christianity. This was a move from the ancient world concept of a separate god for each thing to the medieval view of one god ruling over everything. Each object in the world no longer had its own god or spirit. Because of this the unconscious energy which had been projected to the world as spirits in every object was greatly withdrawn. With this change there was only one god and the world could be seen more as it was, a material thing. This allowed the possibility of a more pragmatic interaction with the world as opposed to dealing with the ruling spirits or gods; it was an early step toward a scientific view of the world, a step that would be honed by centuries of medieval thought.

Toward the end of the ancient world, Romans and Greeks were coming to see their own gods as immoral, a collection of Davids and Calvins; as a result, the status of the Hebrew religion increased significantly in late antiquity. By the time Christianity arrived, Judaism was held in high regard in the ancient world. This esteem collapsed with the revolts in Judea and the Jewish wars against Rome in the early first century, and St. Paul's Christianity provided an attractive alternative without the necessity of circumcision.

Kohlberg's stage three of moral development extends from approximately age ten to thirteen among children in Western countries. Moral behavior is seen as being good or nice, playing the role of a good person, and living up to the expectations of respected people, including parents and family as well as teachers and religious leaders. What actually constitutes being good comes from the values of these people. Rather than the "eye for an eye" reciprocity of stage two, a stage three child feels that you should treat other people as you would like to be treated, as opposed to how they treated you. Punishment is seen as rehabilitation, particularly of the personality and attitude; it is not seen as revenge or paying back a debt. It is only fair to give more to helpless people. The greatest motivator for good behavior is fear of disapproval by the group. The disapproval can be real or imaginary, either producing shame or guilt. These ethics work well when the child is dealing with their family, friends, and social group (teachers, religious leaders) but they are not easily extended outside of those relationships. Kohlberg notes that there is a selfish side of stage three ethics, because the child does not really put himself into the role of the person being helped. What is one person's help may be another's harm, with the excuse "I was only trying to help" covering underlying selfish motives. Kohlberg also notes that a racist can "stretch" what is "nice" to include a great deal of racist behavior.

When this description of stage three morality is considered historically, it is evident that it is a summary of the morality which came with Christianity, specifically medieval Christianity. While this thinking has its origins in the stricter values that appeared in the Hebrew religion after the Babylonian captivity, there is no doubt that Christianity took the ball and ran with it much further and faster than its mother religion could have ever imagined. Christianity is built on a foundation of internalized guilt and shame which can only be dealt with by "being good." The specific commandment "thou shalt not commit adultery" of the Hebrew scriptures became the general moral code of "thou shalt not lust" of the Christians.

But the ideal of "being good" to others is typically reserved for those in the group, with much less desirable treatment given to those outside of the community. Christianity has allowed and even encouraged vicious behavior to be visited on those outside of the group, including pogroms, slavery, and mass murder of those considered heretics, as long as the believer maintained the appearance of "being good" in the community of believers. The medieval church executed any number of heretics, and Jewish people were frequent Christian targets. Slaveholders were considered solid citizens of the American South before 1865.

What stage three morality accomplished was to provide a basic, internalized sense of right and wrong, at least as far as the greater family, the community of believers, the people of a like faith. Before, David tried to get away with "bad" behavior, and he would not have any regret over his actions except that he was caught and punished. Contrast that with Judas Iscariot and Peter; they did not have to be caught for the guilt to start. While this guilt has, for the most part, only arisen when the believer did wrong to someone in their own group or faith, nevertheless, it is an internalized sense of right and wrong, a superior development over simply avoiding punishment in stage two.

Let there be no doubt about what early stage three morality was up against, historically speaking. When we look back now, we think that we could behave quite well with the Ten Commandments of the Hebrews, and all of the guilt and shame introduced by Christianity would not have been necessary. Again, this is the error of modern people assuming that people of two or three thousand years ago thought as we do; it ignores the fact that modern Western people have undergone 2,000 years of work on impulse control. The fine points of history, typically ignored, present a more accurate picture. It was not extraordinarily unusual for a new male convert to Christianity to castrate himself; Origen, one of the more influential of the early church fathers, did so, to avoid temptations of the flesh.[58] Origen's act was apparently not that unusual for the time; Saint Matthew refers to those who "have made themselves eunuchs for the kingdom of heaven's sake."[59] To understand this behavior, you must think of David's morality, of Calvin, and the fact that the ancient world was a flood, a deluge, of impulses, sexuality, and aggression. There were gods for the impulses, including Ares or Mars for aggression and Aphrodite or Venus for sexuality. Sex in ancient Rome was a major industry, and in an ordinary Roman town sex with a prostitute cost about as much as a loaf of bread.[60] Augustine, another early church father, prayed for chastity, "but not yet," and apparently had a significant problem with controlling his lust. Galen, a second century Greek physician, saw passions as diseases of the soul.[61] Saint Paul complained of a "thorn in the flesh."[62] According to Saint Matthew, if your right eye should offend you, then "pluck it out"[63] and if your right hand offends you, then "cut it off;"[64] that's a pretty intense way to get control.

There is a certain desperate yet determined quality to these early attempts at learning self-control. It should be obvious that it was a huge problem of the times, similar to the graven images in an earlier era. Controlling the impulses was an almost impossible task, one with major religious overtones. Maybe the best analogy for our time is the desperate desire of an addict for narcotics.

The changes which would mark the end of the ancient world and the beginning of the medieval world were already present before the arrival of Christianity. Pagan philosophies somewhat in line with Christian doctrine were present in late antiquity, and served to lay a foundation for the coming of Christianity. Epicureanism taught that one should behave so as to have a pleasant life and that one should not do harmful or wrong things. Stoicism emphasized virtue and overcoming emotions, and saw passions as destructive; it was important to care for one's soul and live according to divine will. Cynicism stressed virtue, morality, and freedom from desire. And even Skepticism's arguments against reasoning and rationality helped prepare the way for the coming age of faith. The Isis cult, which had been present in Egypt for hundreds of years, came to Rome in the late second century B.C.E. The religion featured a personal relationship with the goddess as opposed to the communal effects of the more distant traditional Roman gods. Her husband, Osiris, died and was born again, suggesting a new life after death for the believer.[65] These philosophies reflected the beginnings of stage three medieval culture well before Christianity was born, and indicate that the psychology necessary for Christianity was already developing hundreds of years earlier, similar to the gradual growth of the new psychology over recent centuries of our own era.

It is important to emphasize again and again the fact that our forebears did not think like we do. We can deal with graven images without breaking down and worshiping them. We can go to the beach with scantily clad members of the opposite sex and not lose control. We assume that everyone throughout history has been the same as us, and we don't understand why, for example, the ancient Hebrews kept worshiping idols when they were repeatedly told not to, or why some people feel women should wear clothing that completely covers them.

The values of Kohlberg's stage three of moral development are most consistent with medieval Christianity. His stage four morality is much more in accord with the values of Protestantism and the modern West.

I should also note that Kohlberg felt that most American adults were in developmental stages three and four, implying that these stages may also describe end-stage adult morality, as opposed to earlier developmental stages that children pass through.

Stage four for Kohlberg is a law-and-order maintaining orientation. Doing the right thing means doing one's duty and upholding the law and the social order. Duty includes helping maintain the present order. The moral perspective is the establishment, and the establishment defines rules and one's role in life. Maintaining one's honor with the establishment is of primary importance. Particular roles are given additional rights; at this stage, a general, a politician, a physician, or even a husband expect and receive special rights. Punishment is seen as paying a debt to society. For stage four, morality is a matter of defending the establishment against its enemies. Hostility and punitiveness toward dissidents, criminals, and enemies both feed on and feed respect for law, nation and God. This leads to a "love it or leave" attitude toward those trying to "change the system" and an imperialistic attitude toward other countries.

If Kohlberg's stage four morality seems familiar to you, it should. It is essentially the morality of the Western world for the past 500 years. It is the emphasis on the nation-state as opposed to the society of believers of the medieval world, or the clan and city-state of the ancient world. It is the morality of rank and status, with royalty over the upper classes, the upper classes over the lower classes, and the lower classes over the riffraff, all of whom are over non-Europeans. "God and country" are identified as one. As Douglas MacArthur put it, "duty, honor, country."

You don't read about the ancient Hebrews doing their duty. They did what was necessary to keep God off their backs. They repeatedly misbehaved and they were repeatedly punished. (Living on real estate that was on a main route between Asia and Africa ensured frequent armed attention from foreigners, but they felt it was God punishing them specifically.) The ancient Christians did not speak of duty, but rather of faith. A modern person can, after the fact, interpret the attitude of the ancient Hebrews or the early Christians as duty, but that is a modern view. For ancient Christians it was an act of faith, of belief. They believed that they were taken into heaven upon death, virtually an act of magic, and this allowed them to face their demise willingly. Duty does not enter into group psychology in a major way until the rise of the nation-state, a relatively recent concept, an idea which has developed only over the past few hundred years with the modern West.

The ancients would fight to the death to defend their city or clan, but you do not read about them lining up and marching into almost certain death, as did Europeans in World War I, when untold thousands of soldiers marched into machine-gun fire. The identifying of God with country has made the horrific wars of the Western world possible, along with national exploitation of non-Western people. The medieval world fought wars of faith, and the ancient world fought wars to get loot and slaves. It is only the modern West that has fought battles solely for the expansion and preservation of the state. A medieval person would not understand a national war; the pope was the pope, regardless of who was king, and kings squabbling over kingdoms were only something to avoid; taxes would be paid regardless of who was king.

For Piaget, development is a maturation of the intellect, and for Kohlberg development is a maturation of morality. For our third author, Jane Loevinger, development involves the entire conscious mind.[66] She saw the mind as becoming more and more competent through its experiences over time, and these changes take place in a series of stages. These stages are essentially the same as those outlined by Piaget and Kohlberg.

Jane Loevinger – personality development

Loevinger calls her first stage the Symbiotic Stage, because the child does not see itself as a separate being from its mother. Development in this stage is a matter of the very young child learning to differentiate itself from its surroundings, that is, what is "me" and what isn't. The child learns that there is a stable world of objects outside of itself. As an example, a child in this stage learns to keep searching for a hidden object because the child has learned that the object will continue to exist even though it is not in sight, as when playing peekaboo.

Stage two is the Impulsive Stage. It is during this time that the child's impulses help in forming a separate identity. The child comes to realize that it is a being separate from its mother. Loevinger points out that learning to say "No!" is probably key to the transition from stage one to stage two. (Think of the child in the proverbial "terrible twos" screaming "No!" to his mother as she attempts to usher him out of the candy isle of a store.) At the same time, the child is gradually learning control over its impulses through fear of retaliation. There is no differentiation between the impulse and acting on the impulse. Relationships with others are dependent and exploitative.

Children at this age are dominated by their impulses, particularly aggressive and sexual impulses. They feel ruled by their impulses. There are many impulses, including the impulse to eat, to urinate, to defecate, and so on, but anger and sexuality are the most potent. The anger and rage of a stage two child is well known, but there is also significant sexuality during this stage, including "playing doctor," genital touching, and masturbation. There is a reason that the ancients had specific gods for aggression and sexuality, as the Romans' Mars and Venus. For an ancient Greek, any unexplained departure from normal routine was considered to be the work of the gods.[67] Plato described men as being puppets of the gods.[68]

By the second half of stage two, the child has learned that impulses do not necessarily lead to action so that behavior may be controlled, if only briefly. "Why?" is a keyword at this time, showing the learning of connection between cause and event, or impulse and action. Behavior is opportunistic and only controlled by the child's fear of getting caught. Getting caught means the behavior was wrong, so the rule is "Don't get caught." If caught, the child attempts to shift blame to someone else, and if the child should accept responsibility for the misdeed, he is likely to blame it on some part of himself, as "My hand took it." Loevinger feels that externalization of responsibility may explain the imaginary childhood companions that appear at this stage. Relations with others are manipulative and exploitative, and the child is largely concerned with self-protection, advantage, and control.

Loevinger's description of stage two fits with the psychology of the ancient world. The child comes to separate itself from its mother in this stage, primarily through the push of its impulses. Much of the mythology of the ancient world involved male deities coming to dominate female deities. The study of ancient myths makes it clear that the female deities preexisted the male deities who later displaced them. Early Babylonian mythology tells of a fierce and dominant mother deity who was killed by the male hero god Marduk. He divided her into two parts, making heaven and earth with them. These same themes are carried directly into Hebrew mythology with Yahweh dividing the firmament above from the waters below. Virtually all mythology from the ancient world included an earlier mother goddess. (The ancient Hebrews had a mother goddess as well, and we will get to her in time.)

Behavior in the ancient world was certainly opportunistic, and King David serves as a good example. There was no sense of shame or guilt, but only fear of being caught for his deeds. A Roman might have felt shame in the sense of disgrace or dishonor and committed suicide, but there is no evidence of a sense of sin.

An adult fixated in the second half of stage two would be opportunistic, deceptive, and manipulative. Life would be, essentially, opportunistic hedonism. Work would be irksome. My guess is that many criminals are dominated by level two thinking. One occasionally reads of gang members finding salvation in religion, which is a conversion that pushes them into stage three. With this new-found belief, the personality has a foundation on which to develop and build a new stage. This is the same step the ancient Hebrews made after the Babylonian captivity, and the entire ancient world made with the introduction of Christianity. This is the move to developmental stage three.

For Loevinger, stage three is the Conformist Stage, when the child begins to identify personal welfare with group welfare, the group being the family, a peer group or other group which can be trusted (as a religious group). The child internalizes both the group's rules and a need to conform to those rules. Guilt is felt when the rules are broken. The child gains control by conforming to the external rules, and experiences shame or guilt with failure to do so. Social acceptability by the group is critical to a child in this stage, and behavior centers on superficial niceness and a need to conform. The rules are upheld simply because they are the rules of the group. Impulse control is usually rigorous. The conformity is characterized by a lack of logical justification. ("I believe because it is absurd" is attributed to Tertullian, another of the early Christian church fathers.) A person in this stage is well aware of differences between one's own group and outsiders, but much less aware of differences between individuals in the group. There is trust and acceptance for people in the group, but not for outsiders or members of other groups. Rules of the group are seen as what is normal, so that something unusual, such as odd clothing, may be seen as immoral. These individuals tend toward strong sex role stereotypes.

The child becomes much more modest in stage three. Sexual behavior and sex play may continue, but hidden. There is a growing realization that certain activities are not public and are to be hidden.

As the medieval world replaced the ancient world, public baths, latrines, and brothels became private. The frank sexuality of the Hebrew Scriptures, like King David's behavior, was put in the closet in the Christian Scriptures. In contrast to the sexuality of the Hebrew Scriptures, the Christian Scriptures became sanitized. The medieval world needed a replacement for the Venus of the ancient world, and Mary Magdalene was adapted to fill the void. We are told virtually nothing about Mary Magdalene in the Bible, except that Jesus "cast seven devils"[69] out of her. Nothing is stated about the nature of these devils; for all we know, she had a bad stammer, or maybe she was lame. But medieval mythology grew up around her, declaring her to be a prostitute reformed by the removal of her "devils." Venus was transformed into a repentant prostitute to suit the medieval mind-set.

It is notable that Loevinger states that, as stage three progresses, the individual becomes more self-aware and more aware that the ideals of the group are not being met, producing conflict which leads to stage four. Translated into a historical context, individuals became more and more aware that the medieval church was not living up to its ideals, and the conflict produced the Protestant Reformation, a turning point in the establishment of stage four society.

Loevinger's fourth stage is the Conscientious Stage, in which a person lives under self-evaluated standards established through self-criticism. Personal responsibility, self-respect, and achievement are emphasized. The individual is the source of his or her own destiny. Work is seen as a chance to achieve. Strong impulse control remains characteristic, as with stage three. Thinking tends to be in terms of polar opposites. The second half of stage four involves an increased sense of individuality. This is the psychology that developed in the West during the past five centuries.

Summary of development

The three principal authors in developmental psychology have described consistent behaviors in four basic stages. All three authors described a hierarchical system of developmental stages. The stages must be taken in sequences and stages may not be skipped. Each stage has its own characteristic behavior and psychology. A person may be between stages and show characteristics of two stages, the one they are leaving and the one they are developing into. Each stage represents a higher level of development, providing the person with greater freedom and flexibility than was available at the previous stage. Maturity is reached when the individual reaches the level of their society. Development is a product of interaction between the individual and the group, and no one develops significantly beyond the group as interaction with the group is required for development.

Historical development and child development proceed through similar stages. For a child, the differences between the developmental stages are so subtle that they may not be noticed. But when these subtle differences are multiplied by millions of people, they set the tone for the society.

There are remains of each earlier stage in the backgrounds of each individual. A part of us is a prehistoric hunter-gatherer, a Greek pagan, and a medieval believer, and they all serve as the foundation structure for the modern Western mind.

Individual and historical development follow the same sequence, implying that the sequence is archetypal, that is, an intrinsic factor of the mind. Archetypes will be discussed further in chapter 12, but a brief explanation is due here. An archetype is an instinctual pattern, one of the basic structures of the mind. We do not see archetypes, but we see their symbols; the symbol of the Madonna may represent the archetype of mothering.

Developmental psychology has not provided any rationale for the behavior exhibited in the stages. Developmental texts present the stages as a series of odd and unrelated behaviors with no unifying principle. In contrast, development as an archetypal process provides a rational explanation for the unique qualities of each of the developmental stages and their sequence. Without an underlying archetypal process, development is only a series of unrelated behavior patterns. With the archetypal sequence, a logical and orderly pattern becomes apparent.

The next six chapters fill out the behavior associated with the first four stages of development. This will give a sense of the psychology behind the behavior, including the symbols and archetypes associated with each stage. The psychological history of who we have been leads to understanding who we are becoming.

CHAPTER VI

Stage One and the Prehistoric World

The world of the mother

Because the same pattern shapes both individual and historical development, insight into one sheds light on the other. The developmental pattern may be viewed in three areas: a case history of Western people, a case history of an individual, or the development of children in general. The similarities between historical eras and individual development stages show the unique psychology underlying each stage. We begin with stage one.

A newborn begins developmental stage one with minimal conscious awareness and ends the stage with awareness that it is an entity separate from its mother. During this span it is totally dominated by its physical needs, and it is completely dependent on its mother to have those needs met. The child "knows" that it needs certain things including food and comfort, as well as relief from gas, cold, and dirty diapers. It also "knows" that it can only express distress in an effort to get these needs met. The mother-child relationship is central to stage one. It is in this setting that the infant gradually learns that it is a being separate from the seemingly all-powerful mother.

All of stage one occurs before the child's brain has developed the mechanisms necessary to store long-term memories. Because of this the events and occurrences that take place during stage one usually do not become memories subject to recall.

Although the memories of specific events are not saved, the emotional climate of the mother-child relationship does remain. It continues as the person's foundation, their basic orientation toward life, which colors all of that individual's experiences throughout the rest of their life. It is during this time that the infant learns that it is accepted and loved, or that it is merely accepted, or that it is an unwanted presence. That basic orientation permeates all of the individual's later experiences and interactions. The child that is loved and cherished sees the world, and is treated by the world, in a far different manner than the child that is not. One knows that its needs will somehow be met, that the world is essentially a positive place, and that it has value; the other sees the world far differently. This is a fundamental experience for the infant in stage one.

The experiences of this stage remain with the maturing individual, but they are not conscious; they form the basis of the unconscious part of the mind. Jung referred to this as the personal unconscious, so naming it because much of the material involved is related to one's own personal experiences. It mostly contains the shadow so that it is almost identical to the shadow.[70] Jung differentiated the personal unconscious from an even lower level, the collective unconscious.[71]

The personal unconscious serves as the foundation for all subsequent development of the personality. It remains with us throughout life, providing the same buffer to reality that our mothers gave us as infants. It serves as the "basement" of the personality, where material unacceptable to the conscious mind may be stored, and where symbols from the underlying collective unconscious may be transferred to the conscious mind through dreams. As development proceeds, it will hold repressed and forgotten material, perceptions missed by consciousness, material just coming into conscious awareness, shadow material, and other content not ready for the conscious mind; all of these are of a personal nature.[72]

The developmental process throughout this stage is the child learning that it is not a part of the mother, that the child and the mother are two independent beings. The stage ends as the child realizes that it and the mother are separate beings. This awareness is the true beginning of the individual conscious mind; the child becomes truly born from the mother as stage one ends. It is still dependent on the mother, but it is now aware it is a being separate from its mother.

For children in stage one, objects seem to have a life and a will of their own. Morality is avoiding punishment; if you get away with something, then it was not bad. Consciousness is passive and unfocused.

The historical parallel with stage one of individual development is the prehistoric world. Unfortunately, because it is prehistoric, we have no real history of that time and only a very few relics. But we do have a great deal of information about relatively primitive people, and by comparing that with archaeological findings, we have a good idea of the lifestyles of our stage one prehistoric ancestors. They most likely lived in small, extended family hunter-gatherer groups which may have been loosely affiliated with other similar groups. They were probably unassuming people who worked actively to preserve social equality. All food was shared within the group; it was considered wrong to hoard food or even store food. They were slow to anger, and worked to suppress violence. Homicide occurred, but was not socially acceptable; the offender might be forced out of the group. A truly dangerous person might be executed by other group members or by his family.[73]

In *Early Human Kinship Was Matrilineal*, anthropologist Chris Knight reviewed the classical anthropological literature and concluded that the evidence indicates that kinship of early human societies was matrilineal. Early human groups, hunters and gatherers, were probably organized around the mothers and their offspring, that is, grandmothers, mothers, and daughters. Most likely, daughters stayed with mothers, acquiring husbands from other groups. "Bride-service" by the bridegroom, typically providing food to the bride's family, is a fundamental economic transaction in hunter-gatherer groups; the bridegroom would bind himself to the female core of the group he was marrying into. The human exodus out of Africa, which would populate the globe, is confirmation of the matrilineal organization of early societies; the only way early humans could have prospered sufficiently to have generated the greatly increased population required to exit Africa was with very good childcare. And the only way such childcare would have been available was in a matrilineal society where mothers could rely on their own male relatives to protect them from male suitors, by having multiple male suitors, and by having grandmothers caring for their descendants. These requirements would not have been met in a patrilineal society.[74]

Marija Gimbutas and Old Europe

Solid archaeological evidence for matrilineal social organization in the prehistoric world is scant. Years ago, when I began pursuing this subject, the assumption was that the prehistoric world was an earlier version of the ancient world, masculine-dominated and warring, but without writing or cities. This began to change when archaeologist Marija Gimbutas published *The Goddesses and Gods of Old Europe*[75] in 1982, followed by *The Language of the Goddess*[76] in 1989, *The Civilization of the Goddess*[77] in 1991, and *The Living Goddesses* in 1999.[78] She suggested that, beginning in approximately 6500 B.C.E. and continuing for another 3,000 years, the culture of an area of eastern Europe was predominantly woman-centered. She indirectly indicated that matrilineal societies preceded all patrilineal ones.

There have been challenges to her work, as I discuss below. But my overall assessment is that, at the very least, her central themes are valid. Fundamentally, Gimbutas suggests that the culture of prehistory was matrilineal, and hence quite different from the ancient world that replaced it. This is consistent with anthropological data, ethnological data, mythology, and archaeological data.

Gimbutas, using her own work as an archaeologist as well as that of others in her field, studied sites and findings in what is now eastern Europe. She proposed that these findings indicated a widespread culture in an area she called the civilization of Old Europe, a culture that existed from approximately 6500 to 3500 B.C.E. She described this as a civilization because of the artwork, population centers, architecture, metal work, sacred script, and trade connections that were present. The civilization was gynocentric, that is, mother and woman-centered. The social order was probably matrilineal although there remains no suggestion that either sex was subservient to the other. The societies were probably organized around a community temple and were guided by a priestess. Time was perceived as cyclical and nonlinear, that is, the seasons followed one after another without emphasis on years passing. Village sites were not selected for ease of defense or fortification, and there is no evidence of weapons being used against other humans. Defensive structures only appear in the end of the era as it was being destroyed by invaders. Gimbutas found that the religion was that of the Goddess, that is, some form of a Goddess cult, in her roles as Giver-of-Life, Wielder-of-Death, and Regeneratrix. Gimbutas found no representations of a father god from that age.

According to Gimbutas, this civilization was destroyed by invading warriors from the east, horsemen armed with spears, bows and arrows, and long knives. These people had already transitioned from a matrilineal culture to a patrilineal one earlier. They worshiped male warrior deities rather than a goddess.

Gimbutas made her claim for only one area of Europe, and for only one relatively brief period of time. But the idea that follows from this is that there was a matrilineal period of prehistory that preceded all later patrilineal societies, ending at different times in different places. That is saying a great deal, and the archaeological evidence is scant and subject to interpretation. There have been criticisms of Dr. Gimbutas's work, suggesting that she may have over-interpreted the artifacts, that there never was a single mother goddess or fertility goddess, and that there were early male gods as well. *Ancient Goddesses*[79] is an inquiry into the problem.

We do know that there were numerous goddesses in the ancient world, more than one might realize. Mythology indicates that most of the goddesses of the ancient world existed before their male counterparts.[80] It is also clear that there was never one specific mother goddess in the prehistoric world in the same sense that there is the single character Jesus in Christianity. There never was a single cult of the mother goddess like we have the Roman Catholic Church. The idea of a mother goddess or great goddess existing before the ancient world is more complex, and it probably began quite early in prehistory. It probably consisted of many variations of what we call the Great Goddess, as opposed to one specific deity.

The problem with drawing conclusions from archaeology is that it depends on the artifacts it finds. By the time humans developed the technology required to make goddess artifacts durable enough to last until excavation by modern archaeologists, the era of the Great Goddess was ending. The end of the prehistoric world, and hence the end of the world of the Great Goddess, is usually held to be the establishment of the first city-states, as Sumer. But from a psychological perspective, the need for, organization of, and construction of the city-states required that developmental level two thinking (the psychology of the ancient world) was already established in a number of individuals. The city-states were the product of, and not cause of, level two culture and the end of the age of the Great Goddess. I suspect that during this time leaders were functioning in level two and worshiping male deities or a combination of male and older female deities, while the masses of people still clung to goddess worship. Male deities had already begun their rise to power by that point, at least among the ruling elite, and those deities were portrayed by the elite as being founders of the civilizations. Those male deities represented the new level two thinking which was beginning to dominate culture. The level two will to achieve, master, conquer, control, and build is celebrated in the ruins of these ancient civilizations which we can still visit today. The age of the Great Goddess in her own right was already well over when these civilizations began.

The age of the Great Goddess was the huge time span before masculine gods arose, stretching back 100,000 or possibly 200,000 years to the time the earliest modern humans appeared. Her development would have been gradual and subtle. Most artifacts representing her would have been primitive and unlikely to survive, as all physical evidence of human behavior during this time is rare.

It was probably women who first conceived the idea of some greater being as a source of hope and possible help. Women were directly concerned with the great mysteries of life, including fears of death during childbirth, fears of not becoming pregnant and not replacing children who frequently died early; the mystery of menstruation and its similarity to the moon's cycles; the mystery of lactation and feeding infants. These hopes and fears would have been material for meditation over days and months, as in pregnancy, as opposed to sudden dangers for men hunting and gathering. Women probably first looked to their own mother or the older women in the clan for solace. Grandmothers and older wise women were remembered, and their lore was passed down from generation to generation. The compassion of their own mothers was remembered and drawn on in periods of fear and despair. That mother-figure tie would have been at least as powerful as the West's tie to a father-figure god during the past 2,000 years. The spirit of the relationship between daughter, mother, and grandmother developed in untold numbers of clans over a huge time span into forms of a Great Goddess figure. Over time, the clan women would refer to the idea by name, gradually leading to imaginary embodiment and eventual spiritualization and deification of the idea. At some point these clan goddesses may have been made manifest in tangible objects, as carvings or clay figurines, which archaeologists excavate today. But by that time, man's lore, as working metal, firing clay, and making pottery molds, had already begun its climb to dominance, setting the stage for the ancient world, so that the age of the Great Goddess was almost over. The newer masculine lore would have led to newer male gods appearing near the end of the prehistoric world.

There would have been considerable variation in forms of the Great Goddess during prehistory. Each clan would have its own lore and variation, but the underlying motif would have been the archetype of the great mother. Her manifestations were many and varied and they were not seen as being different examples of the same goddess. Even by the time of the ancient world, each family and each city had its own deities. In ancient Greece, one city's Hera was not the same as another city's Hera; only philosophers realized that they were the same. In Naples, Italy, as late as 1864, "each quarter of the city has its Madonna," with insults toward and fights about a neighboring quarter's Madonna.[81] From a psychological and mythological perspective, there is no evidence that there was one specific Great Goddess figure in the prehistoric world, but there were many variations of her.

The physical evidence of events of this time span is quite limited. There are a number of early female figurines, but relatively few male ones, and we know the importance of "graven images" for the early

81

developmental levels. There are myths of the ancient world that tell of male gods replacing or marrying preexisting goddesses. For example, early in the ancient world, the older Sumerian mother goddess Tiamat was slain by the male deity Marduk; by the end of the ancient world the newer male deities "married" the older female deities. Among primitive people, it was not unusual for the mother's brother to be more important to the child than the father, a suggestion of an earlier matrilineal orientation.

In the developmental model, the first developmental stage is characterized by the child's dependent relationship with the mother; the relationship to the father principle has not formed at that time. The psychological and mythological indications are that the prehistoric world was dominated by various goddess forms, all manifestations of the Great Mother archetype. I can't recall having read any archaeological work which indicated that male images were found at a lower level in a dig (that is, from an earlier age) than female images; the reverse always seems to be the case when both are found.

Some of the oldest existing human images are from the late Stone Age (10,000 to 50,000 years ago), including the "Venus" figurines, most notably the famed Venus of Willendorf. Most of the human images from that time are females.[82] I do not believe that to be a coincidence, and it tends to confirm the concept that the earliest ideas of the deity in human form were female. These objects would have been considered to be powerful talismans representing goddesses we would identify as great mother goddesses. I have emphasized the Hebrew bans against graven images and the reasons behind those bans. We today cannot really conceive of the power those objects held because of the extraordinary strength of the Western mind. The modern conscious mind is enormously stronger and more competent than that of our prehistoric forebears. They did not have the immunity to the allure and power of images that we do.

I should say that modern people are fairly immune, but not completely. More than once I have heard women complain that the man to whom they were speaking, "only looked at my breasts and not my face." There are many people today who insist that women remain completely covered because male conscious thinking is not strong enough to resist the lure of the feminine. This is because the pull of the feminine form still casts a powerful spell on the (somewhat) civilized male. Think of the strength of that pull to prehistoric males—it would be seen as irresistible and magic. Thousands of years of civilization have transformed the unadulterated instinct of lust into civilized love with lust secondary. Prehistoric males did not have that control, and saw women and the Goddess as having an uncanny power over them. Add to that the mysteries of menstruation and fertility. Having children was a life and death matter; without reproduction, there would be no children to help procure food and shelter, and the clan would die out. The Goddess ruled their lives through lust, fertility, and death. She was all-powerful.

Gimbutas points out three aspects of the Goddess of the ancient world: Regeneratrix, Giver-of-Life, and Wielder-of-Death. You might think of them as the maiden, the mother, and the crone. The maiden aspect of the Goddess was sexual and represented the power of sexual attraction, as well as the potentiality of anything to be fertilized leading to the birth of something new. The power of sexuality and lust have been civilized somewhat with development; that was not the case thousands of years ago. Even today there are people who believe that sexual intercourse with a virgin might cure disease.[83]

The mother aspect of the Goddess gave life through her fertility; without her influence, animals would not reproduce, crops would wither, and children would not be born. These were life-threatening possibilities for primitive people, while we are usually insulated from these fears by our understanding of science. Lastly, the crone, whom we know as the witch, embodied the deadly side of the Goddess. We have overcome much of our horror and fear of death, of disease, of the unknown, and of the dark; early people did not have the strength of conscious thinking that we do, and they were terrified by the unknown. They did not have modern medicine to stand in the way of disease.

Perhaps you can begin to feel the power goddess images held if you think of the time of the greatest horror in your life, the time of your worst fear, your strongest experience of hunger, the moment of your greatest sexual attraction, and add to that a miraculous healing power, a cornucopia of food for a feast, the fear of starvation, and sum all that into one figurine.

The dark side of the Goddess seems remote from our civilized lives, but I have long suspected that horrible and ghoulish crimes, including serial murders, cannibalism, grotesque mutilations, and sadistic torture, stem from impairment in the first developmental level. We do not understand this class of criminal, and we do not know what to do with them except to execute them or permanently isolate them from society. But these behaviors fit with the darkest side of the Great Goddess archetype. For the infant, as for primitive people, there is an awareness of an arbitrary and terrible power of the mother, be she the personal mother or the Great Goddess. There may be great love for her if she is perceived as bountiful. But there may also be great hate and fear based on the terror that the mother can withhold and thereby destroy. A full sense of the archetype of the Great Goddess includes the extremes of both ghoulish horror and loving bounty, combined with sexual attraction and repulsion.

The Great Goddess was associated with fertility, motherhood, and death, but that is not a complete picture. Ishtar, an Assyrian and Babylonian goddess, ruled sex and fertility, but she also ruled war. It is probably accurate to say that, before the masculine gods became dominant, virtually every aspect of life was associated with some goddess, and all these goddesses represented some facet of the Great Goddess archetype. As the ancient world replaced the prehistoric world, some of the goddesses would have been combined into major roles, as Hera became queen of the Greek gods. Some would have remained separate to represent specific aspects of the goddess, as Demeter was goddess of fertility and Hestia was goddess of the hearth. The arts considered masculine, such as war and metalworking, were assigned to male deities. Gimbutas traces the paths of a number of the old goddesses as they were transformed into their ancient world incarnations in *The Living Goddesses*.

It is not unreasonable to think that some male mythological figures may have been a part of the earlier years of humanity, perhaps as heroic hunters such as the much later Gilgamesh, a Sumerian hero and demigod.[84] But the presence of male figures would not mean that the basic religious tone was masculine. Mary has been dominant for almost 2,000 years of Catholic Christianity, yet it is a masculine religion. In all likelihood, it was women who started the process of religious development, modeled after their own relationships with their mothers. That relationship is the dominant archetype of the first developmental stage, and it probably shaped the organization of prehistoric societies. It is a reasonable hypothesis that the deity of the prehistoric world was some variation of the Great Goddess, but she would have been seen in many forms by the people of the time.

The archaeology of the Hebrews before the Babylonian captivity provides another example of the replacement of the goddess. Archaeologist William Dever explores the subject in *Did God Have a Wife?*[85] He notes that numerous goddess images have been found in the archaeology of ancient Israel, predominantly dating from before the Babylonian invasion and captivity in the sixth century B.C.E. He contrasts the "book" religion of Yahweh with the "folk" religion of Asherah, a female deity. It is his finding that Asherah was the dominant deity of most people of the time, with the worship of Yahweh limited to the few literate people and the ruling elite in the main urban areas. The many rural, illiterate people had their shrines to Asherah and possibly other gods as well; the few urban, literate people had their temple of Yahweh. This changed after the Babylonian captivity, and Asherah, who was probably once a consort of Yahweh, was almost completely written out of the revised scriptures. Dever points out how often those revised scriptures contain references to the priests of Yahweh condemning Asherah worship; she must have been extremely popular to merit such frequent condemnations. She became a Biblical footnote with the passage of centuries. It is not just that the Yahweh cult won out over the Asherah cult after they had coexisted for centuries. Rather, she began to lose status when a new kind of thinking became dominant, men's thinking, mixing copper with tin to make bronze, making chariots, making iron, and making war. I suspect that Asherah is actually much older than Yahweh.

Savina Teubal's observations support the idea that goddesses had a significant presence among the ancient Hebrews before the Babylonian captivity. She suggests that at least three of the matriarchs of the Jewish people, Sarah, Rebecca, and Rachel, were actually priestesses of, or avatars of, some form of a goddess. She feels they lived during the ending of the world of the goddess, as Abraham and Isaac lived in the beginning of the patriarchal world of Yahweh.[86]

Gimbutas felt that people in the Great Mother culture were not warlike, and that war came with the rise of the male deities. Studies of our evolutionary and cultural roots in *War, Peace, and Human Nature*[87] confirm this. The archaeological evidence, the studies of hunter-gatherer societies existing in modern times, and the studies of the behavior of our closest animal relatives, chimpanzees and bonobos, suggest that early humans were egalitarian and relatively peaceful. Chimpanzees do kill chimpanzees from other troops on occasion, but they do not make war on other troops. Bonobos rarely kill one another. There are killings in human hunter-gatherer groups, but they are rare, often the result of the incursion of modern society. All the evidence indicates that our prehistoric ancestors did not conduct war; they had occasional murders, but they probably tended to restraint and reconciliation rather than aggression. On the whole they were most likely less violent than people in the modern West.

There are few remaining hunter-gatherer people left and most have been tainted by outside society. One of these is the San (Bushmen) of the Kalahari region of Africa, now mostly forced onto settlements. They are described as having a "fiercely" egalitarian society. Decisions are made by consensus rather than by authority. Food is not stored; what is found is eaten on a daily basis. Cooperative networks are maintained by affection and equality. Private property is limited to what one can easily carry. Encouraging permanent settlement and work are difficult because they have little interest in the rewards of our society, money and material items, aside from getting money for alcohol.[88]

In his article on early human kinship, Chris Knight notes that the idea that primitive tribes were matrilineal had been rejected in the last century due to—essentially—political reasons. He reports that the matrilineal view did not fit the zeitgeist of the time, and was rejected, despite a preponderance of supporting evidence.[89] I hope that the work of Dr. Gimbutas has not been rejected for similar reasons, but as is clear from our daily politics, there is more than a little resistance to the idea of male-female equality, much less the idea that the feminine was once dominant in any way.

Archaeologist David Anthony both supports and disparages Gimbutas, and the disparagement is apparently due to her suggestion of sexual equality in the prehistoric world. In his book *The Horse, The Wheel, and Language*, he basically supports her scenario of the ending of Old Europe.[90] The book details his work in light of findings of Russian archaeology. The central concept is that a group of people living just north of the Black and Caspian Seas over 8,000 years ago is the source of most of European languages, as well as the languages of India and Iran; they are the very earliest beginnings of our culture. Anthony refers to these people as the Proto-Indo-Europeans; they were once termed Aryans.[91] Their culture began when they learned to domesticate horses, first for food and later for transportation. Once they began to ride, raiding began, and Anthony admits that those raids may have brought about the end of Old Europe, as Gimbutas contended, although he notes that other factors may have been involved as well.

But Anthony has a problem with Dr. Gimbutas' portrait of Old Europe. He disparagingly refers to it as "a utopian prehistoric world of feminine peace and beauty"[92] and a "world of egalitarian peace and beauty."[93] Dr. Anthony has failed to grasp the significance of the difference between the culture of Old Europe and that of the raiding Proto-Indo-Europeans. Raids made by would-be heroes striking out to murder and loot are the early form of the warfare described in Homer's Iliad. Raiding by a patriarchal clan denotes early level two behavior, and in all likelihood, Old Europeans were late level one people, former hunter-gatherers who had settled into permanent agricultural situations. We know that such people were typically egalitarian, and we know that they typically did not conduct violence as a group. They would have been easy prey for the raiders. Dr. Anthony has entirely missed the reason the Proto-Indo-Europeans were able to go on to dominate most of Europe, India, and Iran: they were developmentally ahead of the people they conquered, and were thereby easily able to subdue them. Dr. Anthony's need to trivialize and disparage Dr. Gimbutas has caused him to miss this vital point.

On the other hand, Dr. Anthony's remark that Old Europe was a "world of egalitarian peace and beauty" hits close to the mark. It may have been a world of minimal conflict, but there was minimal progress as well. It did not produce the great cultures, the religions, the laws, or the thinkers that the ancient world did. Probably the only progress was in moving from gathering and hunting to settled agriculture. The angry, aggressive masculine push typical of level two was not present, and millennia passed with very little change. That push would wipe out most of Old Europe in waves of killing and wrecking as the early level two raiders spread their culture. It would be centuries before the civilizations of the ancient world developed out of the ashes of Old Europe.

Dr. Gimbutas is strongly supported by recent genetic research. Studies show a significant decrease (a "post-Neolithic Y-chromosome bottleneck") in male—not female—genetic diversity approximately 5,000 to 7,000 years ago. The most probable cause was violent competition among patrilineal kin groups.[94] That is, there was a long history of gradually increasing genetic diversity before the bottleneck, corresponding to millennium after millennium of peaceful hunter-gatherer groups. Suddenly many male lineages ended during a period of extreme murderous violence, exactly matching the end of Old Europe as Gimbutas described. This violent period marks the beginning of level two psychology; the construction of the walled cities of the ancient world was the result.

Our prehistoric ancestors may have murdered one another on occasion, but it was not until relatively late in the prehistoric period that war developed. The first clear evidence of warfare has been dated to approximately 8,000 B.C.E.,[95] and that point in time is a good estimate of the beginnings of significant level two psychology. (6,000 B.C.E. may be more accurate for the Proto-Indo-Europeans.) 8,000 B.C.E. is not an absolutely firm date, and it may well change with new archaeological discoveries. The important points are that warfare began very late in the prehistoric world, and warfare began quite recently in the overall history of humanity. Warfare is a marker of the beginnings of level two society. Our level one hunter-gatherer forebears were relatively peaceful for millennium upon millennium until level two psychology began to take hold about 10,000 years ago. This is quite recent in the great time-line of humanity, accounting for only about five percent of our total past.

These findings are echoed by developmental psychology. Recall the rage of the four-year-old in the candy aisle after being told "no" by his mother. The rage is due to thwarted instincts, the same instincts which drive the child in the notorious "terrible twos." Rage is not present in stage one children and there is no evidence to suggest it was present in prehistoric people. Rather, it is in the level two mythology of the ancient world that conflict becomes a typical motif. The ancients had deities associated with war; the causes of conflicts in their myths seem so minor that it is easy to conclude that they just liked to fight. Mythological brothers fought over trivial matters; Cain killed Abel, Romulus killed Remus, and Set killed Osiris, all mostly out of petty jealousy. Developmental psychology confirms the findings of archaeology, ethnic studies, and animal studies: war came relatively late to humanity. It is a necessary part of the developmental process in stages two, three, and four, and probably no others. To paraphrase Heraclitus, war is the father of all things for civilizations in developmental levels two, three, and four.

Considering the violence of our written history, the scenario painted by Dr. Gimbutas of a peaceful matrilineal society may easily appear outlandish. This is exacerbated by current political issues, including women's rights and anti-war sentiment. The superficial view of Dr. Gimbutas is that she has mixed relics with women's liberation and hippie communes to produce her ideas. Dr. Anthony's disparagement of the work of Dr. Gimbutas does not appear to be an exception.[96]

However, there is a body of non-archaeological evidence that supports Dr. Gimbutas. We know that hunter-gatherer people tend to be egalitarian, nonviolent, and matrilineal. We know that warfare was not a part of their lives. The concept of a matrilineal (not matriarchal) society does not mean that there was a female Julius Caesar or Douglas MacArthur in command, but rather that families were egalitarian individuals centered around mothers and grandmothers. The evidence will always be scant. But it should be understood that level one culture, as either hunter-gatherers or settled farmers, was a world apart from the level two raiders who conquered them.

It is also notable that Dr. Anthony is not alone among archaeologists in disparaging Dr. Gimbutas.[97] I think this is largely because Dr. Gimbutas was a woman who took a position at odds with the male-dominated mainstream of her field and suggested that male domination had not always been present throughout history. Her success and recognition undoubtedly fueled jealousy among her more insecure colleagues. This was all exacerbated by the attention her work received from feminist authors, and this association poured more fuel on the flames. These issues are ultimately the issues of our time; the treatment of Dr. Gimbutas is not really surprising. I predict that the future will uphold her findings, and she will be remembered long after her hostile colleagues are forgotten.

While there is little doubt that there was never a specific form of the Great Goddess appearing throughout the prehistoric world, it is highly probable that there were numerous goddesses who represented aspects of that archetype. All of these goddesses may be considered some form of the Great Goddess. By the time ancient world religions were first recorded, most of those earlier forms had been lost or condensed into a few lasting goddess roles; many were paired with or replaced by male deities. Not much archaeological evidence is available for humanity's early years, so the ethnological, anthropological, and developmental evidence may be the best there is. The Great Goddess, in various forms, was the dominant deity of the prehistoric world.

It is highly probable that matrilineal societies preceded patrilineal societies in the prehistoric world, becoming patriarchal only after many millennia. Beginning at least 200,000 years ago, thinking gradually developed from primitive, almost animal, conscious awareness into the mind-set of the ancient world, that is, from an essentially unconscious state into thinking that we could recognize and relate to. As with infants, very early humans did not appear with modern mental processes intact, but rather in a basic form. For most of this period, consisting of many tens of thousands of years, early human thinking was a primitive, dim twilight conscious awareness, more unconscious than conscious, primarily instinctual.

Jung discussed the thinking of the "primitive" person in a seminar he conducted in 1931. It was his observation that the primitive person had minimal ability to concentrate and maintain attention. If something did not "catch his instinct," he was unaware. Jung described this as a "passive awareness."[98] These observations were made shortly after World War I; we do not see this today due to the spread of Western thinking throughout the world.

Recall the incident of the posthypnotic suggestion of tying shoelaces I mentioned earlier; think of the unconscious awareness of the act of tying the shoelaces as level one consciousness and the discussion of the events leading to overt conscious awareness as parallel to the transition to level two consciousness. Ten thousand years ago, a person who had achieved level two consciousness would have an immense advantage over his level one peers; it is easy to see why early level two leaders, as the Egyptian pharaohs, were considered gods.

Developmental stage one covers both the first period of an infant's life as well as our historical infancy, the prehistoric world. It is during this time that the infant's conscious awareness is centered in the part of the mind we refer to as the unconscious, the matrix from which focused conscious awareness develops in stage two. This process is exactly parallel to the mental development occurring in the prehistoric world. In both arenas the mother is the dominant figure, either as the actual mother, or as some form of the Great Goddess, and the individual struggles to establish the most basic separate identity.

CHAPTER VII

Stage Two and the Ancient World

The child of the mother

If stage one is dominated by the mother, stage two is dominated by the child's rebellion against her domination as it begins to establish its own identity through the forces of its impulses. Driven by impulses, the child says "No!" to the mother's control and begins to form an identity separate from her. As the child learns control, based on the link between impulse and action, it asks "Why?" to learn of links between other causes and events. Animism, seeing objects as having a life of their own, continues in the first half of the stage and diminishes in the second half. Morality and justice are both seen as equal exchanges between the parties involved.

The ancient world was likewise dominated by impulses; they were personified as gods and goddesses. Mythology of the ancient world reveals male gods supplementing and replacing earlier female deities, although, as a general rule, the earlier mother goddess remained in the background. Laws were seen as an equal interchange, as "eye for an eye" rules. Inanimate objects, that is graven images, were seen as powerful to the point that they might be captured and worshiped by enemy forces, or later, banned entirely as a religious threat (the threat of graven images). Morality was determined by getting caught, not by guilt.

In *The Creation of Inequality*, Kent Flannery and Joyce Marcus use archaeology and social anthropology to outline the transition from egalitarian level one societies to hierarchical level two societies. They review despotic kingdoms and empires in the Near East, Egypt, Africa, Mexico, Peru, and the Pacific, and give a picture of the transition our ancestors made from ice age hunter-gatherer groups to ancient Egypt and city-states in ancient Mesopotamia. The first steps involve the founding of bachelors' huts or men's huts; in time, ambitious males become temporary leaders. The need for leadership may have come about as a reaction to raids from other groups. Ambitious "Big Men" lead the group by persuasion. The group's size increases, from large families to clans, and an "us versus them" attitude toward other clans may develop. Raids and war may be encouraged, with the taking of trophies including heads and scalps. Food accumulation, never acceptable to hunter-gatherer groups, becomes tolerated. Society becomes unequal, although this is initially achievement-based and not hereditary. With the passage of time, the men's huts become temples dedicated to gods. Leading families become royal families with a lineage, often going back to the gods. Rank becomes hereditary, with a hereditary elite; inequality is fixed. Kings may become gods or are thought to have supernatural powers. Despite male dominance, matrilineal elements may continue. Property value and inequality increase through the process.[99]

The separation of men from women, the rise of inequality, the beginnings of warfare, and the beginnings of property ownership all happened at approximately the same time. This is a marked shift from the egalitarian hunter-gatherers who avoided aggression and whose only property was their personal items. Rulers claiming to be gods or descendants of gods occur only in stage two. War and claims of ownership beyond one's personal needs began with stage two and probably do not extend beyond level four; the idea that we "have the poor with you always"[100] is only valid for those stages.

In *War Before Civilization*, Lawrence Keeley cites archaeological evidence to attack the notion of "the peaceful savage" and support his contention that humans have always been warlike.[101] But the evidence he presents is of groups who have already begun the transition from hunter-gatherers to raiding clans. History makes it clear that stage two societies were frequently aggressive, and that may not be generalized to stage one people. It is my impression that Keeley did not investigate true hunter-gatherer societies; rather, he presented a survey of early stage two people and assumed that earlier humans functioned in a similar manner.

Incidentally, an unstated theme of *The Creation of Inequality* is that human inequality is a problem and is not our natural state. This is modern thinking. At no time since prehistoric societies first became unequal and hierarchical as they entered stage two has inequality been questioned or seen as a problem; rather, it has been seen as God's natural order on earth. It is only in relatively recent history that we are questioning the idea of inequality in society. For stages two through four, society's hierarchy has been the central organizing core of developing consciousness. It is only in our time, when this development is virtually complete, that inequality and hierarchy are being considered problematic.

The historical transition from stage one to stage two psychology was marked by the ending of the egalitarian hunter-gatherer stone age and the beginnings of hierarchical societies, metalworking, and warfare. It began with savage men, beholden to savage male gods, wrecking, killing, and enslaving. It brought a dark age as the earlier level one matrilineal societies were wiped out. There would be centuries of warring clans fighting for the glory of war and conquest before the first civilizations appeared in the ancient world. Level two thinking was well-established by the time the first great city-states appeared; the city-states were a product of, not a cause of, level two thinking. Society moved from egalitarian hunting and gathering nomads to organized hierarchical clans, clans which would fuse together to form the first great cities. A good guess for this transition was about 8,000 B.C.E., but the date would have varied a great deal by location. Leaders took power over their fellows. Burials changed from a few grave goods with each person to greatly increased hoards of goods buried with a few males. A permanent military class developed. The older female gods were replaced by, married to, or made sister to (as Hera and Isis) the up-and-coming male gods that represented the new thinking and social organization. Slaves were taken for labor and sex. Booty was sought to decorate dwellings. War was sought to express aggression and to bring glory. Walled cities were built, and the ancient world came into full bloom.

The ancient world

People in the ancient world pursued knowledge, but it was usually heavily intermixed with mythology. The Greeks led the ancient world by establishing basic methods of grasping, defining, and analyzing reality. However, they generally failed to even consider following up their ideas and speculations with practical applications, although there certainly were exceptions such as the famed Antikythera mechanism, an astronomical calculator from the first century B.C.E. It has never been clear why the Greeks were able to define the basic rules of logic and reason, yet were unable to take the next steps in applying those rules; that would not be done until the Age of Enlightenment, more than 1,500 years later.

Why didn't the Greeks develop science and start the industrial age centuries ago? This cannot be blamed on Christianity, which did not appear until approximately three centuries after the zenith of Greek civilization. Relying on slaves for labor did not help, but it does not explain why Greek rational development proceeded strongly and then seemingly stopped. It seems that, for the Greeks, what we call science was only another aspect of their philosophy, as opposed to our concept of science as a study of physical reality. It was a mental exercise which was never meant for the material world; it has taken the West's emphasis on the material world to produce true science. Ultimately, Greek rationalism was true to developmental stage two, asking "why?" but never really pursuing the answer. A stage two child can ask "why" repeatedly, and despite exhaustive explanations, the whole process remains only a mental exercise. So it was with the Greeks.

The West's inherent materialistic bias, a bias toward doing something in the physical world, has created the idea that Greek intellectual progress was blocked, in that they did not produce much from their reasoning. In fact they pursued it as far as their developmental level would allow. Similarly, the medieval Arabic world developed algebra but went no further with mathematics.

The early Hebrews were no exception to the general behavior patterns of the ancient world. Although prophets made repeated calls for them to stop worshiping graven images of various deities, they continued to do so. Yahweh, the God of the ancient Hebrews, was ambiguous, both good and evil, as were most other deities in the ancient world; a totally good version would not appear until Christianity. Raphael Patai, in *The Hebrew Goddess*,[102] observed that the early Hebrews worshiped the Goddess, in the form of Asherah, as a consort of and equal to Yahweh. Throughout the entire existence of the temple attributed to Solomon, images of Asherah were present almost two-thirds of the time; she was worshiped by the Hebrews for six centuries despite the increasing dominance of Yahwist monotheism. As I noted, William Dever reported that archaeology confirmed the importance of Asherah and the polytheistic nature of most of the Hebrews before the arrival of the Babylonians. Dever differentiated the "folk" religion of the masses from the "book" religion of the elite few; the folk religion included Asherah and possibly other deities, while the book religion was focused exclusively on Yahweh. Both authors indicate that the early Hebrew religion was polytheistic. This behavior changed following the Babylonian conquest which resulted in the destruction of Solomon's temple and the captivity. It was then that the seeds of the medieval age began to grow. After the Babylonian captivity (587-538 B.C.E.), monotheism grew to predominance, as Yahweh began to transform into the medieval Great Father God.

I mentioned that Greek philosophical developments, including Epicureanism, Stoicism, Cynicism, and Skepticism, were intellectual forerunners of medieval psychology and Christianity. Note that these schools of thought were prominent at about the same time as the Babylonian captivity and its aftermath among the Hebrews. The philosophical developments of the Greeks and the religious developments of the Hebrews would eventually serve as major foundation stones for the development of the medieval West. But throughout the time of the ancient world, such ideas were only ideals. The reality was domination by the impulses as a child is so dominated.

A Homeric Greek felt he was bound by his fate, a passive instrument of the gods. He could not help his own actions; an impulse or emotion would come to him, he acted, and then rejoiced or grieved. A god had motivated him, either positively or negatively; he was not a free agent.[103]

Brutality in the ancient world was remarkable. If one Greek city fought another, the winners would execute every surviving adult male from the defeated city, and the women and children would be sold into slavery. If one Roman slave rose against the master, every slave in the household would be crucified. A Roman household might have a flagellant on staff, and it was not unusual to beat slaves to death or beat them until they died shortly afterward. Nero had Christians covered in asphalt and used as torches. The Roman arena was extraordinarily brutal, and the brutality was thoroughly enjoyed. People were hacked apart, torn apart by animals, burned alive, mutilated, all as entertainment. Saint Augustine wrote of a friend who was addicted to the games; Augustine made it clear that the friend became like a savage with blood-lust at the games, and he apparently continued for years before Augustine was able to win him away from the games and convert him to Christianity. When the ancient Hebrews began capturing towns in Canaan after their exodus from Egypt, at Yahweh's instructions, they didn't just massacre all of the men, women and children in the towns they captured, but the cattle as well.[104] One of the reasons King Saul lost favor with Yahweh was that he didn't carry through with a complete genocide of an enemy as ordered.[105]

The story of King David and Bathsheba illustrates the attitude toward punishment in the ancient world. As in stage one, if you get away with it, it wasn't bad, but in stage two, if you get caught then you should pay an appropriate price for your transgression. Sin and guilt, right and wrong, are not a factor, but paying the appropriate price if you get caught is. Because of this the heroes of the ancient world are wily characters, as opposed to the "good guys" of the West. They are heroes because of excellent skills of avoiding, tricking, and outwitting, not because they are good or moral. Jacob pretended that he was his brother Esau and tricked their father Isaac to get the blessing intended for the firstborn.[106] The Greek heroes Odysseus and Heracles succeeded by obeying the deities when they had to, by trickery when they were able to use it, by physical strength, and by luck. The ancient heroes were not portrayed as good men or wise men, but as clever men. They did what they had to when the gods were looking, and otherwise did their best not to get caught. This is not the good versus evil morality of the modern West. It is not the morality of Christianity. It is the morality of Bill Watterson's Calvin, and it is the morality of a stage two child.

An ancient Greek might experience shame but not guilt.[107] While there was no guilt or sin, there was a pervasive sense of fate in the ancient world. The best that a person can do is meet fate proudly, because things are really in the hands of the capricious gods. The erratic behavior of Yahweh is typical, telling the Israelites "Thou shalt not kill"[108] in the fifth chapter of Deuteronomy, but in the seventh chapter he tells them to "utterly destroy"[109] every person and every animal in each city they capture in Canaan.

The savagery of the ancient world was routine. The brutality of the Roman games was a part of daily life, not something that only happened in war. This contrasts with modern life, where you may want to see your team win, but most people don't want to see the other team killed. I have heard remarks to the effect that people only go to sports games, automobile races, and so on to see the players killed in accidents, but I think this is really just a derogatory and disdainful belittling of sports fans. The fans like the excitement and the competition, but they want the challenge for each team to return anew next season in a new round of competition. That was not so in the ancient world. We want to see a hard-fought game with the best team winning; they wanted to see brutality and death. We see that brutality in our lives only in very limited venues; combat is typical, and it often results in a medical condition, posttraumatic stress disorder. The ancients enjoyed watching horrors that would cause many of us to develop flashbacks, nightmares, and related symptoms. I have found no evidence of post-traumatic stress disorder symptoms in the ancient world.

The mythology of this time often features the tale of hostile brothers, as Cain and Abel, Set and Osiris, Jacob and Esau, and Romulus and Remus. The hostility between the two was not because of a projected shadow, but due to more basic passions, usually envy or covetousness. Personal and clan revenge is another theme from the times. There is rarely any sense of one side being evil or sinful. The parties may be opposites, as David and Goliath, but they are not shadows of one another, except in the most basic sense.

Motivation for conflict was usually greed—for slaves or booty—but it was not built on hate.

As to sexuality in the ancient world, these were cultures with prostitutes in the temples. Any household slave, male or female, was sexually available to the master (this also occurred in Western slavery, but was covert). Women and children taken prisoner in wars became prostitutes, and by the time of the Roman Empire, there was an abundance of prostituted slaves. Sexuality was as much a part of life in the ancient world as was violence. If the ancients discussed love, they were usually referring to sexual love and not family affection.[110] The romantic love of the modern West was unknown. In Homer's Greece, daughters were commercial assets to be sold to the highest bidders.[111] Agape, brotherly love, was unknown before it arrived with Christianity. If there was love, it probably was sexual, if society allowed. Eros, the god of love, was the son of Aphrodite, and Aphrodite had nothing to do with brotherly love.

Women of the ancient world only had power associated with their family and clan; if a husband wanted to be rid of his wife, she could be turned back to her clan or placed in a brothel; she had no other options. Christianity improved the lot of women with its ideas of the sanctity of marriage and its philosophy of good behavior toward fellow believers. But in the male-dominated ancient world, if there was a problem with your wife, you could get another one, or have sex with your slaves. The critical element was the alliance between families. The modern romantic attachment to specific individuals was not present; if there was chemistry, it was sexual. It was the level two morality of Calvin and King David.

Level two psychology has little empathy for others, aside from the mother and for sexual chemistry; other people are essentially objects. Males might identify with a charismatic hero, be he a Cesar or a general, but this was hero worship, not caring for other people as we understand it. David wanted Uriah's wife, so he had him killed. The ancients enjoyed seeing other people horribly killed and considered it entertainment. Other people were objects; empathy is not learned until developmental stage three.

It is not possible to overstate the cruelty of the ancient world, including the Greeks and Romans and all their forerunner civilizations, as well as the parallel civilizations in the New World, including the Aztecs, Incas, and Mayans. Nietzsche referred to Greek cruelty as "a tigerish lust to annihilate" and added that we would shudder if we knew the Greeks as they actually were.[112] I would add that it was the same for the Romans, except that they were perhaps more disciplined.[113] This was not the anonymous mass murder of modern warfare, but individual cruelty, and joy in that cruelty, that we only see in people we consider psychopaths.

Both the Greeks[114] and the Romans[115] were sexually ambivalent. This was not modern homosexuality, in which some individuals are attracted to individuals of the same sex. Rather, it was based on societies in which males associated with males, and women were either sequestered for the production of offspring, or in the lowest strata of society; occasionally some became courtesans. It was a psychology we associate with pre-adolescence, when the boys play with boys and avoid girls. In Rome, prostitution of women and children was central to Roman society and was practiced on an industrial scale.[116] There is every reason to believe that every other civilization in the ancient world, since its earliest years, made the same use of captive women and boys; it was for the Homeric Greeks.[117] For the Romans, any male sexual behavior was acceptable as long as one was not passive or being penetrated; that was for women and slaves (male or female).[118] Nietzsche describes the festivals of the ancient world as involving "extravagant sexual licentiousness" including a "horrible mixture of sensuality and cruelty."[119] This was obsessive, wildly unrestrained instinctual behavior as opposed to any rational choice of partners.

I suspect there was a higher probability of male sexual ambivalence in all level two societies, as the feminine is associated with childbearing and mothering, not companionship, and hence a threat to be avoided by sequestering females and only consorting with males. This is somewhat suppressed in level three.

The impulse dominated mind

It is as difficult for us to realize impulse domination in the ancient world as it is to realize a similar impulse domination among young children. We cannot really understand the torrents of libido that drove the ancient world, just as we cannot really understand the impact of overwhelming impulses of aggression and sexuality to a stage two child. We think of the games in the Roman arena as a forerunner of the modern football game, oblivious of the murderous blood lust that dominated the Roman crowd. Adults expect children to control their impulses and may not understand the rage children experience when those impulses are blocked. But the stage two child and the ancient world are a long way, psychologically speaking, from the modern adult and the modern West. The same impulses motivate the stage two child as motivated the ancient world, but the situation in the child is much more tame because it involves small children instead of mature adults, and because children are dominated by the larger adults around them.

The child in stage two is forming an identity through expression of the impulses despite what others may think; imagine a four-year-old demanding candy, saying "No!" when mother refuses. This child may become furious, driven by rage. The child cannot control the anger; it controls him. For a stage two person, it is as if a deity has taken over, first with the aggression and then with rage when the aggression is blocked. It is not until stage three that the child learns to control impulses by internalizing group values. Stage one ends with the child's awareness that it is a being separate from its mother; it still is entirely dependent on her and without an identity apart from her. It is in stage two that the first true conscious individuality is formed, and it is all based on impulses. When the child driven by its impulses demands candy, it is making its first steps toward forming an individual identity through the push of personal desires. The child personally wants the candy despite the wishes of the mother, and is establishing itself as a separate person from her in doing so.

A child possessed by rage can sincerely say, "I hate you, I wish you were dead," and later, when no longer angry, can sincerely profess love to the same person. The Romans could imprison, torture and enslave people and later make them citizens. Even the angriest child can be brought to friendship with a gift; diplomacy in the ancient world was almost solely a matter of gifts for rulers.

While the ancient world saw vicious competition and warfare between cities and kingdoms, they did not hate one another for years on end solely for the sake of hate. Like children, they hated others to the extent that they wanted something from them, that is, loot, trade, or slaves, but it went no further. It is interesting to contrast the ancient Roman attitude toward Jewish people with the Nazi attitude. The Romans grew increasingly displeased with the Hebrews after the revolts in Judea in the first century; they devastated Jerusalem and scattered the Jewish people, causing the great Jewish Diaspora. One of those Hebrews, Josephus, a member of one of the rebellious sects actively fighting against Rome, was captured. He managed to avoid execution, and eventually became a noted Roman citizen. We know him as a major historian of the ancient world.[120] By contrast, the Nazis rarely spared Jewish people and never allowed them to become citizens or important members of Nazi society. (There were a very few Jewish "honorary Aryans" and they were not granted any significant place in Nazi society.) This ongoing hatred on ideological grounds was unknown in the ancient world. The ancients would certainly hate you until the battle was won, but the matter usually ended there.

Political organization in the ancient world was essentially that of the extended family or clan. The dominant male of the clan, the one with absolute control over his wives, children, servants, slaves, and client families, met in a senate or congress with his peers, the heads of other families. If there ever was any democracy in the ancient world, it was among this group of equals, the heads of the dominant families. The dominant male of that group then ran the city, and the entire ancient world was organized in such city-states. Typically, the political head of the city-state was also the chief priest, at least in name. The head of the family was the primary priest for the family gods, and the head of the city was the primary priest for the city's gods, with the city organized as, essentially, one large family or clan group.[121]

The sensual world of the ancients was repressed in its entirety by the medieval world that replaced it. Similarly, for the child developing into stage three, the impulsiveness that began in the "terrible twos" gives way to being "nice" and the identity formed in stage two is repressed. What happens to the personality formed in stage two? We have a hint from the "Calvin and Hobbes" cartoon strips: it remains inside as the inner child, the little kid inside, the part that still likes to play, tease, enjoy, and have fun. This aspect of Western psychology has become more accessible to us over the past century. The modern West is discovering its ancient world roots as it discovers its inner child.

The inner child

The inner child is the source of much creativity. I imagine that it was the inner child thinking that it would be terrific to fly that inspired Leonardo da Vinci and the Wright brothers. Da Vinci dreamed of the engineering required to fly, and the Wright brothers accomplished it. The adult ego in each of those men listened to the inspiration from the inner child and did the work necessary to make the inspiration into a reality.

When Freud wrote about this part of the personality, he referred to it as the "id," an almost completely unconscious part of the mind that was the origin of the demands for immediate satisfaction of primitive desires stemming from instinctual impulses. The idea of the id came from a more strait-laced Europe of over a century ago, when impulses from the inner child were seen as something to be controlled. The West has become tremendously more accepting of and open to sex over the past century (helped in no small part by the discovery of effective birth control and treatment of venereal disease). Today, a Victoria's Secret catalog in the mailbox is commonplace; a century ago it would have produced outrage. Freud's id was seen as a threatening, seething cauldron of wicked desires; now we know it as the sometimes naughty part inside, a part that we are familiar with and which provides a great deal of joy in life. Our society is much more accepting of play than a century ago, both sexually and otherwise. Adult play, adult naughtiness within bounds, adult humor have all left the basement of repression and have become a part of the adult conscious mind, a part separate from the ego.

Esther Harding, an American Jungian, referred to the inner child as the "autos," which she described as a developmentally early focus of consciousness dominated by the drives; Harding did not place this in the negative light Freud did.[122]

The degree to which sex has come "out of the closet" in the past 100 years is another indicator of how we are changing. Seventy-five years ago it was only discussed in medical books, and now it is discussed publicly in the media. It is rapidly becoming just another human function, although an important one. Venus is resuming her place after spending almost 2,000 years in either the gutter or the nunnery.

The fact that this material has come into conscious awareness does not mean that there is no unconscious, but rather, that much of what was unconscious a century ago is now more available to conscious thinking. A large amount of what was considered shameful, disgusting, and so forth, then, is accepted now, within limits. The idea of "within limits" implies that the modern conscious mind is strong enough that it can let the internal child out to play, yet keep it within boundaries acceptable to society. Each individual's ego has strengthened to the point that it can set limits without the need for society to do so. I think that it is remarkable how much play has entered adult lives over the past century. I assume that part of this is that we have more free time than did adults of 1900. There was entertainment, such as theater and music, but it was not play so much as entertainment. We play, and we do it a lot, and it demonstrates how the inner child has come out of its closet and become a part of our lives. It is no longer the threatening id of Freud's day, but an important part of happiness in our lives.

The increase in importance and awareness of the inner child and its pleasures over the past century reflects an ongoing increase in the strength of the conscious mind as this once-repressed material is brought into conscious awareness and enjoyed. Whereas the Western mind was not strong enough to allow this 500 or even 200 years ago, it has strengthened to the point that this is no longer a threat. The limits are firmly set, modern conscious thinking is firmly in control, and the inner child may play freely within those limits, for most people.

An interesting phenomenon that psychologists have observed is that, over the past few decades, traditional neurosis has been seen less and less frequently, and personality disorders have been seen more and more frequently. The behavioral patterns referred to as personality disorders become more understandable if they are seen as the eruption of a wounded inner child into daily conscious awareness. One sees rages, impulsive sexuality, suspicion, mistrust, detachment, hostility, explosiveness, and other behaviors typical of emotionally injured children. These behaviors push aside and break through conscious controls, so that the individual may break into a rage, for example, despite all attempts to control the situation. These behavioral patterns have appeared more frequently in recent decades because, as a group, we have developed a strong enough conscious mind that the controls on the inner child have loosened. As the inner child has become more conscious, the wounds of the child have become apparent as well. This is parallel to the increased emphasis on play and diminished emphasis on control that have occurred in Western society over the past century or so.

The internal child of developmental level two is a source of joy for an adult who has it under good control. But the level two child has yet to learn that control, and begins to look for approval from adults who have already mastered it. For the ancient Romans, the feeling was that freedom could be gained by suppressing the impulses through Christianity. For both, the next step is developmental level three.

CHAPTER VIII

Stage Three and the Medieval World

The world of the father

Perhaps the greatest transition in Western history to date was that between the ancient world and the medieval world. We think of civilization entering the Dark Ages with the fall of Rome, and that was somewhat true for western Europe, although the eastern arm of the Roman Empire survived quite successfully for a millennium as the Byzantine Empire. The Roman emperor Constantine the Great legalized Christianity in the early 300s, and it spread until both eastern and western Europe became devoutly Christian.

The transformation from the ancient world to the medieval world was not a simple matter of taking up a new religion, but rather a complete transformation of the social organization and psychology. The entire order of life changed in just a few centuries, as society took control of the impulses that had previously dominated it. Christianity gradually achieved dominance over the pagan religions and eventually replaced them because it reflected the values of the people; it did not reach initial dominance through force. Psychological change caused the change in religion, and Christianity succeeded because it most accurately reflected the new consciousness of the time.

One of the most defining characteristics of the new sect of Christianity was a renunciation of the world. Early Christians accepted horrible martyrdom in the Roman arena rather than renounce their faith. A young married couple might live together virtually as brother and sister with little or no sexual contact. As Christianity spread, large numbers of

107

people chose a life of monasticism and rejected the world as it had been structured for thousands of years. In the early years of Christianity the deserts of the Middle East were particularly attractive to those seeking escape from the temptations of society and the persecutions of their faith. The eastern Roman Empire tended to produce desert recluses, usually male, while the west tended to produce cloistered nuns. An interesting character of the times was Simon Stylites, a religious recluse in the Syrian desert. Simon fastened himself to the top of a pillar where he lived his extremely ascetic life, attracting numerous pilgrims. Simon was only slightly extreme among the religious hermits. This sort of behavior was unheard of in the ancient world where sex and violence had been intrinsic to life: suddenly they were rejected.

In a very short time historically speaking, primarily between 100 and 300 C.E., the Roman world changed from numerous deities and religions to one. Even with the advent of Christianity, there were multiple orientations and interpretations of what Jesus taught. In this short period of time all of the other religions and non-orthodox interpretations of Christianity were swept aside and replaced with one church and one dogma. The new religion assumed power and centralized control unknown to any religion in the ancient world; in time those who failed to adhere to the new belief might be executed. The new church became a power in itself, equal to, if not stronger than, the civil government.

The coming of Christianity marked the end of the age of the city-state and the beginning of the age of faith. Christians began looking after other Christians, giving the poor food and clothing. By the end of the sixth century, Christians had lost their age-old allegiance to their cities, and formed a new allegiance to their fellow believers. Religion provided a deeper sense of community identity than the city had. They were no longer fellow citizens, but fellow believers.[123]

For the ancient world, love was primarily physical and sexual; it was something that could be found in a brothel. Christianity and the medieval world developed agape, that is, spiritual love or brotherly love, the love Christians have for their fellow believers. This was not modern romantic love, but a sense of empathy for those in the social group, that is, the society of believers. It was accompanied by rejection of those not in the reference group, nonbelievers.

Attitudes made an equally sharp turn in that short time span. Early Christians emphasized virginity and sexual abstinence, something almost unheard of in the ancient world. Abstaining from sexual contact was seen as gaining freedom; we can now understand abstinence as freedom from dominance by the instinctual drives which had ruled the ancient world. In a short time span, virginity, sexual abstinence, and even abstinence in marriage came to be seen as godly. The ancient world had seen sexuality as necessary for maintaining the family; suddenly sex was something to be avoided if at all possible. Similarly, at least for the Romans and Greeks, the human body had almost been a deity in itself, beautifully copied in marble and bronze. With the arrival of Christianity, the body became a source of shame, something to be covered.[124]

Yahweh of the Hebrew scriptures was changed as he entered Christian scriptures. Throughout the Hebrew scriptures he was described as an ambivalent character with both good and bad, or dark and light, aspects. You will recall that he proclaimed "Thou shall not kill" at about the same time he insisted the Hebrews "utterly destroy" the people they overran when entering Canaan. Christianity split off all of Yahweh's evil side into Satan (like Jesus, one of the "sons of God"[125] according to the book of Job), and transformed Yahweh into the father and son team of good gods of the Christian Scriptures. Dark and light were to be utterly separate for the next two millennia. All evil was assigned to Satan and human beings, all good to the godhead.

The teachings of Jesus were very much in the Jewish tradition, and were it not for Saint Paul, Jesus would have probably remained a minor Jewish rabbi. Saint Paul and other early Christians wove more and more of what was then the new psychology into the teachings of Jesus. The rebirth of the soul in a heavenly afterlife was added; this was not a part of traditional Jewish teaching. The biggest psychological change was a pronounced emphasis on separation, a split that would remain characteristic of Christianity for the next 2,000 years. Sinners were separated from believers, the saved from the damned, spirit from flesh, good from evil, the thief on the right from the thief on the left, sheep from goats, the Jews from the Gentiles, and so on. All this meant that the believer must separate from his or her lust, anger, impulses, naughtiness, sexuality, greed and any other of the "base" impulses, to be "saved" and join the society of believers.

A person's value in the ancient world was not much more than that of their physical body; it was a pleasurable diversion to watch others torn apart by animals in the arena. The idea that each person had an eternal soul led medieval people to value their fellows more than the ancients had. While this increased valuation was only for those of the faith, it did mark the beginning of empathy for one's fellow human beings.

Religion in the ancient world, including that of the ancient Hebrews, was a matter of performance. It was what you did that was important, not what you thought. "Thou shalt have no other gods before me" or "Thou shalt not make unto thee any graven image" are examples. As long as the sacrifices were made, as long as the rules were kept, everything was fine, despite what one believed; belief was never an issue. It is only with the arrival of Christianity that one's mental attitude became an issue. The principle became one of not doing and not thinking wrong things in general (at least to other Christians), rather than not doing specific prohibited things. This required a mind-set of correctness, as opposed to awareness of a specific set of laws and taboos. This mind-set was the tool used to suppress unacceptable drives into the unconscious.

It can be said that free will came with Christianity. Generally speaking, the ancients felt that their fate and their behavior were in the hands of their gods. If you felt lust or had sex, it was due to the influence of a deity, such as Eros. The best you could do was to accept your fate, whether positive or negative. With the arrival of Christianity, fate was still in the hands of the deity, but the individual had free will in their reaction to what fate presented. Christians were expected to make the right choice in response to their fate. Thus the ancient might be condemned by fate, but the Christian could be condemned by their mind-set when facing their fate. For example, rape was widespread in the sack of Rome in 410 C.E., but Saint Augustine made it clear that the Christian mental state of the victims meant that they had not sinned.[126] It wasn't until the modern West that the idea of making one's fate developed.

Early Christians were joyfully filled with God the Father, some to the point of welcoming death to be with him. They found great comfort in their newly formed identification with the world of the fathers, specifically, the church fathers. Many were anti-materialistic and frequently desired to distance themselves from the realities of their world. This was a dramatic change in psychology from that of the ancient world. It parallels the sudden conversion of some gang members in our time. If the groundwork has been laid beforehand, the change from one level to the next may occur suddenly; the change from level two to three may be a sudden religious conversion. The conversion of Saul the persecutor of Christians to Saint Paul the preacher of Christianity occurred this way.[127]

These sudden changes occurring in a brief period of time represent a major psychological reorientation of society. Saying that this change was only a seizure of power by the church says nothing, for while the church did gain power, it did so because it expressed the thinking of a population whose attitudes had changed. The church became more and more popular as society changed; it did not seize power. There are a number of specific factors which played a role in this reorientation: the loss of faith in the old gods, the huge disparity between the rich and the poor, and so on, but there is no one suitable explanation for this huge change except to say that the Roman world became medieval as its consciousness moved from late level two to early level three. There were competing sects at the time, with values vaguely similar to Christianity, but they are largely forgotten; Christianity best matched the newly arrived medieval consciousness.

The medieval world

The medieval mind worked to separate itself from anything considered undesirable. The bright white light of the heavenly Father was chosen over the darkness of Satan and the lower world of Hell. The upper part of the body was preferred over the lower portion, with its filth and lusts. Earthly smells, as the odors of feces and sexual functioning, or even burning sulfur, were associated with evil and Satan, while airy, perfumed scents were associated with good. Life was divided in half, and the less-than-desirable half was thoroughly repressed. St. Augustine took this so far as to say that evil did not even exist; rather, what seemed evil was only an absence of good. The unacceptable was completely repressed.

The heroes for the medieval world were the saints and the old wise men of The Book. Knowledge was focused on the Bible and religious texts; ideas were vanity except for wisdom that brought the soul closer to harmony with God. Real knowledge was rare and superstition was prevalent. Earthly life was seen as a mere prelude to the real life, which began after death. The physical world, including the human body, was disparaged. Human beings were inherently sinful, as they were born out of disgusting, lustful sexual intercourse. Augustine wrote that we are "born between urine and feces" and thus born sinful from the start. Women were in particular disrepute, because they were the object of desire that caused the problems in the first place; consider the wickedness of Eve. Punishment was oriented toward the physical body, the seat of the impulses and desires, so that those who misbehaved were tortured or burned. The body was but a desire-ridden, temporary container for the heavenly soul. Fasting, self-flagellation, and similar self-imposed disciplining of the physical body was thought to produce spiritual change. The spirit could be refined by disciplining the body. The underlying theory was not so much based on hatred of the body as an attempt to purify it.[128]

The preference of some societies to keep women covered from head to foot even today is a remainder of the medieval mind learning to control the impulses; mental control was not fully established and external aids had to be used. The medieval mind lacked the ego that needs to prove it has mastered its impulses. The sight of naked flesh may be threatening to the medieval mind; impulse control is not completely learned so that the threat of loss of control is always present. Because it was a threat to medieval consciousness, it was considered unholy. Medieval logic dictated that females emitted rays that captivated and seduced men, so women were to be completely covered to shield men from this dangerous radiation.

For the medieval person, bad events were proof of God's displeasure. When Attila the Hun invaded and devastated Europe in the early medieval period, the people of the time saw him as God's instrument of punishment, referring to him as "the Scourge of God." We might compare Attila and his Huns with the Nazis and think that they were bad men, but we do not think that if the Nazis bombed your city it was because God was giving you punishment; we thought the Nazis were evil people doing evil things.

The child of the father

Parallel to the change from the ancient world to the medieval world is the child's entry into developmental stage three. It is then that the child begins to work to conform to outside rules so as to gain control over the impulses that previously dominated its behavior. The child becomes concerned about being good and doing the right thing in the eyes of the approving group, possibly including parents, teachers, close relatives, officials, church members, and such. In doing so the child is internalizing both the group's rules and the need to conform to those rules. At first the child wants to meet the group's expectations to avoid disapproval. But later the child wants to avoid shame or guilt feelings even if the group is unaware of the behavior because the group expectations have been internalized. The child wants to appear to be "being good" to the group, even when the group is not watching. On the other hand, those outside of the reference group, people of a different race or social class for instance, may not be treated so well. By internalizing these controls the child develops its own freedom, finally free from the demands of the impulses. Free will begins with the establishment of stage three controls.

This stage starts with conscious suppression of unacceptable material from the mind and progresses to unconscious repression of unacceptable material. That is, the process shifts from conscious choices not to misbehave to automatic responses without conscious deliberation, so that acceptable behavior becomes second nature and unacceptable behavior is not considered.

Where stages one and two were dominated by the mother, stage three focuses attention away from that relationship to the group that sets the standard for "good" and controlled behavior, typically a religious group or other respected authorities. It is in stage three that the dominant factor is non-maternal authority; the child passes into the world of the father, or the fathers of society. Ideally the representative of this is the actual father or father-substitute, but could be the disciplining side of the mother in a single-parent family. The child wants to please authority and endeavors to meet the expectations of authority. There is little sense of self-gratification in this aside from pleasure in pleasing authority; recall that the child had only recently developed some limited sense of self in stage two through expressing impulses, and now those same impulses, and their gratification, must be suppressed to please authority and avoid guilt. The controls learned in this stage are termed the superego.

The stage three formation process produces a remarkable change in children, as they suddenly become interested in societal approval and being "nice." It was equally dramatic as our civilization left the ancient world and entered the medieval world. Much of the material from the ancient world was repressed, thrown aside, or forgotten. Pagan temples were destroyed. Sexually explicit statues that had been quite acceptable in the ancient world were ridiculed, deemed disgusting, and destroyed. Much of the knowledge of the ancient world was put away or forgotten.

The same process was repeated in the people themselves, as the new Christian faith served to repress their impulses and desires, making them into "nice" Christians and splitting off their "sinful" sides into the unconscious. This resulted in a great split in the minds of Western people, a split which is an essential dynamic of the psychology underlying Christianity. Christianity did not cause this split to occur, but rather, served as the cultural expression of the underlying psychology.

With each stage of consciousness development, the mind becomes stronger, more independent, and more individual. It may seem unusual to think of being more independent and individual when considering the superego, which is a wholesale incorporation of parental and societal values, all of the "should" and "should not" rules we were raised with. But when you recall the domination by the impulses in stage two, with the child screaming for candy, or the unchecked blood lust and sexual libido of the ancient world, the importance of the superego becomes clear. It serves to dampen and control the demands of the inner child. And it also serves, in turn, as the foundation for the modern mind, which can listen to input from the underlying centers of consciousness and choose the best course of action without being overwhelmed by the impulses.

The stage three child begins to identify with the others in its group, as did the people of the medieval world. This is only for people in the group and not for outsiders, so outsiders do not get the same treatment. But the child does begin to value other people at this point. This was not true in the ancient world, as it is not true for a stage two (Calvin) child. Stage two children are manipulative and exploitative, and any adult remaining in that stage would probably be considered a sociopath. That was life in the ancient world: Romans wanted to see people in the arena killed; King David wanted to have sex with Bathsheba and had her husband killed. This changes in stage three because the child wants to incorporate the rules and be accepted by important others, and so the child begins to actually care about those other people, at least those in his or her own group.

For this reason, society for the stage three child is its reference group, including its parents, the authorities it looks up to, and possibly religious leaders. In a parallel fashion, in the medieval era the primary social structure was the society of believers, that is the church.

In the inner world, the superego is formed during stage three. The superego puts the brakes on the impulses; this means denying part of the mind. Stage three is the first stage in which the individual learns to deny behavior and be "nice" as opposed to following the impulses of stage two. Stage three is when the group passes from the minimally controlled libido of the ancient world and enters the medieval society of believers with its asceticism, hair shirts, monasteries, and convents. Most of the impulsive libido of stage two must be suppressed and shoved into the basement of the mind, the unconscious. With this split, consciousness is freed from domination by the impulses.

The superego is the internalization of the moral standards of our parents in particular and society in general. The "rules" it incorporates vary from society to society, hence its group or collective nature; for this reason Jung referred to it as the collective consciousness[129]. Another word might be one's "parent" or internal parent. In many ways it is a collection of values and rules from parents and other authorities. The term superego is most frequently used to describe these basic "should" and "should-not" rules that we live by.

Jung's expression "collective consciousness" implies the thinking of the group we adopt as we mature into being members of our society. It is our collection of rules of right and wrong, our respect for laws and for society's values, our internalized ideas of acceptable public and private behavior: don't cheat, don't steal, don't kill. The rules vary somewhat from group to group; some feel that dogs are pets, and some feel that they are food. A world in which the only conscious awareness was superego collective thinking would be a medieval world, where life is lived according to the "We should" rules of the group, with minimal emphasis on "I want" or "I will."

At first, the stage three child only wants to meet the expectations of others, as the parents, so as to avoid disapproval. But as this stage continues, the child has internalized values to the point that he or she wants to avoid guilt feelings even if others are unaware of the behavior. For true Christians it is not good enough to avoid sin; the ideal is to avoid even thinking about sin. This means extraordinary control over the impulses, and a parallel loss of contact with much of the inner child.

For a child in developmental stage three, or an adult in the medieval world, the mind is composed of three distinct sections. The unconscious formed in stage one—the thinking of the prehistoric world—is at the base, occasionally providing hints and guidance in dreams. Above that is the internal child from stage two—the thinking of the ancient world— expressing the impulses. And at the very top is the newly formed layer, the superego, the thinking of the medieval world. In stage three, the superego largely represses the internal child into unconsciousness.

116

The great split in consciousness

The repressed material may then be "found" in projection. This is the material of the shadow, the repressed part of the mind. I have discussed how parts of this material are usually projected onto other ethnic groups, other religious groups, other social classes, and so on. The projected material is the shadow, a part of the mind that forms in stage three. People in the ancient world had minimal, if any, psychological shadow; they were what they were, without a sense of sin to cause them to repress certain parts of themselves. Shadow psychology began with the medieval world.

Similarly, stage three children reject much of the stage two inner child. They also reject certain other people, those not belonging to the reference group. These are the groups that typically carry the shadow values for the child. The more problematic the repressed material (the angry, licentious, or greedy inner child), the greater the feeling of revulsion felt toward the people carrying the shadow. This ongoing hatred, loathing, and disgust for other people was not known in the ancient world, nor is it a part of a stage two child. Hate forces a person to be the opposite of whomever is hated, facilitating adaption of a positive role.

The split of the conscious mind from the internal child and its impulses brings enormous control over the instincts. But the cost is the development of a shadow and the projection of the shadow onto one's fellow humans. Historically, this is at the root of the mixed blessing of Christianity; it civilized northern Europe, but at a cost of great suffering for those who bore the shadow.

The past 2,000 years of civilization has been relatively accepting of violence, but much less so of sexuality. These two most powerful impulses were represented by important deities in the ancient world. Aphrodite and Venus were transformed into Mary Magdalene, a supposed repentant prostitute. But Ares and Mars were left pretty much alone, despite the Christian directive to turn the other cheek and not hit back.

One reason for the medieval acceptance of violence is that aggression is an aspect of control. One is being aggressive to part of one's own being when denying impulses and desires in order to "be nice" and meet group expectations in stage three. In the past this was accomplished by forcing people to accept the group's religious values, removing those who did not, and attacking nonbelievers. For the child undergoing this transition, much of the inner child must be repressed to form a conscious orientation acceptable to the group. A large portion of the well-developed conscious mind must be cut off and forgotten. This internal act of violence is parallel to the violence toward medieval individuals who were not acceptable to the medieval society of believers.

The stage three child learns that a part of the personality must be repressed to meet the expectations of society; this forms the shadow part of the mind. At the same time, he or she also learns to put on a "good" or socially acceptable facade when interacting with society, as it becomes clear that some behavior is acceptable, and other behavior is not. The child learns to appear as a "good" person acceptable to society, presenting a mask of acceptability when interacting with society. Jung termed this facade the persona.[130] It begins development in stage three as an appearance of being proper according to the group's rules. The persona strengthens as the shadow is repressed through stage three so that the stage three child comes to be identified with the persona. The persona—what is shown to the world—is almost the opposite of the shadow—what is hidden from the world. For stage three, neither is well defined; complexity of both will increase markedly in the next developmental level.

The child at this stage wants to appear to be good and acceptable to the adult reference group. For the medieval person, the persona was a facade of goodness, virtue, and holiness, and that facade was more important than the social role, be it king or peasant.

The repression and control of the internal child is a normal part of developmental stage three, but it must occur in its own time in the maturation process. Developmental problems occur when an overzealous parent sees a stage two child as uncontrolled and wicked, and attempts to force stage three behavior onto the stage two child by severe punishment and abuse. Instead, the internal child is only wounded and left feeling powerless and inferior. As an adult, that person may be driven by the wounded internal child to compensate by gaining power in society, or by abusing others. The ideal is to help the stage two child deal with their impulses until he or she develops stage three controls through their own maturation.

The birth of the soul

The medieval person realized, albeit unconsciously, that they had lost a part of themselves as consciousness was split. As a result the concept of the immortal soul was developed extensively, an immortal wholeness created in God's image.

The Hebrew scriptures indicate that life after death was either nonexistent or minimal. According to Psalms, there was no thought of giving praise to Yahweh in the afterlife because the dead were unable to do so.[131] Other verses suggest a continuing but hardly blissful existence after death; the Witch of Endor helped Saul consult the ghost of Samuel, who arose from his subterranean existence.[132] For the Greeks and Romans, the spirits of the dead lived in an underground afterworld with minimal activity. It was only in the late ancient world that the idea of the soul living a blissful afterlife entered mainstream thinking, just in time for it to be incorporated into Christianity as a major theme. It developed at that time because it provided an image of wholeness that was being lost with medieval psychology, which split the Western mind in two.

The medieval contribution to the West

The thinking of the medieval world is easily dismissed as a grim interlude between the brilliance of the ancient Greeks, and to a lesser degree the Romans, and the modern West. The Renaissance is seen as an intellectual reawakening that led the West to the industrial revolution and our modern world. It is as if Western humanity went to sleep after the brilliant golden age of Greece (500 to 300 B.C.E.) and the Roman world that followed, and did not reawaken until 1500 C.E. With that awakening, our ancestors seemingly took up where the ancient Greeks and Romans left off, building the modern West after a thousand-year medieval nap.

But that is not the case: the intervening medieval era fostered the necessary development from the questioning-but-not-acting ancient world to the questioning-and-acting modern West. The Greeks were not capable of the applied, practical intellect necessary for the industrial revolution. Neither the Greek nor the Roman intellect was capable of what would later blossom in the Renaissance. The Renaissance was not a "rebirth" of ancient culture; ancient world art forms were the form of the message but they were not the message itself. It was the birth of a new culture out of a long period of medieval development.

Christianity provided the basic structure for the medieval world of belief, as Christianity was in the process of defining itself throughout the era. Debate centered around determining what constituted Christian doctrine. Education of the time consisted of the quadrivium (arithmetic, geometry, music, and astronomy) and the trivium (rhetoric, logic, and grammar). Of these, rhetoric and logic were the most critical because they were necessary to debate and define doctrine, to integrate knowledge from ancient writers, like Aristotle, into Christian thinking, and to align doctrine with the writings of the early fathers of the church. Religion and philosophy were rigorously argued as doctrine was developed to support faith; as a result, reason was keenly developed.[133]

The use of logic and rhetoric led to the development of more sophisticated critical thinking. It was disciplined thinking of the best minds of the times within the structure of Christian faith. It gradually developed into the rigorous thinking that, when applied to the outer world instead of religious issues, became science. During what appeared to be a medieval hibernation between the end of pagan Rome and the Renaissance, a metamorphosis occurred. The medieval world provided a period of discipline that led from the speculative thinking of the ancient world to the applied reason which would build the West.

The modern world's opening chapters, the Renaissance and the Reformation, came out of a long period of Christian medieval development. The foundation for those opening expressions of the modern West was the level three medieval Christian world; but the building that arose on that foundation was not medieval.

CHAPTER IX

Stage Four and the Western World, Part 1

The modern West begins

By the end of the medieval world, the basis for the modern West was in position. A strong superego held the impulses, drives, and needs of the internal child and the unconscious in place. The foundation was ready for the development of the ego. It would be the most sophisticated mental development history had ever produced: mental facilities that would conquer many diseases, go to the moon, split the atom, and wage warfare on a scale unknown to our predecessors. It would produce romantic love as well as racial hate. The development of the ego in the internal world corresponded to the development of the nation-state in the external world. They are the engines that drove the West to master the world, beginning around 1500.

The West's earliest differentiation into a new culture began after the breakup of the Roman Empire. As the ancient world ended, the Roman Empire split into eastern and western halves and the western division settled into what was to become medieval Europe. Rome remained the religious center of the West, and in many ways the political center as well. But north of the Alps, a new way of thinking was beginning to take hold. The people of the area were pagans who were converting to Christianity. While they had cities, they were less city-oriented than their fellow believers to the south. That led to a new concept: a society that had cities but was not based on them, as opposed to earlier societies that were centered on one city. The emphasis on a region, as opposed to a specific city, would in time lead to the nation-state and the idea that a religion could be held by a people without a relation to a specific city. Medieval Christianity provided the stepping stone from the city-state of the ancient world to the nation-state of the modern world.

Perhaps it was due to the north's distance from Rome that the thinking and ideas that would lead to the modern West began to appear in Northern Europe. Soon after the year 1100 C.E. the seeds of stage four thinking appeared; they would fully blossom about 400 years later. It was in the twelfth century that European thought started to show signs of change. The stories of the Holy Grail, King Arthur and the Knights of the Round Table, and other knights and quests began to spread.[134] The idea of courtly love and courtly behavior started to be circulated by troubadours. Reason had been a servant to faith for medieval scholars but the roles were beginning to reverse.

The West's twelfth-century steps away from medieval thinking have been noted by historians. Charles Radding observed that reliance on authorities began to lose favor while emphasis on one's own logic increased during this time. Trial by ordeal, as opposed to trial by jury, began to fall out of favor, and the idea of personal intent became an issue in law, so that murder with malice aforethought became a more significant crime than an accidental killing. It is noteworthy that Radding described those changes as being parallel to the developmental changes outlined by Piaget.[135,136] Colin Morris reported that one of the most important developments of the era was the "discovery of the individual," with increased emphasis on individual evaluation, salvation, and initiative.[137] Caroline Walker Bynum stated that although this was not modern individualism, it was an increase in confidence and optimism due to conforming to the life of Christ in an attempt to serve as a model for others;[138] it was a movement of individual actions. She reported an increased focus on holy relics during that period, which led to more interest in devotional art but also led to rejection of such images;[139] centuries later we look back at this as the beginnings of our conflicts with extremes of materialism. Bynum also reported that people became fascinated with the idea of change.[140]

King Arthur and his knights

The Arthurian romances and their ideals of courtly behavior helped civilize the nobles of northern Europe, who had remained relatively rustic although effective warriors while high civilization was carried by the medieval Eastern Roman Empire and the Arab Empire.

Stories about King Arthur, the Round Table, and the Holy Grail not only carried the theme of courtly ideals but added the idea of an earthly purpose for each knight, an individual quest and individual meaning. Each knight served his earthly leader and fought for an earthly kingdom. He fought individual enemies and sought his ladylove. At the same time the troubadours, wandering minstrels, were composing and presenting songs of romantic love, a love between a specific lover and his or her one true beloved. While all of these ideas grew out of the medieval world, they were not medieval. They reflect the central ideas of developmental stage four. These ideas represented a new way of seeing the world as individualism began to replace medieval traditionalism.

The core of the Grail stories was an individual quest by a knight. Although Christian purity was emphasized, this was not a medieval group task but an individual's own quest. Reading such tales would prompt the question, What is my personal quest? The implication is finding meaning in earthly endeavors rather than in the afterlife in heaven. There was a job to be done here and now. Interest in the Grail stories marked a shift in interest from life in the hereafter to life on earth in the present.

Much of the knight's task involved overcoming his shadow, an enemy knight. In contrast, for the medieval world, the task had been to stay separate from the shadow. With the Grail stories the task shifted to actively engaging the shadow so as to conquer and control it. The Grail stories echoed the crusades and the group enemy, the Moors; the stories also told of specific, individual enemies conquered by individual knights.

The knight was not at the top of the system, but he was still identified with it. He worked to support and defend the kingdom, instead of only subjugating himself to it. Enemies of the kingdom were to be ruthlessly destroyed. That is, the knight found his position in the social hierarchy, identified with the system, and fought to uphold and maintain his society.

It was not a fight to defend the faith, but a fight to defend an earthly establishment.

Part of the knight's quest was finding his true love. Such love might be for an ideal, unattainable love object, such as his queen. This was the beginning of the Western tradition of romantic love, and it was entirely new to the world.[141] The ancients had erotic love, the Christians had agape or brotherly love, but never in history has there ever been the idea of the unique love of one person for another specific individual. Sexual love and brotherly love are both indiscriminate, but romantic love is quite specific.

The medieval world placed a strong emphasis on the salvation of the soul for life after death. It remained an issue as the West left the medieval world, but where the "soul image" really became the focus of enthusiasm was in romantic love. Lovers found their soulmate, their true love, or their "other half" in their beloved. The soul of the medieval world became the love object in the Western world, something one was to find on this earthly plane, not in the next life. True romantic love could only be with this one special person who was the living embodiment of the soul on earth.

The knight's search for his beloved became the romantic novel, which eventually became standard fare for Western teenagers. Adults living in the West are now much more realistic about love, but it is still the "spell" of romantic love that leads one into a long-term relationship, wherein one may, with luck, find out what love really is. The central part of this process is finding an aspect of one's own unconscious in projection in another person. When someone fits the projection, it seems like one's soul or "other half" has been found.

Of course, you do not find your unconscious in the beloved, but rather an embodiment of the opposite sex of your conscious attitude. For a woman this is the animus, and for a man this is the anima.[142] The animus or anima is an unconscious part of each of us, usually found when projected onto the lover. The lover as a real individual person is not truly known until time has passed and real love hopefully has developed. That is when they see their partner as the person they really are, and the animus or anima projection is somewhat withdrawn.

This is all rather theoretical, but it is important to recognize what became of the medieval passion for saving the soul. It became the Western passion for finding the beloved.

Both the shadow and the anima or animus are aspects of the unconscious, and both are initially found in projection, carried by the people one loathes on the one hand, and the people of the opposite sex that one loves on the other. Neither appears in the developmental process until stages three and four, when the socially unacceptable parts of the mind are "cut off" and repressed. They are then found "out there," in projection, embodied by living people that one finds repulsive or attractive.

The central character of the Grail stories was King Arthur, an earthly ruler who sent knights out on their quests. It is notable that the central role was a king as opposed to a pope or religious leader; this reflected the coming change in importance of those roles. Historians Will and Ariel Durant noted that the central issue of medieval politics was the supremacy of the pope over kings while the central issue of modern politics has been the conflict of nation-states no longer under papal control.[143] When Charlemagne became emperor of the Holy Roman Empire in 800 C.E., he was crowned by the pope. By the sixteenth century, Henry VIII had broken with Rome and founded the Church of England on his own terms. As the medieval age of faith waned and the Western age of reason developed, the power of the church diminished as the power of the king, and later the state, grew. Primary allegiance would shift from faith to king and country.

An earthly hierarchy is built into the Grail stories. The king was at the top over the knights and nobles, who were all above commoners. Leaders and leadership are also intrinsic; the king led the nobles, the nobles led the knights, and the knights led the commoners. Stage four people want to lead or be led, and they want to know their place in the system; these principles are central to supporting and upholding the social order. This subordination of the individual to the leader in the external world is parallel to the subordination of the internal child and the superego to the ego in the internal world during stage four.

Values of the West

The values that arose early in the Western world are those of developmental stage four. The individual shifts the focus from a position of pleasing authority and "being nice," to the task of forming an individual identity and assuming authority in life. Reason and logic begin to dominate thinking. Knowledge is sought as a pathway to power and importance in the group, rather than pleasing the group. Romance becomes a central theme.

In stage four, as in the modern West, there is an emphasis on the individual and individualism as never before. We take this for granted and assume that it has been true for all of history, but that is not the case. People's roles in the ancient world were felt to be the result of fate, whether to be poor, rich, or slave. One author goes so far as to state that the people of the ancient world "knew nothing of individual liberty" as each citizen was entirely subordinate, body and soul, to their city.[144] In the medieval world as well, people were seen as locked in their fated roles, roles to be played out until death, when they would join the hosts of angels in heaven. A medieval person would say that they would accomplish a task, "God willing"; a modern person would commit to the task and follow through regardless. There is a much greater sense of making your own destiny in the West than was ever the case in the past. We have each become the Grail knights going out on our quest in our daily lives.

Rank in the stage four hierarchy is defined by one's position in the hierarchy, that is, one's role in life. While heredity or luck may get you the job, it is the job itself, be it monarch or street sweeper, that gives the primary definition of who a person is in Western society. This is reinforced by the ego's need to build strength and self-esteem, something that work provides as we acquire knowledge and competence. The ego is given to work and the role it implies, as the inner child is given to appetite satisfaction and play; the modern person demands work, while the ancient Roman demanded bread and games.

The persona, the facade one presents to the world, becomes one's role in society in stage four. If I meet you socially, I present myself as a psychologist, although that is not who I really am; that is only my role, my social facade. The persona, the face one presents to the world, begins to develop in stage three, but it is largely limited to a mask of a good, socially acceptable person. Stage four individualism and its emphasis on individual accomplishment cause the persona to develop into an individual role in the social hierarchy, be it butcher, baker, or homemaker. This is central to stage four ego development. It is the front that allows the individual ego to mesh with the demands of the group. That mask also serves as a skeleton or framework for the developing ego; behind the mask of butcher or homemaker the ego develops as it fills out its role in life.

Society's hierarchy is actually a hierarchy of personas, a ranking of the various roles in society. The persona of king outranks the persona of nobleman, which outranks the persona of knight, and so on. The higher the role, the more power that person has. The physician role outranks the plumber role, and has more power and more rights. This distribution of power and authority is intrinsic to the stage four hierarchical society.

The problem with the persona is that it is easy to think that I am my persona, not that it is just a role I fulfill. This is termed identification with the persona. It is normal for a young adult, but it becomes a problem in the second half of life. The person who remains overly identified with their role in life is unable to differentiate their social role, be it plumber or dermatologist, from the inner person they really are, their ego. That makes figuring out who they are more difficult, but it is even more problematic in that it ties the individual's identity and self-esteem to their position in the social order. It is then easy to feel that a person higher in the social structure is better than someone lower and vice versa, so the banker feels superior to the carpenter. That wasn't such a big deal a century ago, but in our time it leads to an inflated sense of self-worth for the more powerful and successful, and a deflated self-valuation for those lower in the hierarchy. It makes it difficult to recognize one's shadow because the shadow is seen only in projection to other people in the social hierarchy, rather than as a part of one's own mind. If one can only see oneself as a lawyer or gardener, how can one realize who one really is?

The level four association between the persona, role identity in society, and work suggests the probability that work will become much less important as level five society develops and the need for the challenge of ego development diminishes.

In the first half of life, in early and middle adulthood, the ego develops by identifying with its persona. By developing its role in life, the ego is strengthened and tied into the social structure. Individuality in stage four is emphasized as never before in history even though a strong group identification continues. The knight was willing to sacrifice his life for the kingdom he served, and uncountable soldiers have done the same since. This is not a sacrifice for a chance to get loot or slaves in the ancient world, or for the faith in the medieval world, but to support the political system. The Western individual feels a part of his or her political division, be it kingdom or nation-state, and feels it important enough to defend and sacrifice for, even self-sacrifice. The idea of loving a country would have seemed foolish to a medieval person; such love was reserved for the church. An individual from the ancient world would have understood a love of the city-state, which was essentially a family of families. But the person from the ancient world would never have understood swearing allegiance to a nation, an entity which would seem to be only an area on a map, a government hierarchy, but not a clan or extended family.

The stage four allegiance to the system led to the rise of the nation-state. The system that Western people began to identify with was their nation. There might be fondness and devotion for a particular ruler as had been the case in the ancient world and the medieval world, but with stage four the primary identity began to be with the nation, as Britain or France. This was the order that each person felt a part of, to which each person felt a duty and responsibility.

Stage four develops a partial individualism, one still strongly rooted in group identity. The West's individualism, strong as it is, is swept aside by national identification, as when the country is involved in a war. When the passions of war arise individual concerns are forgotten and personal identity becomes swept up in that of the nation-state.

CHAPTER X

Stage Four and the Western World, Part 2

The beginning of the nation-state

After 1500, Europe's social organization began to change from kingdoms with diverse populations into nation-states with more homogeneous populations. The English gave up their claims to parts of France, and the French people began to identify with greater France and the French king, as opposed to separate provinces and rulers. National identities began to develop, with citizens beginning to feel they were a part of the nation-state and not just subjects of the local nobility.[145] Most European states began to centralize power, largely due to war. By 1660 European wars were fought primarily on the basis of national interest rather than religion.[146] Personal power began to be projected to the king, who was seen as living symbol of the political system one identified with, and not just the local noble who ruled by force of arms. The power of central governments began to increase as church power waned. Primary personal identity began to shift from transnational religions to the nation-state. Looking back, it is clear that a new age of history was beginning after 1500.[147]

With this increased power of kings came a royal hierarchy, similar to King Arthur and his knights, but vastly expanded. Kings became monarchs. There were any number of royal positions: courtiers, knights, the noble families, earls and dukes, knights, squires, and on and on. With this came a large hierarchy and a rank-order system. All of these people became part of the extended systems of the kingdoms of the West. They became a part of and actively supported it. This is the behavior of a stage four person: not merely pleasing authority, but maintaining and supporting it. Because of this, stage four thinking tends to be quite authoritarian. Each individual knows where he or she stands in the ranking, and hence has power and control over those below. People rarely have equal status in a hierarchical society; even if two individuals have the same rank, one would have seniority due to age or time in service. Hierarchical ordering of society begins in stage two and reaches a zenith in stage four.

The stage four person projects a great degree of personal power to those above him in the hierarchy, with increasing power projected to those nearer the top of the heap. The monarch was seen as next to God.

The stage four hierarchy showed little mercy in building the nation-state. It would lead to an upper class that would march its enlisted lower-class soldiers into almost certain-death battles, use the press gang to "recruit" any lower-class male found outside his village, and execute lower-class people or transport them to distant colonies for minor legal offenses. Because they did not own land, the poor could be fenced out of common areas and allowed to starve if the nobles so chose. Less advanced people could be enslaved or eradicated. Early stage four people felt little, if any, empathy toward those they dominated; those people represented the shadow and the shadow must be mastered. It is only in later stage four that empathy for people carrying the burden of the shadow begins to develop.

Position and power have been held by those born to it, but there was also a gradually increasing emphasis on performance. Just as King Arthur's knights were held in higher esteem if they conquered more enemies than their peers, people in the West have been seen more positively if they have been successful. This was not so much so in the medieval world. For a medieval person, such a thought would represent vanity and pride. Not true for the West. The concept was that a knight in favor with God would prevail over a knight in a lesser degree of favor with God, and therefore be more godly. Material success on earth began to be seen as evidence of godliness. This was new for the West.

The result was a gradual shift toward earthly accomplishment and materialism. The emphasis was no longer on the next world, as had been the case in medieval society. For the West, the emphasis was on achieving here and now. God rewarded the good with success. The good citizen felt the need to maintain the social system and achieve. The material world began to be much more important than it ever had been in the medieval era. More power and more knowledge would make one more successful, and this formula would make our world.

Western thinking leaves the medieval world

Stage four materialism takes two forms. There is a focus on the material world itself, ranging from an interest in scientific explanation of physical phenomena, to the physical body and its health, to money and physical things one can own. The second focus is on a material explanation of the world; tears from a holy statue explained as condensation of moisture from the air, or spirit possession in a séance explained as hysteria. The latter is rational thinking, as opposed to stage three faith, and when it is refined it is the scientific method. It is not possible before stage four.

The changes that began gradually after 1100 C.E. became earth-changing after about 400 more years, beginning around 1500. Copernicus showed that the earth rotated around the sun, moving us away from a mythical position at the center of creation and into the reality of scientific knowledge. Columbus discovered new worlds unknown to the Bible. Luther began the Protestant Reformation, removing the Roman Catholic Church as intercessor between humans and God and replacing it with an individual relationship to the deity. Henry VIII broke with the Catholic church and founded the Church of England, placing the nation-state above the church and furthering the spread of Protestantism and nationalism. Art began to portray classical subjects, reflecting the rediscovery of classical learning, as opposed to medieval religious subjects. Sandro Botticelli's "The Birth of Venus" (circa 1486) marked a return of the sensual side of the feminine after a millennium of picturing her as the maternal Mary. The work of Leonardo da Vinci and Michelangelo marked the high Renaissance, a sea change in our art and knowledge. Ferdinand Magellan's expedition of 1519-1522 circled the earth proving it to be round. Vesalius founded modern human anatomy, basing his work on actual autopsy as opposed to repeating notions of antiquity. Shakespeare wrote plays about complex characters with contradictory motivations, as opposed to single-trait characters of earlier works, reflecting the complex motives of the ego. His plays emphasized that one makes one's destiny, as opposed to the fated life of the medieval world.

As the power of individual reason grew, it pushed faith and medieval reasoning aside. By the sixteenth century, the great medieval scholar, John Duns Scotus (who died in 1308), was rejected and even ridiculed. All we have left of him now is the word dunce.

The West began to leave the medieval world after 1500. We left the shelter of the medieval Catholic Church, which was so powerful it could supposedly get a sinner's soul out of hell, with enough prayer and donations. We left the shelter of the group approach to belief, forcing each person to consider his or her personal religious beliefs. We left the shelter of a mythological earth-centered world, just as God had supposedly made it, and moved into a less secure position, rotating around the sun. Many of the old comforts and securities were lost. Of course, they were only mythological securities, which is true of any security we dream up, but it was security. Humans had to face living, reproducing, and dying with more independence, but less security and more loneliness than they ever had before. Individuals were much more independent and on their own than at any earlier time in history.

The shift could be briefly described as a change in thinking from "we believe" to "I know," the result of the developing ego. It has been termed a "cognitive revolution" occurring between the mid-twelfth century and the seventeenth century.[148] Destiny came to be seen as being in the individual's hands, rather than in their fate, or as Shakespeare put it, "The fault, dear Brutus, is not in our stars, But in ourselves."[149] Will and intention replaced fatalism and tradition. Causality replaced fate; the West learned to think rationally. With the realization that failure was also possible, probability entered thinking. If the success of an endeavor was not determined by fate but by probability of success, then insurance and alternative planning became possible. Events and behavior had discoverable causes as opposed to the whims of fate; cause and effect replaced miracles. Making plans of action replaced consulting prophecy. Shakespeare's works presented radically new concepts, as character causing destiny, and intention leading to action, as opposed to fatalism. A medieval person would easily accept spare bones as being those of saints, and loose feathers as having fallen from angels' wings. Modern people think much more logically; compared to medieval people, all Western adults are scientists.

Knowledge consisted of both fact and fantasy in the ancient world. The Romans believed that a race of people who had only one large foot lived in Africa. They accepted this and presented it as fact on maps, yet never investigated the story to see if such people actually existed. Julius Caesar claimed that he was a descendant of Venus. The ancient world did not have the division between myth and reality that we have today; their knowledge was much more like that of a child. This changed somewhat in the medieval world, as the details of faith were argued extensively among theologians. But for the average medieval person, if it was said that a holy man had not eaten for fifty years, or drunk water in three years, then that was fact, as everyone knew holy men did not need food or even water.[150] If it was reported that a dead holy man, lying in state, awakened from the dead, and rebuked mourners for worshiping his body, it was taken as fact; everyone knew holy men can perform such feats. Rationality as we know it, and the need for rationality, developed somewhat during the medieval period, mostly among scholars in regard to issues of religious dogma. But modern Western development produced rational thought honed to its keenest edge by the scientific method. It is one of the West's great gifts to the world.

Time became much more important as the modern West unfolded. During the medieval era, time was seen as beginning with creation, continuing cyclically through the church calendar year after year, more or less the same, and ending with judgment day. Otherwise time held little meaning. Individual days were only important as religious days or as indications of when to plant and when to harvest. Likewise, individual hours were only important as times for prayer. But with Western thinking came real clocks and a need to know the time and date. Time became something to control, with accurate clocks, accurate appointments, and the use of clocks for accurate ocean navigation. Suddenly much more was going on in life besides planting and harvesting.

The stage four thinking of post-Reformation Europe began to leave the mythological world of angels and demons and see the world as it really is. This permitted our ancestors to develop better tools, accurate counting and measurement, accurate perspective in art and engineering, better mechanics, and a better grasp of physical reality. From this we have gained huge improvements in our equipment, food, medicine, architecture, knowledge, and ability to make war.

After 1500 the West used its new tools to conquer the earth, including colonial exploitation and slavery. Sympathy for the exploited people was not there, or only superficially so, until relatively recently. Occasionally there would be suggestions that some group of non-European people should not be treated so badly, but the general trend was toward ruthless exploitation that was seen as God's mandate for the earth. The newly discovered people were darker than the Europeans, they were less technically advanced, and they were not Christians. Therefore they were obviously dominated by Satan and suitable for exploitation; it was God's will.

Slavery had been virtually eliminated in medieval Western Europe,[151] but was used extensively in the Western exploitation of the New World. Black people had been present in the ancient world and they were seen with respect, especially in late antiquity.[152] They were seen by Early Christians without any negative bias, solely as other Christians.[153] It is only after about 1600 that Africans began to be portrayed in a negative light, virtually as beasts.[154]

By 1680 it could be said that to be black was to be a slave in the English colonies in North America.[155] By 1776, there were two colors, black and white, and two statuses, slave and free.[156] Race based slavery is a product of the modern West.

Capitalism flourished with this mind-set. It arose in the medieval world, but its growth was explosive in the West. It did not develop in the ancient world where contracts, profits, and bribes were more likely to go to cronies and relatives rather than to the ablest provider. It did not flourish in the medieval world with its denial of material values and denigration of money, finance, and interest. Thriving capitalism is a feature of stage four historical development. It requires a business-oriented middle class and a sense of identity with the system rather than catering exclusively to one's family or clan. It requires a sense that material values and profits are good, and an independent, inventive mentality to make or do something that will produce a return on investment. It thrives in a materialistic society with ideals of progress; new and better goods could be produced for a receptive market. It thrives in the intellectual freedom of the West, because of individual needs to compete, apply knowledge, and achieve.

At the same time more and more knowledge was accumulated, to the point that many diseases have been conquered. Better farming knowledge led to the ability to overcome hunger and famine. The conquering Western mind extended its control over almost all of the earth. All of this was made possible by the new psychology of the West. It allowed rational, factual thinking unperturbed by belief and tradition. As thinking moved away from belief and toward reason, it allowed facts to dominate the mind's view of reality, as opposed to beliefs. Reality could be grasped, studied, and manipulated to a much greater degree than ever before. It was only with the stage four psychology of the Western mind that rational logical thinking and the scientific method became possible.

Protestantism and the West

Rational thinking demanded materialistic answers, as opposed to explanations involving angels and saints. Protestant religion associated godliness with materialistic success, not success in the next world. Combined, these factors made the West the most materialistic society ever.

The Protestant religions that came to dominate the West reflected this new thinking. It has been suggested that the West's orientation toward materialism and success is due to the Protestant religions, hence the expression "Protestant ethic[157]." But the Protestant religions developed out of the same psychology that produced Shakespeare and Western science. It has not formed our psychology; rather, our psychology has formed it. It is a religion that has developed out of our way of thinking and our psychology, just as the ideas of Copernicus and Shakespeare did.

For people of the modern West, Catholicism, Judaism, and other forms of worship are all virtually Protestant sects. The Catholics believe the pope is important and listen to him a little bit, when it fits with what they want to believe; other sects don't listen to him at all. Most sects accept Christ, but Jewish people don't. Mormons have an entirely different scheme of things. But we're all Protestants, because that is our underlying psychology of individual will and choice, earthly achievement, and materialistic (both in the sense of material goods and non-spiritual thinking) values. While superficial beliefs vary widely, the fundamental values do not; from a psychological point of view, modern Western Protestant religions, modern Catholicism, and modern Judaism are much more similar to one another than they are to medieval Roman Catholicism or medieval Judaism. All are strongly based on Western psychology, the so-called Protestant ethic, and all are miles from their medieval roots. The psychology underlying Protestantism defines the West, and there are very few native-born Western adults who are an exception to this.

It is interesting to watch the upsurge in Protestant sects among newly arrived Latinos in the United States. A recent immigrant from Latin America informed me that he had left the Catholic church and joined a Protestant group. He told me that he now reads the Bible (as opposed to the priest reading it for him), that the Catholics worship idols (statues of Mary and the saints), and that he knew of a priest in the old country that had sex with nuns there. These are almost the same arguments raised by Protestants in northern Europe 500 years ago, and they are becoming important to a people who seem to be leaving an almost medieval peasant world and who are now seeking a place in the modern West. I have repeatedly observed a strong desire for a job and a trade among these people. I recall a young man beginning his trade telling me "I am a plasterer," proud of his new identity. He found a Western identity, as opposed to the typical generic "field worker" identity in the old country. This all reflects a newly established ego orientation, a need to have a skill, knowledge and position, and to control one's own fate, rather than the fatalistic traditional society left behind. It is the same process that northern Europe went through in the Reformation. It may be a different time, but it is the same developmental process.

For a medieval person there was little difference between God the Father and Jesus, God the Son. They, along with the Holy Ghost, were seen as distant, unapproachable, and strict. They were essentially viewed as one distant unit. Little emphasis was placed on Jesus and less on the Holy Ghost. While there was a familiarity with the stories of the life of Jesus on earth, he had left earth and was reigning with God the Father in heaven; the familiarity ended with the ascension into heaven. The personal relationship with Jesus typical of the Protestant West was not present. God was seen as three beings, but all with the agenda of a strict, stern and unforgiving father, and there was little differentiation between those beings. God was essentially a Great Father God. In these respects, medieval Christianity was more similar to medieval Judaism than to modern Christianity. Jesus, as part of God, came to earth, but he went back to heaven, and he was there with his father, ready to return and give out horrible punishments to the damned.

While the three forms of God were relatively distant and inaccessible to the medieval Christian, the saints, especially Mary, were not. The saints were seen as approachable, much as modern Christians have come to see Jesus. The idea of Jesus as a "personal savior" would never have entered the mind of a medieval person. But the saints were not gods; they were ordinary mortals who had supposedly led exemplary lives, had died, gone to heaven, and could intercede between those living on the earth and God. Living holy people also served the same purpose, to a lesser degree; touching the robe of a devoted hermit might cure a disease, for example, and medieval Judaism was similar in this respect. These humans, dead or alive, served as a bridge for the great medieval gulf between God and ordinary mortals.

The arrival of Protestantism was supposedly the "Reformation" of the Catholic church. But it is with Protestantism that the central character in Christianity became Jesus, making Protestantism an entirely new religion when compared with the medieval church. God the Father, along with the saints, faded into the background. Jesus became the model for human behavior. Everyone could now read the Bible, something previously open only to the church hierarchy, and Jesus was the savior, not the church. The individual became responsible for his or her own soul.

But this is not the real reason for Protestantism or the Reformation. The real reason was the huge shift taking place in the psychology of Europeans as they left the medieval world and entered the modern West. Hundreds of years (1100 to 1500 C.E.) of gradually increasing emphasis on individual will, earthly achievement, and materialism required a new religion and a new deity. Jesus became the center of religious attention. While he was God, he was also human, and thus to some small degree he was just like us mortals—almost one of us.

This shift was made because Jesus could be interpreted as matching the new psychology developing in Europe. He was an individual who faced his challenge and conquered it. The Protestant Jesus was the first of a long line of "good guys in white hats" for the West. He became the model for behavior, the conqueror of death and Satan. Each follower would be "a good soldier of Jesus Christ"[158] who would do their own conquering on this earth rather than waiting patiently for the next world as their medieval counterparts had done. Jesus became the ideal for action on the material plane. Jesus had faced his task, assigned by God the Father, of being crucified and dying, descending into Hell and harassing Satan, and coming back from the dead. He took concrete action on earth rather than just "being good" and waiting for the next world. He set the standard for heroic behavior for the West. It was no longer sufficient to simply "be good"; you had to prove yourself in this world. You had to act. Belief remained in the background, but action moved to the foreground.

A great split in the Western mind had begun with early Christianity; you were to be on the good side of the fence, and Satan and nonbelievers were to be on the other side. This reflected the separation of the medieval mind from its shadow. But Jesus took this a step further when he "descended into hell"[159] during his period of earthly death, and in doing so defeated Satan and death. This was a minor point for medieval Christians. But for the Western mind, the model changed from just separating from the shadow, to conquering and controlling it. The new model was a heroic orientation toward overcoming and dominating the shadow, a line of thought that had been growing in the Grail romance stories. It would be acted out in innumerable ways, from conquering disease to conquering non-white people. Competition, conquest, and control in the material world were built into Western psychology from the beginning. It is inherently a psychology of winners and losers.

The Protestant ethic has been associated with the rise of capitalism. It encouraged work and the accumulation of wealth so that capital investments could be made. The ethic is the expression of the underlying psychology of level four, identifying with Jesus and overcoming Satanic sloth, as opposed to simply behaving and waiting to go to heaven. The material world and materialism became positives, as opposed to the medieval view of the world as only a place of temptation. But this new orientation had a dark side: success became associated with godliness. Material success and successful enterprise became subtle measures of God's favor. The rich and successful were blessed by God for their goodness, the poor less so, despite claims of the poverty of Jesus. It is the West's psychology of winners and losers, and the poor continue to be abused in the West, because they are the losers.

The entire orientation of the West changed as it left its medieval roots and began to form a world that we can recognize as being familiar to us now. The newly-formed Western mind was not dominated by libido and impulses as was the case in the ancient world; it could accept impulses as they were now under well-developed superego controls. It was not constrained by rigid belief as the medieval world, but allowed a large degree of individualism which could operate in harmony with belief yet not be dominated by it. It needed to confront and control the shadow, and was not content to only be separated from it. It wanted active involvement with the material world and rational explanations for its phenomena. These changes represented a completely new consciousness, that of Western culture. The psychology developed a new part of the mind, something that had never been developed before, a part based on earlier developments but superior to them all: the ego.

CHAPTER XI

Stage Four and the Western World, Part 3

The psychology of the West

The development of the ego and ego psychology is the direct result of the past few centuries of Western culture; it paralleled the development of the nation-state over that time. The West's exploitation of the non-Western world helped spread this psychology over the world, a process which began to gain speed after World War I and accelerated more after World War II. Western consciousness has become the rational thinking of much of the world.

The ego is the part of your mind that is you: the controlling center of your thoughts and behavior, your conscious mind, your sense of "I." It has access to knowledge, memories, and sensations, but it is not these things; they are its resources. If you think that "I like this" or "I dislike that," then that "I" is your ego. It does not include your unconscious mind. It does not include your inner child (your inner Calvin or Susie) and it does not include your superego and its rules. The ego is to the inner world as the nation-state is to the outer world; they are both built with the same processes using the same symbols.

I have identified the parts of the mind with various characters. The unconscious is the prehistoric person, the inner cave man or woman who provides hunches, intuitions, coincidences, and dreams, based on a fundamental, almost organic, view of life. Jung referred to this as the 2,000,000-year-old man.[160] Then there is the inner child, the inner King David or Bathsheba, or Calvin or Susie (of "Calvin and Hobbes"). The inner child is strongly tied to the impulses and is the source of spontaneity, play,

141

creativity, naughtiness, and childish anger. Next is the superego, best identified as the internalized values of one's society, the values that should be kept, and must be kept, for a society to interact in trust and harmony. The superego could be imagined as a medieval monk or nun, or possibly as an internalized version of the rules learned from one's parents: directions for behavior, what you should and should not do, or laws defining harmony between citizens. Finally, there is the ego, the real you, the central part of the conscious mind which must deal with the other parts and decide what action to take. The ego is the layer of the mind formed in the latest developmental stage. It is the "I will" that allowed the West to conquer the world. It is the will that set Columbus off to discover a new world, Luther to establish a religion based on a personal relationship with God, and Shakespeare to write plays depicting individuals forming their own fates. It is the seat of the will that got us into space and to the moon. It is portrayed by the myth of the hero in the white hat who defeats the villain in the black hat and gets the "girl."

When ego consciousness first appeared historically, as when it first appears in a developing young person, the ego was weak and needed exercising and proving itself to gain strength. Medieval thought and superstitions were rejected, as Henry VIII rejected the Catholic church. After Henry's time Catholics were seen as superstitious and the Catholic church was perceived as having an anti-reason bias. In England there was a fear that the Catholic church would smother scientific thought if allowed to return to power. Similarly, a young person at the same developmental point may reject parental authority or church authority, and embrace an outside identification, such as military, scientific, or police training, to develop their own ego stance. The "being nice" of stage three is rejected in favor of gaining mastery and power. An achieving young person, following a career path suggested by admired teachers and attending Bible study classes, decides to pursue a different course in life. A slothful, dependent young adult living with his or her parents moves out, becomes quite work oriented, and voices animosity toward supposed welfare cheats living off of the system. Dependence on authority, by either trying to please or passive-aggressive submission, might be replaced by a new identity. The values that had been embraced in stage three, typically those of parents, teachers or religious leaders, may be rejected and replaced by a more independent authority. A different political party may be chosen, or some other previously respected parental value rejected, in developing independence.

The West developed ego strength by building a strong social hierarchy, with the upper classes having social control over the lower classes, with slavery, and with wars. Defeating and controlling others, particularly those seen as symbolic of the "darker" aspects of the personality, was a path to ego strength. This developed to the point that upper-class officers could march ranks of lower-class soldiers into almost certain death on the battlefield; World War I was the high point of this. Non-Western people of the world could be ruled, enslaved, or even murdered with absolute belief in the correctness of the action. The Western ego was determined to control as much of the world as possible at any price, and it largely did.

The superior control that developed in the outer world was also developed in the inner world by the ego. In stage three, the superego had developed control over the impulses. This provided the basis for the ego to establish itself as total master of the mind and allow stage four individuality to develop. The ego no longer needed to obey the rules as slavishly as the superego did, but it could decide actions on its own, using the rules yet behaving independently. It could allow the impulses some freedom yet still maintain control.

Armies and slavery are more obvious examples of ego functioning, but the same ego-building events were occurring at a more modest level in daily life. Work, particularly skilled work, became more and more important, beginning with the guilds. Work requires the ego to master some school of learning, be it carpentry or surgery or running a household, and being able to dependably carry out the tasks involved. The entire structure of the West became one huge process of ego development. And the West has carried the machine, the ultimate extension of the ego, to heights unimagined ever before in history, expanding the power and control of the ego even further.

In the 1500s, only a few leading intellects, Galileo for example, had begun to develop the capability for the rational thinking characteristic of level four; the masses of people were firmly entrenched in level three medieval thinking. With each century that has passed since, increasing numbers of Western people have developed into level four and the rational thinking it entails. This means that the average intelligence quotient (IQ) has gradually increased over time. This does not mean an increase in fundamental "brainpower"; our brain has been physically about the same for many thousands of years. It does mean a huge increase in the ability of individuals to use their intelligence in a focused, problem-solving manner.

The ego is the latest, best, and strongest development of the mind, but it is not alone in the mind. The conscious mind also includes the superego and the inner child, and they are separate from the unconscious mind. Each of these parts has their own contact with and views of external reality, as well as their own thoughts and emotions. They motivate action in their own right, in addition to the will of the ego. When you feel the impulse to throw a snowball or flirt, that's your inner child; when you stop yourself because you suddenly realize you're breaking the rules, that's your superego. If you have a dream about the snowball, that's your unconscious speaking.

All of these parts relate to external reality. They each have their own logic. Each is important in its own way. But there is only one body to act and one mouth to speak, so the question becomes, which part determines behavior? The part that is primarily me, the one that I identify with the most, is the ego, the part usually in ultimate control. Its role in an emotionally healthy adult is to take the input of the other parts and determine an ultimate course of action.

It is no surprise that the vast bulk of psychotherapy is oriented toward strengthening the ego in some way or other. Ideally the ego is in good harmony with the other parts, perhaps with the "final say" as to one's behavior. It is important to receive the hunches from the unconscious, the playfulness, spontaneity, and creativity of the inner child, the rules from the superego, and balance all of that with the ego's planning and will. There are problems if there is too much ego control or too little. A person with too much ego control appears as a machine, with no spontaneity and no rules. Mental health problems usually involve too little ego strength. Traditional neurosis involves a relatively weak ego being overwhelmed by an overly negative superego with too much control. Personality disorders are usually caused by a weak ego being overpowered by a dominating internal child, so that the person is almost a child in an adult's body. Psychosis (excluding organic disorders such as schizophrenia) is caused by an overwhelming of the conscious mind by the unconscious as may happen after extreme psychological trauma. Drug therapy ideally follows the same principle of ego strengthening.

The movie "Amadeus"[161] (1984) can be interpreted as a creative inner child (Mozart) impeded by a punitive superego (Salieri) with no protection from a passive ego (the Emperor). The healing effects of the ego getting in touch with a suppressed or repressed internal child are major themes of the movies "Up"[162] (2009) and "Hugo"[163] (2011).

The ego and its problems

We think of the superego as the most judgmental part of the mind; the recordings of your parents and other authorities telling you that you should do this, you should not do that, and so forth. But the most judgmental part of the mind is not the superego. The superego values are the basic values of society. Jung referred to the superego as the collective consciousness, the group shared values for our behavior. They are the glue that holds any group larger than a family or clan together. You should not kill your fellows, you should not steal from them, you should be a good neighbor, you should be faithful to your spouse, and ideas like that. They are not the severe judgments that one ordinarily associates with the superego.

The real culprit is the ego itself. It is constantly comparing itself with others, judging itself in comparison with others, not accepting itself as being as good as others, or otherwise criticizing itself. It does not have the group security of the "we believe" medieval stage three society. Stage four society puts the burden of salvation on the individual, although in a framework of group belief. The unspoken truth of stage four hierarchy is that the nearer one is to the top, the nearer one is to God. This puts tremendous pressure on the individual, coming from the individual's own ego, to compare against others, to strive for success, to amass the physical rewards which should be coming to a "heroic" stage four person. This can fuel insatiable performance demands on oneself and cause huge feelings of inadequacy. The only solution is the self-acceptance which occurs in stage five. It is in stage five when the ego realizes that it is not the center of the world, that it can accept its fate, and accept itself with compassion, as it learns to accept its fellow human beings with compassion. But self-acceptance is not a big part of stage four. As a group, stage four people are probably the most self-critical, socially isolated, and lonely people in the entire developmental process.

The ego's drive to dominate and control pushed the Western mind and Western people to dominate the entire planet. As noted, the British Empire encircled the globe by the early 1900s; the United States is now attempting the same feat. It is only very recently, historically speaking, that we have come to realize that our drive to conquer the earth has actually put our planet and our existence on it in ecological jeopardy.

The seeds of ideas that will lead to demoting the ego from its position of absolute power germinated during the Enlightenment and began to grow in the eighteenth century. New ideas began to filter into the Western mind, including Jefferson's idea "that all men are created equal."[164] That idea grew out of the Western tradition but it is not a part of the Western tradition. It was almost entirely disconnected from the reality of the world at that time, a world with huge class differences and slavery. But the seeds were planted. Those seeds brought us to the huge changes occurring in our time.

The ego has arrived at the end of its development. It has ambivalent feelings about giving up the power it has achieved, although it knows it must do so to continue consciousness development. A new psychology and new ideas have grown strong enough to challenge the old, leading to the social conflicts of our time. It is at this critical point that we find ourselves.

CHAPTER XII

Symbols of Development - Symbols of History, Part 1

Symbols and archetypes

The developmental process is archetypal, made up of a sequence of archetypes which manifest in a pattern of symbols. To make that clear, it is necessary to understand what archetypes and symbols are.

Earlier I defined archetype as the most basic of psychological processes. Archetypes are instinctual patterns that make up the basic structure of the mind. They are a part of the human mind just as hands and feet are a part of the human body, more or less the same in each of us; in this respect they are inherited. They are the building blocks of the very lowest part of the unconscious mind.

Archetypes are an inherited tendency to develop thoughts along certain lines; they are parallel to the inherited tendency to develop hands, feet, or ears. We don't inherit hands or feet, but we do inherit the patterns to develop them; it is the same with archetypes. The importance and emphasis of particular archetypes, and the relationships between them, vary from person to person.

Archetypes may be described as the basic elements of what it is to be a living being. If you take the basic essence of life and divide that into its natural parts, you would have the archetypes. That basic core was then most likely modified by eons of human experience. Perhaps archetypes predated *homo sapiens*, beginning with our earliest hominid ancestors, if not earlier. The instinctual aspect of archetypes suggests a connection with all animal life.

Archetypes are parallel to instincts; perhaps archetypes are instincts, or possibly images of instincts. You don't see an instinct, but you do see ducks flying south in the winter. Likewise, you don't see an archetype, but you see symbols which are manifestations of the archetype. You do not see a mother archetype, but rather symbols of mothering, as a mother nurturing her children or an artist nurturing his creativity. When the mother, the witch, the fairy godmother appear, or themes of positive or negative nurturing arise, you know that the Great Mother archetype is activated and influencing events.

You see, or dream, a symbol, not the associated archetype. The archetype is the energy behind the symbol. Yahweh of the Hebrew scriptures, God the Father of the Christian Scriptures, and Allah of the Koran are all symbols of the Great Father Archetype. We relate to the symbols, but the archetypes are the underlying motivating forces.

Archetypes are the building blocks of the lowest strata of the unconscious mind, the collective unconscious. The next layer, the personal unconscious, usually serves to insulate us from the collective unconscious and the archetypes. The personal unconscious may translate archetypal material from the collective unconscious into symbols human consciousness can understand, as in dream images.

All of human life can be defined symbolically, as life is essentially an interplay of the archetypes. Each person must deal with the continual presentation of symbols on the stage of their life, as they interact with the archetypes which are dominant in their character. This view of symbols as representations of the archetypes and their interactions is one of the gifts of Jung's psychology.

Each archetype typically has two basic faces, polar opposites, as "good" and "bad," or light and dark sides, and each also has many manifestations and variations. These numerous aspects then interact with other archetypes in their various aspects, producing an infinite number of possible combinations, but a relatively limited number of basic themes. For example, the good mother nurtures and promotes her child, and the bad mother starves and devours her child. Infinite variations of the two basic faces of the archetype are possible. When manifested as the Great Goddess, she had the basic forms of the maiden, the mother and the crone, each of which could have the positive or negative face. These basic forms have been elaborated and developed into numerous themes, including the love goddess, the virgin, the siren, the prostitute, the deadly prostitute (through disease or murder), the prostitute with the heart of gold, the redeemed prostitute, the nun, the tomboy, the demanding mother, the forgiving mother, the dependent daughter, the father's girl, the homely girl, the evil step-mother, the frigid wife, the over-sexed wife, the witch, the fairy godmother, the Amazon, the non-sexual partner, and on and on.

The developmental stages have an archetypal basis and are manifested by symbols. Each stage is dominated by one archetype from the sequence and its symbol. Symbols for each stage in the sequence determine all facets of that stage. For the individual, they determine the child's view of their parents, the child's view of themselves in relation to their parents, their thinking, their entire worldview. For the great periods of history, the same series of symbols determine the form religion takes, how the society is organized and governed, and how the society as a whole thinks. The stages determine the part of the mind being developed, both in the individual and in a period of history, and the symbol serves as a guide in that development. The archetype associated with each stage determines the myth for the entire stage in every aspect of that stage.

For example, during the medieval era the underlying archetype was the Great Father archetype and the dominant symbol was God the Father. The accompanying mythology incorporated the Hebrew and Christian scriptures, and expanded on them with the traditions of the saints.

The myth of a society is the glue that holds it together. There are roles for each aspect of that myth, and people act out the roles with conviction. If the myth involves witches, some people will be witches, or at least believe they are. If the myth holds women to be of lesser intelligence, then they will behave accordingly and be seen accordingly, whether they are or not. (For example, the supposed difficulty women have with mathematics is probably largely, if not entirely, culturally based.[165]) If the myth involves the class system, members will cite "breeding" as conclusive proof that any upper-class person who can add two plus two is superior, while every peasant must be somewhat simple minded, and everyone in the system will accept it as fact. If the myth dictates that minority people are of lesser intelligence, then the best research and the best testing of that society will prove it, because it is part of the structure of consciousness of the group.

I have portrayed the stages as proceeding, more or less, along similar lines throughout the entire developmental phase, until a new stage begins. But that is not quite correct; behavior is not consistent throughout each stage. Observing the stages is much more like observing the spectrum of light, beginning with red, fading into orange and then yellow and so on. While there is an orange band, part of it is red-orange, and part of it is orange-yellow. True orange is only in the middle of the band.

It appears that the first part of a developmental stage is a determined establishment of the relevant psychology. During this time the new principles gradually but surely establish dominance over the old. Historically, behavior based on a new psychology dealing with dissidents has been more forceful in the first half of a stage, as the stamping out of paganism by early Christianity. The first half of the stage involves the establishment of the appropriate internal psychological and external religious and political structures. In the second half of the stage, the new psychology becomes the established psychology and is no longer threatened by new ideas. Because of this security, new ideas are allowed to enter. These new ideas gradually alter the psychology of the stage, lay the groundwork for the next stage, and eventually lead to the next stage.

For the West, the height of level four thinking was probably around 1800, with Mozart, Beethoven, macho military uniforms in bright colors, Field Marshal Arthur Wellesley (Duke of Wellington), Admiral Horatio Nelson, upper-class officers marching lower-class enlisted men into battles of pre-mechanized warfare, and stamping out the upstart Napoleon. It was about that time that elements of the new psychology began to filter into the Western mind.

Symbols and archetypes of the developmental stages

The child in the first stage is dominated by the mother, and while maturing in that stage gradually learns that he or she is a separate individual apart from the mother. The corresponding mythology of the prehistoric world was centered on a Great Mother Goddess.

The child in stage two, dominated by impulses, learns to separate himself or herself from the mother to satisfy drives. The parallel mythology of the ancient world featured male deities who replaced or married more ancient female deities. The hero tricked the gods to achieve his ends but always eventually succumbed to the Great Goddess in death.

In stage three, the child enters the "should" and "should not" world of the father and the social group, and identifies with group values to form internalized controls of the instincts which had dominated behavior in stage two. In stage three mythology, god the father completely replaces god the mother, and the hero follows the will of the Great Father God; this was the psychology of the medieval world. In this stage the father principle replaces that of the mother, and the Great Father God absolutely replaces the Great Goddess. The Goddess, who took the dead back to her bosom for rebirth, was completely replaced by the Father God who abolished the Great Goddess by promising eternal life in a world after death.

In entering stage four, the former child enters our adult world. Enough "should" values are incorporated in stage three that the young person can use these as a basis for forming an individual destiny within the reference group. The young adult establishes a strong sense of "I" and begins to overcome adversity and establish his or her place in society, upholding society. For society, the Son of God becomes the focus of religion; rather than passively being good, one must actively carry out deeds to achieve acceptance. The Son of God performed heroic actions in accordance with the will of God the Father, including his descent to Hell and harassment of Satan.

The first two stages are dominated by either the mother or a mother goddess. Despite all their masculine bravado and masculine deities, the Greeks, the Romans, and most of the ancient world recognized an earlier mother goddess. Although she was usually shunted aside, she was there, at least in the background. Remember that the ancient Hebrews had Asherah, and that the Hebrew scriptures were edited by later Yahweh priests who were not dominant until after the Babylonian captivity; yet vestiges of Asherah still remain in the Hebrew scriptures, and it is clear that she was a major deity for the Hebrews at least until the time of the Babylonian captivity. Osiris was a primary Egyptian deity but it was his sister and companion, Isis, who had the power to bring him back to life. One of the earliest Egyptian deities was the creator goddess Neith, worshiped since the first dynasty or even earlier.[166]

The second two stages are dominated by the father, either in society as the realm of the group's authorities (the world of the fathers), or by the father god for the group.

The first and third stages are alike in that they are totally dominated by the parental figure, either the mother or father. Heroes of these stages are totally at one with the mother or father god. Prehistoric priestesses served the Great Goddess and medieval saints led lives in accordance with the Great Father God.

Stage three involves a complete rejection of stage two consciousness. Stage two behavior is that of a "bratty" child in the "terrible twos"; recall Calvin. The stage three child rejects earlier thinking and behavior entirely, and focuses on being "nice" and being accepted by authority, particularly group authority, the voice of "the fathers" of society. Similarly, when Europe entered the Christian medieval world, almost all remnants of the ancient world and its paganism were rejected. Stage three is based on a complete rejection of nearly all that came before, with an overriding emphasis on "I am not that" referring to rejected shadow values.

I suspect that the child's entry into stage one is just as drastic a change as the entry into stage three. If there were a "stage zero," a stage before birth, it would be one of absolute harmony of all the archetypes without polarization, with no sense of oneself as an individual being and no sense of others. It would be an entirely instinctual life in a world of timeless being, with no conflict, love, or growth. This would be life in the collective unconscious. Leaving that timeless world and entering stage one consciousness, something that begins when the first vestiges of conscious thinking occur, perhaps when the first breath is taken after birth, there would be a huge change, a complete repudiation of previous consciousness. Therefore it is reasonable to say that both stage one and stage three feature a complete change from the previous stage including a complete rejection of the consciousness of the previous stage.

So, there is a pattern of stages one and three, the odd-numbered stages, marked by behavior that is entirely focused along a new line of development and a complete rejection of earlier consciousness. These two stages are each dominated by a parental archetype and the individual develops in a close relationship to that archetype.

The second and fourth stages, the even-numbered stages, are alike in that both push the dominant parental figure to the background, where they serve as a reference base. With that base the individual works somewhat independently in an effort to form additional individuality. Heroes in stage two ancient world were wily and sly males, like Odysseus or Jacob; they knew they could not completely disobey the gods, but they could get what they needed by trickery. Similarly, the fourth stage is still under the sway of the father, but the personal father, or the Great Father God, recedes into the background as the hero strikes out in the world to overcome his or her shadow. The Son of God conquered Satan on his own, while still following the will of the Great Father God.

Each stage develops out of the stage before, so that all conscious awareness ultimately comes out of the instinctual world of the collective unconscious, the fundamental depths that underlie all consciousness. It is as if human conscious awareness is the bloom on the great collective unconsciousness that is the basis for all human life, if not all animal life, on our earth.

The first stage child is at one with the mother, and the third stage child is at one with the father, or the world of the fathers, being "good" and doing as expected by the group. In the first stage the child wants to be fed, comforted and accepted by the mother. In the third stage, the child looks to the father, or to a paternal authority, for acceptance, guidance and support.

The second stage child says "No!" to the authority of the mother in an effort to establish individuality. The fourth stage young adult leaves the authority of the personal father and proves himself or herself in the wider world to form an identity, usually one separate from the personal father and the father's group. In both cases the relevant parent provides the foundation and guidelines (negative or positive) for the independent growth that occurs and the young person moves in a personally chosen direction away from that parent, but the relevant parent is always the foundation for the stage's growth.

At the beginning of stage one, the infant's conscious awareness is centered entirely on the mother, but when the stage ends, the infant realizes that he or she is a separate, although much lesser, being than the mother. In myth, the newly developed conscious thinking was symbolized by the arrival of a male deity, perhaps the son of the Great Goddess. Stage two mythology begins when a male deity becomes immortal like the Goddess.

By the way, this first birth of conscious awareness seems to set the standard for all later heroes; they are usually males, whether or not they serve the masculine or feminine principle. No matter how masculine the old consciousness may be, it becomes a feminine matrix giving birth to the new consciousness, a new son. The old consciousness is the womb of the new, and the masculine new consciousness is distinctly different from the old; yang is born from yin, and in this case the old is always yin. That is not to say that there are no female heroes, but the typical developmental hero in mythology is male.

I noted that in the early mythology of the ancient world, the Sumerian deity Marduk slew the older mother goddess Tiamat, and later in the ancient world the newer male deities "married" the older female deities and assumed more important roles. The masculine gradually supplanted the feminine principle throughout the ancient world, but it never achieved complete mastery. On the other hand, it developed enough strength and confidence that it no longer required slaying the older goddesses; marrying them to transform them into controlled wives was sufficient.

While the feminine's power began to diminish in stage two, it is with stage three and the medieval world that the feminine is completely pushed aside. She was repressed into a lowly position as the Great Father God assumes total power. She has power only as an ideal mother, as the Virgin Mary, and then her only power is that which is allowed to flow through the dominant male. The feminine is allowed to come back to a greater degree in stage four, as the beloved, the ideal love, but she must forever stand on the sidelines of life in the position of cheerleader for her knight, the one who actually does the achieving in life. This ethic has locked women into very specific roles and has made it most difficult for men to develop awareness of their own feminine side.

In stage four, God the Father in heaven is pushed to the background as God the Son takes the position of importance. This is the conquering hero that has served as the model for the development of the West. God the Father was dominant in the medieval world, and God the Son became the central symbol for the West.

The change of our time

From the beginnings of stage two to very recent times, the conscious mind has largely developed by identifying with masculine values and suppressing the feminine. Once stage two begins, feminine values become secondary to masculine values, continuing through late stage four. Women are seen as temptresses, of lesser intelligence, as weak, and generally incompetent; this is all in an effort to support the conscious thinking that was being developed. Conscious awareness up to our time has, figuratively speaking, been built by the masculine treading on the feminine, built on the backs of women. That is now ending. Stages two, three, and four are dominated by the masculine. Masculine dominance increases through stage two, peaks in stage three, and gradually subsides in stage four; this process is neither right nor wrong, but a fact of nature. As we leave stage four, the feminine is returning to a position of status that it has not held for thousands of years.

Western society is losing strongly defined sex roles, as it is becoming more acceptable for men to be aware of their feminine side and vice versa for women. Men are gradually coming to see women as individuals in their own right, as opposed to projections of the male's feminine side, the anima. Women are coming to behave as they will as opposed to acting to fit male expectations. This acceptance of the opposite sex as who they are, rather than who they should be, means that the anima and animus are beginning to be integrated in the individual; this is a stage five trait. Rigid sex roles are most likely present only in stages two through four. Sexuality is becoming more of a spectrum, versus the specific sex roles of our past.

Likewise, it is highly probable that organized warfare is only a prominent feature of the stages dominated by the masculine, that is, two through four. The rate of violence has been diminishing steadily for centuries and there is every reason to believe this general trend will continue; in fact, the decline in violence may accelerate through better handling of shadow projection.

Another characteristic to consider is introversion versus extroversion. An extroverted personality style is characterized by a primary focus on the outer world, with little value placed on the inner world. These people typically have many friends, prefer to join in with the group, and prefer group activities for both work and recreation. They may seem superficial to introverts. In contrast, for an introverted personality the primary focus is on the inner world, with little value placed on the outer world. They prefer to work alone, or with as few other people as possible. They typically do not like crowds and large gatherings; they are not good "mixers." They usually have fewer friends and emphasize individual values. They may seem shy or stuck-up to extroverts. Most people are more or less between the extremes.

The stage three medieval world was more introverted than either the stage two ancient world or the stage four modern West. When one thinks of the medieval world, thoughts turn to nunneries, monasteries, contemplative religious orders, religious hermits, and intensive focus on salvation of the soul. Those were inner world concerns. Concerns of the ancient world were primarily focused on the outer world, including conquering, getting booty and slaves, and watching the games in the amphitheaters. The West has a similar extroverted outlook, largely focused on business, war, and entertainment. All of the great ages had their introverted and extroverted aspects, but it may well be that the even-numbered stages, two and four, are more extroverted, while the odd-numbered ones are more introverted. If this progression is correct, then we can expect the next great age to be more introverted than the West has been, shifting emphasis from stage four shadow conquering in the external world to stage five shadow integration in the inner world.

Both stage three and stage four are concerned with building the conscious mind by dealing with the shadow. Stage three builds the superego by entirely suppressing the impulses and drives that characterized stage two. The material denied by the superego forms the shadow, which is first constructed in stage three. Stage four feels more confident and takes the projected shadow as something to be controlled. Lower-class people, slaves, and people of color are accepted as shadow-bearers, but never as equals; they are to be controlled and manipulated to serve the ends of those higher on the social hierarchy. Stage five completes the shadow problem by integrating the shadow. Stage three forms the shadow, stage four manipulates it, and stage five integrates it into consciousness.

The sequence of the central symbols of the first four stages of the developmental sequence are the Great Mother Goddess, the children of the Great Mother Goddess, the Great Father God, and the son of the Great Father God. For the individual, the sequence is mother-centered, child of the mother, father-centered, and then child of the father. At the beginning of each developmental stage, the appropriate archetype becomes activated, and the relevant symbol becomes a focal point. For the developing child, the appropriate parent or parent surrogate becomes more important. For the group, the symbol of the archetype becomes numinous, that is, it is seen as having supernatural wonder and becomes a vision of the deity, so that it serves as the core of the group religion and a guiding ideal for behavior in the stage. As each stage ends, the orienting symbol gradually loses its luster and the symbol representing the archetype associated with the next stage begins to appear more numinous and enticing, presenting a greater mystery to be solved in life. The only thing permanent in the process is the process itself, eternal change, stage by stage. Each stage begins and each ends but the process continues. It has brought us to this point and it will continue to carry humanity into the future.

CHAPTER XIII

Symbols of Development - Symbols of History, Part 2

The God-image

The West has passed through four developmental stages to date. The relationship between the individual and the God-image, the symbolic expression of the primary archetype of the stage, has been central to each stage. This process has been termed the continuing incarnation of the God-image.[167,168] Our image of God has changed as our psychology has changed and our consciousness has developed.

Some form of God-image has been present since well before the first cities of the ancient world were founded. Whether male or female, one god or many gods, it has guided the course of civilization since. A civilization may be defined by its God-image and religious orientation. It is only in times like ours, times of change and trouble when religions falter that religion is disparaged. It is disparaged because the old form is weak and dying. It is no longer numinous but has lost its sheen and become shopworn so that it does not hold the world together as it once did. Ask an ancient Roman about how his gods lost power and status as new religions, including Christianity, began to seep into his world.

For each of these four stages of development, the relationship of the individual to the God-image has been exactly the same as the corresponding relationship between a child and his or her parent. In the first two stages the mother dominates, and in the second two stages the father dominates. After these four stages, childhood ends. Our time marks the ending of childhood psychology and the beginnings of true adult psychology. Stage five is the first stage without an encompassing group myth; rather, the group myth dictates that each individual must find his or her own myth. Think where that leaves the God-image: God can no longer be conceived of as a great father in the sky or a great earth mother. Yet some form of a God-image has been with us for an extremely long time, well before the first city-states of the ancient world. It will continue, but in a different form; that is what has always happened in the past.

The subtle nature of change

Remember that the differences between the stages are subtle. Recall that no one noticed that children thought differently as they aged until Piaget's findings in the early 1900s. Medieval Catholics were perceived by their Protestant peers as being less rational, but their differences usually boiled down to political struggles. Similarly, psychological differences today are attributed to differences in politics. In conversation, a person may respond from the internal child part of their personality, perhaps being playful or flirting, without being regarded as unusual. Likewise a response from the superego, as telling someone how they should behave, is usually not regarded as unusual. On occasion, it is possible to become aware of material from the unconscious, perhaps when meditating on a dream. The differences in the stages are neither intense nor profound, and possibly not even noticeable when considered alone. Children typically mature with minimal difficulty, while both parents and schools pay little attention to developmental stages. It is only when these subtle differences are multiplied throughout an entire society, to the point that they color the thinking of the entire group, that they become historically important.

Complexes and archetypes

Earlier I discussed a sequence of parts of the mind that develop during the stages: the personal unconscious, the internal child, the superego, and the ego. These parts develop by maturing under the guiding symbol for their respective stages, combined with the actual experience the child has with the respective parent in the stage.

Each part of the mind is actually a bunch, a clump, a collection, a grouping (or what have you), of thoughts. Jung termed this a complex, that is, a complex of ideas.[169] The personal unconscious, the internal child, the superego, and the ego are actually bunches, or rather, complexes, of ideas. Think of what makes your ego or superego what it is; each is, fundamentally, a huge complex of ideas, thoughts, memories, feelings, goals, sorrows, joys, and so on. All of those ideas make up the person you are. You, as a conscious being, are a complex of ideas. And each part of your mind is likewise a complex which operates with its own separate agenda.

At the center of each of these parts is the appropriate archetype, combined with the experiences the individual had in life with his or her manifestation of that archetype. The central archetype for an infant in stage one is the Great Mother. The personal unconscious forms around that archetype and the infant's personal experiences of the archetype's manifestation, the infant's mother.

If the infant perceives a nurturing mother, the positive side of the Great Mother archetype dominates the formation of the personal unconscious. A complex of feelings, mostly positive, will build up around the core of the archetype, from the positive experiences with the mother, to form the personal unconscious. As an adult, that person has a more nurturing and supportive relationship with the unconscious. The reverse of this happens with a negative perception. In that each archetype has both a positive and a negative aspect, how the archetype is experienced depends on the relationship with the real mother.

When the child is in stage two the archetype is the son or daughter of the Great Mother, and the complex that will be the internal child is formed. It gradually builds up in a complex of ideas, experiences, and feelings, around the core archetype and the experiences the child has with its mother as impulses push the child toward autonomy from the mother.

In stage three the dominant archetype is the Great Father and the developing complex is the superego. That complex forms by integrating experiences, feelings, ideas, and thoughts around the core of the Great Father archetype and experiences with the personal father, or the world of the "fathers," the authorities in the world.

For stage four the archetype is the heroic son of the Great Father and the complex being developed is the ego. It is in this stage that we start to become individuals. The developing ego copies the myth of the heroic son of the Great Father to strengthen itself, forming a complex of experiences, ideas, and knowledge, around the archetypal core.

It is clear that the parts form around the appropriate archetype and the personal experience of the parent in each particular stage. But what actually occurs in that process is not at all clear. Siblings, even identical twins, can be raised by the same mother and father, and yet have different experiences of their parents. For some children, no matter how nurturing the mother is, it is never enough. Is this because the mother is somehow secretly not sufficiently nurturing, or is this an insatiable need the child was born with? After all, no mother is perfect, and if the child expects to see the negative, some negative will always be there to experience. This is the "nature versus nurture" problem, and the developmental model does not resolve the question as to which is predominant.

It may be that we are born with an archetypal pattern already intact, a pattern which leads us to perceive reality according to that pattern. Such a person might perceive authority as being overly strict, and if this strictness is not found in the personal father, they might push society until they find it in society's authority, the police. On the other hand, the archetypal potential may be neutral, so that the experience of the symbol of the archetype in life is the only cause of personality development. That person's father relationship would entirely form their perception of authority. Perhaps it is a combination of both. Perhaps the inborn archetypal pattern is so strong that it can evoke the appropriate behavior in the parent. Or perhaps the parent's behavior is synchronistic with the child's archetypal pattern; this is my guess. But no matter what is the ultimate cause of a psychological pattern, it is a fact that each individual has his or her own personal pattern with an archetypal core, and each must deal with it in his or her life.

For example, everyone has mother and father complexes, but some are more problematic than others. With a difficult father complex, one meets it in projection in one's own father, then in older males and authority figures in life, with the possibility of becoming a difficult authority figure later in life. I have my bully issue to deal with, either bullying or being bullied. It is as if nature gives each of us a selection of archetypes at birth, some in their positive guise and some negative, and then nature leads us to interact with those archetypes as we live out our lives.

Consciousness development

Each part of the mind that forms in the first four stages is a structure that consciousness uses, but these parts are not consciousness itself. You could think of consciousness as being behind the mind, or as using the mind as its framework, but consciousness is more than the sum of the psychological parts. There are three reasons that lead me to this conclusion.

First, the stages of consciousness are the pattern or mold that directs the development of the parts of the mind. If increasing consciousness were only a matter of increasing ideas and experiences, for example, in the internal child, development would never proceed beyond that stage. The mind would only have one developmental stage and it would grow by gaining more and more knowledge; we know that is not the case. When each stage is complete, something provokes the mind into developing a new level of consciousness as the old one has reached maturity. That requires an agency outside of the mind, and I assume that to be consciousness itself. As consciousness matures, it finds itself more sensitive to ideas associated with the next developmental stage, as it prepares to accept or reject that development.

Second, as I will discuss below, stage five consciousness does not involve the creation of another "part" of the mind. Stage five consciousness develops an entirely new stage, but the mind only integrates what has already been created. Consciousness makes a significant step, but the underlying psychological change is an integration of existing parts, rather than the construction of new parts typical of the first four stages. That is, the pattern of development varies, and is not always just adding another layer, as it would be if it were a routine process like a tree growing more limbs.

And third, modern Western people develop through the early stages relatively rapidly. A prehistoric person spent a lifetime in stage one. A modern person rapidly develops through the early stages and enters stage four in their teenage years. Modern consciousness does not need prolonged time in the earlier stages, as it has already developed those stages; consciousness can easily and quickly develop through the early stages to reach maturity. Consciousness can quickly construct the "parts" of the mind necessary to build a modern personality, and it only slows down when there is no further developmental path to follow. It is not the construction of the earlier parts of the mind that takes the time once a certain level of consciousness has been established in a society. What takes time is when consciousness develops in the final stage for that society. That implies that the process is consciousness itself developing rather than just adding more associations to the existing complexes in the mind.

Consciousness guides the development of the mind, and uses the mind, but it is not the mind. It is the power behind the throne. Consciousness develops through its interaction with the mind and the mind's development.

Social structure

The structure of government during each age reflects the structure of the group's consciousness. This is because the symbols that provide framework of the mind in the inner world also shape society in the external world. The form a government takes corresponds to the centers of consciousness for each stage. The people correspond to the personal unconscious, on which consciousness develops. There was no center of consciousness for prehistoric people and there was no government.

A person of the ancient world had one center of consciousness: the internal child. Likewise, societal power had one center, the head of the clan or extended family. The organization of the time was that of the extended family or clan with the head male serving as both clan head and chief priest. There was no conflict between church and state because the two were identical. Each family was a small government with the head of the family having absolute power over the family. The city assembly was composed of the heads of the families. The leader of the ranking family was the city head. That person served as both head of the city's political organization and as the city's chief priest.[170] The ranking male was the only center of power in the external world, reflecting the one internal center of consciousness, the internal child.

For the medieval person, there were two centers of conscious awareness: the superego, and what remained of the inner child after suppressing much of it and constraining the rest. These two centers of conscious thinking were reflected in the power establishment of the medieval world, the pope and the king. For most people there was little identification with the king as we now identify with the nation-state. Rather, the king was secondary to the pope, an authority to be submitted to for temporal matters only. The people were much more members of the faith and the church rather than being citizens of a particular kingdom.

Modern Western governments typically have three independent sections: legislative, judicial, and executive branches, reflecting the three conscious sections of the Western mind: internal child, superego, and ego. We fashion our world, including our governments, in our own image, or rather, in the image of our mind.

The level one child has not learned to differentiate itself from the mother, much less other people. In a similar fashion, level one prehistoric people had little individual identity so that they were egalitarian, vaguely identified with the group. There was no societal hierarchy. It is only in stage two that a sense of separation from others becomes established, and the aggressive impulse leads some to a drive to gain power over others. It is in stage two society that social hierarchy begins. The ancient world reflected this psychology, with stronger males and more politically agile individuals taking control over others and establishing a hierarchy of power in society. In the ancient world, power was held by family and clan heads, and later by heads of the city-states. This continued in the medieval world, with the medieval church added to the power structure.

In both the ancient world and the medieval world, the hierarchy was relatively limited, with most people submitting to the few ruling powers.

This expanded greatly with stage four and the nation-state, in which many citizens felt that they were a part of the social hierarchy. Everyone supported the king, and now, everyone votes, and hence everyone is a part of and upholds the national social order. With level four the system is no longer something only to be submitted to; rather, the level four person identifies with the system and defends it. The hierarchy expands to include almost all of society. Everyone votes, everyone is a member of a political party, everyone has a social role, everyone gets drafted, at least in theory. We all are the nation-state except for the people carrying the shadow; voter suppression is but one method of excluding them.

The power hierarchy, including both physical power and social power, begins in level two and reaches peak in level four. Those stages each require an "other" to overcome or control to act out the psychology of the level and make that psychology manifest in the world. The social hierarchy is the product of that need. Level five psychology features a desire to merge with the "other," resulting in a dissolution of the social hierarchy in that stage. In a similar fashion, objectification of others is greatest in level two, gradually diminishing with development, and finally resolving in level five.

Our time in history

We have now entered a time when the stage four conquering hero is beginning to be seen by mature adults with apprehension. The West has conquered distance, it has conquered disease. It has conquered other people. But the cost of this conquering is beginning to be apparent. Non-Western people are tired of being conquered and are fighting back. The earth has been conquered to the point that its ecological health has become a concern. Distance has been conquered with motorized vehicles to the cost of our resources and air quality. We have conquered everything except conquering and we just can't seem to kick the habit.

Or, to put it another way, we are at the end of stage four, having fully developed the ego and its psychology. The ego is the strongest, most determined, most capable, most controlling part of the mind ever produced. Think of the West and its drive to power, conquest, and control. Think of the British Empire upon which "the sun never set." Think of the current American drive to have the world surrounded by military bases, with control established over the entire planet and outer space as well. This is the fully developed ego, tolerating no bounds, completely determined to rule everything and everybody in the outer world, and control every aspect of the inner world.

Never in the history of the world has the human mind ever had the strength and capability of the modern West. Never.

The modern ego does not want to give up control at any cost, yet it must to continue developing. In many ways the ego would choose death over the loss of control and power it has achieved in stage four. The ego's resistance to further development is compounded by the fact that we are in transition between stage four and stage five, that is, from an even-numbered stage to an odd-numbered one. In our developmental past, the rough parallel to our current position was the movement from stage two to stage three, when the ancient world ended and the medieval world began. We are in a parallel situation now. That was a difficult transition, and the one we are in may be even more so.

There are a number of similarities between stage two and stage four, just as there are similarities between the British or American empire on the one hand, and the ancient Roman Empire on the other. Both stage two and four are marked by an aggressive approach to conquest and control of the external world. The transition of the modern West to stage five could parallel the dramatic transition of ancient Rome when the external world and its materialism were rejected, often in favor of inner lives in monasteries and convents.

Since the transition from stage four to five is parallel to that from stage two to three, this suggests that the changes of our time will be another turbulent transition, somewhat like the one the Romans endured. We are moving from a masculine society based on an unequal social and sexual hierarchy to a society that is almost exactly the reverse. The difference is considerable, and that implies major changes in the West's social structure, exactly what we are living through.

CHAPTER XIV

The Self and Development

Individuation and the Self

The central symbols of the first four stages of the developmental sequence are: the Great Mother Goddess, the children of the Great Mother Goddess, the Great Father God, and the son of the Great Father God. That sequence is the basic framework of the first four stages of individual and group development. We are leaving stage four. The logical question is, what's next?

Jung termed adult personality development as individuation.[171] This includes becoming aware of and integrating one's shadow, and becoming aware of one's contrasexual side, the anima or the animus. This corresponds to the two greatest social changes in the past two centuries of the Western world, racial integration and the increasing equality of women. These external world correspondences, both contrary to the West's central myth, led me to realize that individuation is the individual version of the path Western civilization is taking. The new psychology is individuation, just as Jung conceived it.

Individuation includes a third process, and that is becoming aware of one's Self.[172] The Self is the apparent goal of individuation.[173] It only occurs to individuals through their relationships to others.[174] It will be a central part of the new psychology; at this point in time it has only begun to enter general thinking.

The Self is probably Jung's most difficult concept to understand, and that is because most people have no experience of it in normal living. There is no parallel concept in other systems of psychology. The whole idea seems

169

somewhat mysterious or even mystical, but that is not the case and understanding it is central to understanding the new consciousness.

The Self is the most important of all the archetypes. It is the archetype of wholeness at the center of one's being. Almost the only time a person might experience the Self is in dreams, visions, or hallucinations. Hallucinations of that type are rare, even among the insane. Visions of that sort may appear to individuals in emotional turmoil, particularly if they are withdrawn or isolated, and that is still rare. Dreams with the Self as a motif are most likely to appear. People may draw Self representations, usually circular in form, possibly in an effort to center themselves during times of intense emotional turmoil.

The Self is not yourself. It has nothing directly to do with the conscious mind at all. It is outside of conscious thinking. It is separate from you, a "higher" part in you.

First of all, the Self is a psychological concept, another "part" of the mind; it may or may not be more than that, and you can have your own personal interpretation. The Self has typically been perceived as an image of God, but Jung has made it clear that he is not talking about God, but rather, humanity's image of God, in that it is impossible to know what God really is.[175] If you want to enhance that definition and think the Self has a religious connotation, that is your business. If you want to think that the Self is a bit of God in each of us or the soul, so be it, but all one can say scientifically is that it is a psychological construct arising from the depth of the mind. It is clear that it is bigger than the ego and it controls the ego's destiny. It shapes the development of one's consciousness and ego. It seems to decide life, destiny, and death for the individual. Perhaps it is the ultimate source of consciousness. The Self has nothing to do with what I want, but everything to do with what life gives me. Exactly what else it may be is difficult to say.

The Self is not a theological concept, but an empirical fact derived from psychological observation. All ideas of all deities are always perceived as some form of the Self archetype; it is only through the archetype of the Self that we can experience the idea of the deity. If someone wishes to add a religious connotation to this psychological concept, that is their interpretation, but it was not Jung's intent or his definition. The really critical point is not to confuse the Self with the ego.

The Self appears as a deity appropriate to each level of consciousness development in the outer world. First the Great Mother, then her children, later the Great Father, and then his son, have served as central images for the myth of the times. These are all forms that the Self has taken as it was perceived in a group form, a collective image, as the human race was maturing, just as a child may perceive the appropriate parental figure as a Self manifestation.

The Self is older than the ego[176]; it directs the formation of the ego and other parts of the mind, and controls the entire process of consciousness development in the inner world. It appears to direct much of one's fate in life, as it is in the interaction between consciousness and the events of life that consciousness develops.

The Self and the God-image

In less troubled times, each person feels a link to the God-image of the age. This gives a feeling of living in accordance with God's will, of following God's will on earth. It is living in accordance with the myth of the times, and it is the basis for the feeling of having meaning in one's life. Prehistoric people lived in accordance with the Self in the form of the Great Mother, living their lives in accordance with her will so that she would provide for their needs. An ancient Greek might feel the wrath of Ares flowing through his veins as he engaged in combat, realizing his connection with his Self as personified by the god. Early Christians felt joyfully filled with God the Father as they established a relationship between their consciousness and the Self in the form of the Great Father archetype. Protestant Christians felt the same joy in their connection with the Self as the heroic Son of God. In each of these ages, the Self has appeared as a group image.

The West is now leaving the age of a group image of the Self and God. We now begin to address the Self individually; each person can now form a personal relationship with the infinite within. We can't get salvation from the Great Mother, from Jove or Zeus, from God the Father, or the Son of God any more. Christ is no longer carrying our cross; now each person must pick up and carry his or her own cross. Our childhood, with parental forms of the deity, has ended. The new image is something like a bit of the divine inside each of us, the Self. It places more responsibility for personal behavior on the shoulders of the individual than Christianity, with its forgiveness of sins, ever did. Jung referred to this as "a Christification of many" and added that it requires that the ego maintain a relationship with the Self as opposed to an identity with it.[177]

Connecting with the Self brings meaning to one's life and a feeling of belonging in the world and of living in accordance with divine will, which humans have experienced for eons on end. We are entering an era when this involves an individual manifestation of the Self, not a group image.

The Self does not demand praise, worship, or proselytizing. It just presents us with our life and fate, and it is up to each of us to confront the reality given us as morally as we can. That's about it. If you are lucky you might get feedback in your dreams.

A positive relationship with the Self gives the ego a feeling of acceptance and belonging, a sense that one's life is one's proper path in the world. The ego that feels connected with the Self can accept others. It recognizes its Self as the center of its world and that every other person's Self is the center of their world. It respects itself as being in harmony with the Self at the center of its world, and respects others as being in harmony with their Selves at the centers of their worlds.

Probably the only time the Self might be an active entity in a person's life would be through dreams, usually in a time of emotional crises or significant psychological change. Typical motifs include a circle or an impossible combination of opposites. The circle might be divided into equal parts. I recall a dream of a large and powerful underground engine, formed in a circle, with parts so arranged that it would be impossible to construct in reality. The sun is another such symbol; a realization of the Self was indicated in a dream which revealed that a new solar array had been installed on the roof to collect energy from the sun.

There are traditional group Self symbols that may appear in individual dreams. Mandalas from eastern religions are Self symbols, and sand paintings by Native Americans frequently are. A round church window, called a rose window, may be a Self symbol, as well as symmetrical geometrical images, or images of a supernatural divine child. The image may contain an impossible combination of opposites.

Although the average person has little if any idea of the Self and its meaning, the myth of the individual ego in relationship to the Self has entered Western conscious awareness. It is central to current mythology and some very popular stories which I will discuss later.

It appears that the entire focus of stage five is on shadow integration, anima or animus integration, and forming a relationship with the Self. The latter could be as simple as the realization of a "higher power," as advocated by Alcoholics Anonymous. It may be a sense that the Self and not the ego is the center of one's psychological universe, like the earth rotating around the Sun.

Psychological thinking

Contrary to the four earlier stages of development, stage five does not involve construction of a new part of the personality, but rather involves a connection with already existing aspects of the mind. The first four stages of development are stages of personality construction in which the basic personality structures common to all humans are formed. These are stages of construction, stages of childhood, with guidance from parental archetypes. The later stages are stages of individuation, in which the four basic structures serve as the foundation for true individualism.

I have associated psychological thinking with reconciliation with of the shadow, but it is more than that. It includes awareness of all of one's unconscious, not just the shadow, which is only one aspect of the unconscious. It includes parental complexes, sibling conflicts, the anima or animus, and other issues as well. It is only with psychological thinking that personal conflicts are realized as fragments of one's own personality so that projections to others may be withdrawn.

Without psychological thinking, these conflicts are unresolvable struggles with some other human; one continues to wrangle with issues with one's mother, father, or siblings, but the issues never resolve. This maintains a person in the role of the son, the daughter, the father, the mother, the sister, or the brother, prevents the achievement of independent adulthood, and maintains psychological dependency.

With psychological awareness, the task becomes one of dealing with one's own parental or sibling complexes. This allows a detoxification of relationships with others in one's life and leads to a maturation out of the role of parent, son, daughter, or sibling, and into adulthood. It is only in this process that true independent adulthood is possible. It is the same with anima and animus; as long as they remain unintegrated and in projection, one's partner cannot be seen as the person they really are.

A level four person keeps the shadow in projection psychologically and needs to see people carrying their shadow projection in a secondary position in the external world. When a level four person is confronted with the ideas of having a shadow and shadow psychology, the usual response is to ignore the idea completely and continue to try to figure out who is the bad or wrong person in a given issue. For example, if such a person tells you of a conflict they had with another individual, they will repeatedly come back to the question of who was at fault. You may attempt to explain that the other party symbolized some of their own denied qualities, as a character in the drama of their life or a character in their dream, or a character in the myth of their life, but that idea will be ignored. It always comes back to the issue of who was at fault, who was the guilty party, who was to blame, who is the shadow and who is the good guy. Racial difficulties follow the same model; there is always the suggestion that some innate racial inferiority caused the issue. And there is always a hint that you have been told about the issue not just to establish guilt, but to assume the role of justice and punish accordingly; and if you look at it more closely, you see that the underlying hint is that you are to be the parent who decides and punishes. The issues of blame, fault, and guilt maintain the childhood position and blocks growth into independent adulthood. Determining who is the wrong person, the shadow person, is central to Western psychology as that decides who is in the right; it prevents shadow integration.

It is a painful blow to realize that the less than desirable traits you dislike in others are part of your own personality, and it takes humility to accept it.

Stage five of development takes the ego out of the central position in the mind and places the Self there. The ego retains an important position, just not the central position. That change is subtle but real, similar to humanity's realization that the earth rotates around the sun and is not the center of the cosmos. The ego is not the center of the mind, but secondary to its central source of life, the Self, and everyone's Self is likewise the center of their being.

Developing awareness of the shadow, of the anima or animus and the unconscious, and the Self, brings the mind closer to a state of wholeness. A realization of the shadow means that finding who is at fault is less important than learning the meaning of the conflict in life. Accepting my own shadow makes it much less likely that I will judge another person and more likely that I will accept them as they are. It lessens my need to defend myself so that I can more easily accept others and myself.

The developmental process

I suspect that the developmental archetype has a total of seven stages, each dominated by its own archetype. Seven is a traditionally sacred number and is associated with initiation in mythology. There is a correlation between the stages and mythology of the seven days of creation, and there are numerous references to the number seven in the Hebrew and Christian scriptures. There is a correlation with astrological interpretations of the seven planets (but not in their natural order). The stages correspond with the seven traditional chakras of southwest Asian yoga philosophy.[178] William Shakespeare's "As You Like It" refers to the seven ages of man.[179]

Another argument for seven total stages of consciousness is that stage five appears to be complementary to stage three. The goal of level five is the integration of the shadow, the anima or animus, and a realization of the Self; this is a reciprocal of, or complementary to, stage three, with the formation of the shadow and the anima or animus as the soul. Following that logic, level six would be complementary to level two, with a goal of consciousness integrating the unconscious, and level seven would be complementary to level one, with a goal of consciousness integrating with the collective unconscious. This is approximately parallel to the three stages of the alchemical process discussed by Jung.[180] We can only consider these concepts theoretically at this point in our development.

It also appears that, for humanity as a whole, the developmental process may be accelerating. We were hunter-gatherers for one or two hundred thousand years. Ancient World psychology began in approximately 8000 B.C.E., and lasted a little over 8,000 years. The medieval West lasted about a 1,000 or 1,500 years, and the modern West is beginning to end after only 500 years. Improvements in communication over the centuries only partially explain this acceleration.

The old myth based on the Self's group image as son of the Great Father God is dying, and a new myth is being reborn with the personal Self as its central image. Psychology, history, and religion are all pivoting to a new course as the childhood of humanity comes to a close.

CHAPTER XV

"Things fall apart..."

Difficulties triggered by the West's success

The stage four consciousness of the West began the subtle but relentless change to stage five about three or four centuries ago; it is only in our time that this has become obvious. There has been a gradual acceleration of ideas and events that have led to the difficulties of our time. There are two basic sources for these problems. One is the idea of equality of all people, the first seed of stage five that was planted during the Enlightenment. Stage four is not one of equality, and though every Western country claims equality of citizens, we know it is not true. The second source is the intrinsic rationalism and materialism of stage four itself; that is the topic of the next chapter.

Stage four consciousness has enabled Westerners to think more rationally than ever before; the power and accomplishments of Western science and engineering, over only about 400 years, attest to this. The basic myth that has guided Western consciousness is the story of the hero, acting in accordance with the father's will, defeating his shadow and then finding his true love. But there are subtleties in the myth that are problematic. It is the male hero that does the action; the female is the reward, not the actor. The myth requires that someone play the role of shadow and be defeated and controlled; stage four people are intrinsically prejudiced against people in that role. There is an intrinsic prejudice in favor of those seen as being in the hero role. The myth dictates inequality of the people involved, with people carrying the shadow and females below the male hero, and the hero in a hierarchy of achievers. Success is realized on the material plane and in the material world. Two things should be clear here: equality of individuals never enters the Western myth, but materialism does.

The equality problem

By 1700, Europeans had established a strong and resilient social structure that would grow to rule the world. Social values, religious values, and political structures had grown to a position of confident strength. The earth had been mapped out, at least in its essential details. Many aboriginal people had been subjugated. Religious faith was strong and secure. The world was there for the taking, just as, according to the faith, God had decreed. The stage four social structure that had mastered the Western world was moving to dominate the entire globe.

Underlying the external social structure was an equally strong and resilient psychology. The Western mind was so well established in its psychology that it felt comfortable in allowing new ideas to enter, permitting it to greatly expand its scope of vision over the next hundred years. We now refer to this era as the Age of Enlightenment. Rationality, scientific knowledge and progress made great strides during this time, as they replaced beliefs, superstitions, and traditions left over from the medieval world. The new ideas of the Enlightenment were not compatible with the medieval mind, and they could only be entertained by the Western mind once it had fully developed out of the medieval world.

One idea that took root at that time was that all people are equal. Then it was a far-fetched ideal, only considered by a few philosophers, but it would grow. In time it would help lead to the end of the dominance of Western consciousness, because it is a direct opposite of the core values of Western consciousness. If all people are equal, then the people carrying shadow projections are equal to everyone else: slaves are equal to their masters, poor to rich, lower class to upper class, females equal to males; shadow values cannot be projected to equals. That would mean the end of shadow psychology, the end of male dominance, and the end of social hierarchy; it would mean the end of all of the basic premises of the West.

It would lead to the end of Western psychology. And that is exactly what is happening.

When the idea of equality of all people first entered the Western mind, it was not threatening, because the class structure was so pervasive that no one really understood what true equality meant. It is analogous to us thinking about what it might be like to live without petroleum; oil and its byproducts are so pervasive that it is almost impossible to imagine what the world would be without them.

The class system was so much a part of 1776 reality that the founding fathers of the United States could declare that all people were created equal, an obvious and blatant untruth, and not really realize the full extent of what they were saying. These were idealistic notions of equality, ideals really meant only for free males of the same social class, although they were proclaimed for all people.

When the era of the Enlightenment opened, Europeans had already ruthlessly conquered and exploited significant parts of the Americas and the native populations. An extensive trade in slaves had been organized. There were few complaints about the barbarity of the Europeans' behavior, and those were routinely ignored. The focus was on profit, followed at a distance by saving the souls of the natives and the slaves by spreading Christianity. Native civilization and traditions were seen as works of Satan, so that the destruction of those works was also seen as a positive. Success in battle and success in trade meant that one was living in accordance with God's will. From a psychological point of view, conquest and success reinforced the developing egos, and the barbarity of such behavior was easily rationalized and denied.

In other words, the realization of the true horrors of slavery and conquest, as well as the destruction of indigenous populations and civilizations, was avoided by mental tricks. By rationalization, the ego takes some self-serving idea, such as "I am only doing it to bring them to Christ and save their souls" and uses it to deny the brutality of the slave trade. By denial, the ego refuses to recognize the effects of its behavior, declaring that slaves are better off in captivity than they were before. The ego is extremely skilled at denial and rationalization. The poor are only poor because they are lazy. The working class should be on the job for long hours because it keeps them out of mischief. The rich have their money because God has found them to be more deserving. The poor have many children because they are sexually depraved. The nobles have wealth and power because they have royal blood and are chosen by God. The upper class is the product of superior breeding. These themes are all derived from the Western myth, ideas which "everybody knows" to be true so that you don't need to think too much about the underlying reality.

Denial and rationalization are skills necessary for developmental stages three and four. The medieval mind learned to deny its viciousness toward nonbelievers, alleged witches, Jewish people, and anyone else who was not sufficiently "steadfast in the faith."[181] It rationalized that, despite pain to their physical bodies, tortured individuals were better off because their souls would be saved. Stage four followed right along; slavery brought the superior people both heathen souls to be saved and "savages" to be subjugated and civilized. In both stages, the individuals in the ruling groups are so identified with their peers that they are not able to allow themselves to feel the pain of those outside of the group.

As stage four progressed, denial and rationalization began to not work as well as they had. As the ego strengthens it doesn't need to deny and rationalize as much it did earlier. It becomes strong enough that it can look beyond its denials, and realize the truth of its behavior. The ego begins to realize the facts beyond its rationalizations, denials, and projections. The denied ideas tend to enter conscious awareness. For the group these values first began to appear during the Enlightenment. During that time a number of humanitarian ideas and ideals began to filter into the Western mind. Included in these were ideas of the rights of men, rights in relation to the monarch, ideas of religious freedom, and the idea of human equality. In the American Declaration of Independence of 1776, Thomas Jefferson wrote "that all men are created equal." It was an extremely idealistic statement at the time as many of the signers of the declaration, including Jefferson himself, held slaves. Nevertheless, it set up an ideal that would continue to resonate through history. It was not compatible with stage four Western thinking, which was, and remains, hierarchical.

The French Revolution demonstrated what would happen if controls were removed before the individuals involved had developed sufficiently. To the French revolutionaries, the shadow was everywhere, everyone was suspect, and anyone could be an enemy of the people. They attempted to rely on reason, but reason failed, and a bloodbath resulted. The question of equality versus hierarchy was not settled, as the revolutionaries were unable to resolve the opposites in their own psychology. After the Revolution had passed, France returned to a monarchy. In a similar fashion Communist revolutions confirm that you cannot escape your psychology; Communism just establishes another group as the ruling class, except the new one is usually more vicious. In the American Revolution, the United States had only advanced from a system of English royalty to a system of American semi-royalty, based on a property-owning upper class; it did not attempt to advance to real democracy. But the ideals of the revolution were not lost.

By the early 1800s, slavery had come to be seen by many as unacceptable. There was also a growing awareness of the plight of the poor, the reality of child abuse, and the ill effects of child labor. The reality of these aspects of the group's behavior started to be less deniable. The dark side of Western society began to filter into conscious awareness. Abolitionist movements arose. A feeling for people carrying the shadow for the group meant that a corresponding sense of the personal shadow was developing in the inner world.

The sympathy felt for shadow-carrying people increased through the early 1800s. England outlawed the slave trade in 1807 and abolished slavery in 1833. Many of the stories by Charles Dickens, a mid-nineteenth century English writer, reflect a dawning awareness of the abysmal conditions in which the lower class lived. In the United States, Harriet Beecher Stowe's *Uncle Tom's Cabin*,[182] published 1851, evoked a similar sympathy for slaves. The United States Civil War was essentially over the issue of slavery (secession due to the slavery issue for the South and preventing Southern secession for the North). Many in the north saw slavery as morally wrong and agreed with Julia Ward Howe in "The Battle Hymn of the Republic" that God was "trampling out the vintage where the grapes of wrath are stored"[183] by means of the Union Army in the Civil War. Slavery ended in the United States with the Emancipation Proclamation in 1863. Racial problems grew after the Civil War, but the problem was no longer between citizens and slaves, but between citizens and disenfranchised citizens.

Sympathy for shadow-carrying people in the external world reflected a growing need to reach out to the personal shadow in the internal world. Consciousness had been cut off from a great part of itself since the great split imposed by Christianity. As noted, that part was projected onto aboriginal people and the primitive in general. After the discoveries of Columbus, and despite a ruthless exploitation of the non-European people discovered, sympathy for the "noble savage" gradually developed among Europeans. Jean-Jacques Rousseau (1712–1778) contrasted the natural goodness of primitive people with the decadence of civilization. The status of the American Indian was raised to that of a noble icon once the Indians had been destroyed or forced onto reservations. Writers and artists, as Herman Melville and Paul Gauguin, portrayed non-European people positively and even heroically. An attraction to the non-European has gradually taken hold in the Western consciousness. African influence on American music has grown, from ragtime to blues and jazz, to rock and roll, to hip-hop.

Equality of the sexes was an additional trend stemming from the idea of human equality. The fight for women's suffrage began in the middle 1800s. Women's suffrage became law in the United States in 1920 and in England in 1928.

As I indicated, these movements are not in accordance with stage four psychology; backlashes against equal rights for women and minorities confirm this. Both equality movements indicate a change away from stage four psychology, and both give an indication of what we can expect in stage five psychology. Stage four thinking does not really accept the idea that all people are equal because it is authoritarian and hierarchical by nature. It is strongly oriented toward social status, be it economic class, money, "old money," nobility, rank (military or otherwise), skin color, or any other possible way of having some form of seniority over one's fellow human beings. It certainly does not accept the idea that people carrying the projected shadow are equal, so that integration of shadow people into mainstream Western culture has been, and remains, a struggle. Stage four men see women as love objects, mothers, wives, girls, or prostitutes, but not equals. Stage four women do not see themselves as equals. The issue continues: the United States failed to adapt an Equal Rights Amendment to the Constitution.

The underlying stage four psychology is based on the ego defeating and controlling the shadow. It is almost impossible for the stage four ego to see the shadow as an equal. Likewise, the feminine is to be wooed by the conquering, heroic stage four masculine, but she is not his equal.

The argument over a woman's right to choose abortion is really an argument over women's equality and has virtually nothing to do with children. Despite all the clamor over protecting the "unborn child," it doesn't take many years working in the social service and mental health systems to realize that children are often society's discards. The cost of educating children is a frequent target in government budget battles, and it is no secret that many children in the United States go hungry. Pregnant women and working mothers are routine targets of discrimination in the workplace.[184] The real issues all revolve around maintaining stage four psychology. The masculine must remain dominant over the feminine to maintain the myth, and thus women must be kept in a controlled, secondary position. Women must be kept in their roles of virgin, mother, or prostitute; she cannot be free or equal. And the symbol of the divine "unborn" child must be maintained, an inner Christ image, a Self symbol which is always in potential and "unborn" and not brought into the reality of the individual mind, a characteristic of developmental stage five. It is this mythical "unborn" image which is held in esteem, not the real "born" child.

Democracy and the shadow

From a psychological perspective, the stage four ego is capable of considerable independent thinking, but it still retains a great deal of group orientation, as it is very involved in upholding and maintaining the group's social order. Because of this, it is identified with the group, with the nation-state, with its place in the system, with the status quo, and with authority figures. The group identity makes self-sacrifice for the nation relatively easy, for example, supporting the wars of the nation-state. Such an ego sees itself as a part of the system on some level, leader or follower, private soldier or commanding officer, but a part of the social group nevertheless.

Finding one's place in the system is intrinsic to the idea of membership in and support of the system. And place is always associated with rank and position to the stage four person.

Rank and position evolved out of the European class structure and are intrinsic to stage four psychology. Higher ranking people, such as politicians, movie stars, medical doctors, and so forth, get more respect and status. In Europe, this is based more on ruling class lineage, but being rich helps there, too. Working class people get less status, but they have their own identifications, as with their favorite sports team, with whom they identify and gain a degree of status. The people carrying the group's shadow who form the bottom of the social structure get the least respect. To a degree, anyone lower on the stage four hierarchy carries the shadow for his or her superior, but the real shadow bearers were the non-white people and slaves, the bottom of the heap. It is difficult for the stage four ego to look at any other person and not consider the relative status of that person in the social order. The idea of equality of people is antithetical to stage four thought. A huge amount of the individual's personal power is projected to leaders and anyone considered higher in the social structure, and an equivalent degree of respect is expected from those below in that structure. This projected power is the basis of the strength of the nation-state; leaders of these states have enormous power as a result.

European rank and social structure were based on proximity to royalty. Kings and queens have been around for a long time in one form or another, but they became the heads of extensive hierarchies of royalty in stage four Europe. This remained the case in America until the Revolution, when royalty was replaced with the American upper class. In Europe it lost most of its power to legislative bodies. While it lasted, the monarchy was central to European politics. It is notable that countries without a king or queen felt it necessary to have one. If the king was somehow lost and no heir available, a suitable person from a royal family in another country would be chosen. Someone from the correct class from another country would be chosen over a local person whose breeding was not quite up to par; the mythology of "royal blood" and class took precedence over any nationalistic feelings.

The position of king or queen for Western countries was extremely important because it was the head place in the entire hierarchy of the country, and proper "nobility" and "royal blood" at the top of the hierarchy legitimized the entire nation-state structure. With a proper king or queen in place, there was a proper social order to support and defend, a need central to stage four psychology. This was the system that was maintained and upheld by the stage four ego. The stage two clan ties that established the city-state could not hold the nation-state together, nor could it be held together by the faith that was the glue of the medieval world.

The monarch served as the final authority for the country. There were a few liberal monarchs and any number of conservative ones, and there were various factions attempting to influence the monarch, but the ultimate orientation of the country was that of the monarch. If the monarch was Protestant or Catholic, so was the nation. If the king was liberal or conservative, then so was the country. That ended when absolute monarchies ended. And when they ended, the West took another step toward its own end.

Conservatism is associated with resisting change and maintaining traditional ideas. Liberalism may be described as more open to change and accepting new ideas. In essence, the conservative point of view is what yesterday was, and the liberal point of view is what tomorrow might be. The problem is that neither is a true assessment of today; neither describes the current moment, the problem right now. The conservative ideal is the myth of a glorious past, a past viewed through rose-colored glasses, and the liberal ideal is a similar view of an idealized future. A real, factual, unromanticized view of the past is not the conservative agenda, which is based on an idealized past that never occurred. Likewise, no one knows what the future might bring, and it is another illusion, another myth. The more conservative or liberal an individual is, the more likely it is that present problems are seen inaccurately and mythologically, making an optimal solution less likely.

All of us are liberal or conservative to some degree; it is human nature. And everything has a past and a future. There is no completely right or wrong answer, despite how it was done in the past or how it could be changed for the future. A decision must be made, and both liberal and conservative decisions are sometimes right and sometimes wrong. These two sides are always present for every issue. With a monarchy, the orientation was always that of the monarch. There were never two sides to an issue; there was only the side of the ruler. Any opposition was removed and perhaps even executed. With democracy, that is no longer the case. The group must allow for liberal and conservative biases and arrive at a decision without executing those who disagree.

From a psychological point of view, democracy requires that most of the individuals involved are mature enough to realize that there are two sides to every issue and decide accordingly. Democracy in the external world requires democracy in the internal world. There must be enough maturity in the conservative to be able to tolerate his or her liberal shadow, and vice versa for the liberal, and to be able to compromise with the shadow. This occurs almost exclusively in a mature stage four society; the West has only been psychologically capable of democracy for a few hundred years. By contrast, an earlier society could, at best, have an advisory committee or senate that could entertain opposing views, but the final view would be that of the head of the church or state. Democracy in the ancient world was only a democracy of the heads of important households. It follows that democracy cannot be transplanted to a society that has not developed to the point that it is psychologically ready for it.

It is also true that democracy, like human equality, grows out of stage four, but is also antithetical to stage four psychology. Democracy is the result of the development of psychology which will eventually replace stage four. A democracy demands at least two political parties, that is, it has two sides to every issue by definition. Inevitably one side is the shadow of the other, and thus the viciousness of liberal versus conservative politics. But also by definition, each side must tolerate the other, and hence, some degree of shadow toleration and acceptance is required for the system to work. Because of this it is not surprising that many people in the history of the West have had difficulty accepting the right of an opposing political party to have political power or even to exist. We have only managed enough maturity to continue such a system for a relatively short period of time, historically speaking, and there are still many who feel that those in the opposing political party are actually enemies of the state.

Nevertheless, having a democracy means learning to tolerate the shadow, that is, tolerating people who are the "other" to some degree, an idea fundamentally at odds with stage four thinking. The process has gone on reasonably well for about two or three centuries. It is only in our time, with the current revolt against any shadow acceptance, that the word "liberal" has become a profanity for some, and the opposing political party is seen as virtually traitorous; I will return to this momentarily. But for over 200 years, democracy has gradually advanced shadow acceptance.

Integration and equality

Issues of equality have continued to gradually gain momentum with the passage of the past two centuries. Historically speaking, this time frame is the blink of an eye; psychologically speaking, the change is huge. Change of this magnitude and speed only occurs when there is a change from one developmental stage to the next. The twentieth century was a time of particularly increasing change, and the sudden resistance to change which has arisen in recent years confirms the importance and strength of the process.

I have heard complaints that the progress of racial integration is abysmal and that not much has actually changed since the American Civil War. Such a complaint vastly understates the degree of the problem before 1861. Only about 150 years ago, the United States allowed one human being to own another so that many human beings were legal property; that behavior required a huge amount of psychological denial and rationalization. Numerous people believed that God approved of slavery and even more felt that slave people were inferior beings. Many whites fervently opposed to slavery still felt African-Americans to be inferior people. The American Civil War may have been against slavery, but it was not for racial integration. Yet despite the fact that racial prejudice continues, few people now have the extreme biases that were common in 1860. We no longer have great numbers of people who think that God approves of owning and selling other people. Most Americans now feel that everyone is entitled to the basic rights of citizenship. Like it or not, the United States and the West are integrating. The integration we have today could not be imagined in 1940, much less 1860. The possibility of an African-American president could not have been taken seriously in 1980, or even 1990. We are changing; you can like it or lump it, but it is happening. The supposed lack of progress is really a lack of realization of just how great the problem was in the first place, and how great it continues to be. It involves an entire change of consciousness.

Although there has been progress in achieving racial integration and sexual equality, it is clear that we remain far short of these goals. The difficulty is the size and nature of the problem itself. It is not just a matter of integrating schools or ensuring that women have equal employment opportunities; it is a matter of a complete change of Western psychology. Basic Western thought is absolutely antithetical to the idea of any true sense of equality, much less equality with minority people or males with women. Integration and women's rights have been approached as if they were only minor additions to the current rules, but that is hardly the case. Those changes mean that our world is being overturned. That is why these problems have been so difficult for us and why the issues continue.

The huge and swift changes of the twentieth century mean that we have entered the ending years of Western psychology. The very foundation of who we are is changing rapidly. No wonder people have resisted integration, sexual equality, and other measures of equality. It means the end of the world that was.

Viewed psychologically, these trends also reveal much about stage five psychology, the psychology we are developing into. The first point is that the shadow is not projected to other people but is integrated, just as our society is gradually integrating racially. The symbol of the nonwhite person as separate and inferior is no longer socially acceptable in the external world. This means that projection of one's own shadow is no longer acceptable in the internal world. This implies psychological awareness, the knowledge of my own dark side, my own shortcomings, my own inadequacies. If I cannot find my shortcomings, my ignorance, my sexuality, my anger, my inadequacies in others, I must find them in myself.

The second point is that this new psychology is not ego oriented. The ego has developed over the past five centuries by projecting and controlling the shadow. This was done by maintaining superiority over the lower classes, dark people, slaves, and anyone else lower in the social hierarchy. Now the ego has to learn to accept the idea that it is just as adequate, or inadequate, as anyone else. It is neither better than others nor worse than others, as we are all equal. All of the unpleasant material once projected to ethnic minorities must be accepted as part of one's own personality. It is a hard lesson. The ego will lose its position of utmost importance in the internal world as the Western ego is in the process of losing its absolutely dominant position in the external world.

Any social integration is a difficult process. Newcomers of a different color, a different accent, a different social class, or from a different mother-country must be accepted into a preexisting arrangement of society. Shadow psychology easily becomes an issue, particularly when the new people are of a different skin color. But what is an integration problem for most countries is central to American psychology and the psychological change that is intrinsic to what America is.

The stark division of the races was not especially prominent in America before the revolution of 1776, but it was certainly strong by the early 1800s. By that time, probably due to the large numbers of Africans imported as slaves and segregated from mainstream society, two separate cultures had developed. That separation led to a national psychology based on the difference between the two groups. American culture defined its white majority as proper, upright, and superior, and defined its African-American shadow as all that was less than proper, even less than human. The result was a national psychology with African-Americans as the primary carriers of the shadow for the nation, and a national problem of shadow integration. It is a psychology that began with almost absolute separation of the ego from the shadow, and gradually grew to encourage shadow integration. It produced two cultures subtly tied to one another, two parts of a complex whole, orbiting around each other, at first kept separate, and now gradually growing together to form a new culture.

By comparison, Europe has accepted a relatively few people of African ancestry and scolded Americans about their racial problems, but has done little about their own segregation. The position of people of African descent in Europe is more like the position of people with red hair in the United States; it seems to make little difference to their status there. (This excludes the newly-arrived African immigrants who have difficulty integrating due to reasons beyond their race.) But at the same time, Europe contains large Muslim populations that appear to have little interest in truly integrating into European culture, and vice versa. Both groups tolerate each other, but neither appears to want any further degree of integration. True integration results in each party giving up some of their identity and assuming some of the other's, and I have the distinct impression that very few Europeans, both non-Muslim and Muslim, desire this. European integration remains at the level of the "separate but equal" racial doctrine put forth in the United States Supreme Court decision of Plessy v. Ferguson in 1896. Each group wants to keep their own identity. If you really integrate, values intermix and a new social identity is formed. To me, that is not happening in Europe.

Some societies may have integrated relatively well, although lighter skin still may outrank darker. But these people have not separated into two cultures, each the shadow of the other, holding a great potential for psychological growth when integration does finally occur.

The early separation policy destined the United States to eventually deal with shadow integration on a large-scale public level. There are enough African-Americans to have a huge influence in the formation of society, but not enough that the majority feels overwhelmed. This is synchronous with the current developmental level of the average American, who has enough ego strength to integrate their shadow but not feel overwhelmed by it.

Hand-in-hand with external integration, the personal shadow is integrated in the inner world. Each person gradually integrates their own dark side internally, as they integrate socially in the outer world. Every American feels this to some degree; it is subtle, but real, and is always present in interactions between Americans of different racial groups. It is America's fate to work through the integration problem, both in external world racial integration and inner world shadow integration, on a large scale. It has made the issue of shadow integration central to the United States; this is not just a matter of new people moving into the neighborhood, but it is redefining who we are. This is a matter of a major change in psychology, a great process fundamental to the United States. It is leading to a new America.

The third point is that sexual equality implies an end of the romantic ideal, including the achieving knightly male and the woman as love object on a pedestal. Traditional romantic love, finding one's "other half," has meant finding someone who somewhat matched the projection of one's own anima (for the man) and animus (for the woman). To maintain the relationship, each person had to make themselves fit, more or less, their mate's ideal, rather than being themselves. This required the sacrifice of individuality to fulfill another person's ideal and society's roles. And typically, it was the woman doing most of the sacrificing as she took the traditional female role.

Sexual equality means the end of tying women into roles defined by the male's projected anima. It means the end of the old myth of the untouched virgin female waiting in a castle as her knight conquers in the world. Internally, it implies an awareness of one's unconscious, with its opposite sex anima or animus, as being a part of one's own personality, not a projection onto another person as an ideal love. That is not to say that people won't continue to fall in love. But as noted before, the romantic songs of the troubadour of ten centuries ago are now more important in the world of teenagers and young adults than in that of older adults. Our assessment of potential partners has grown to be more realistic and less idealistic. Each partner has more freedom to be himself or herself in the relationship, as opposed to living as the other partner's ideal.

The idea of the untouched, virgin bride is rapidly diminishing in the West. The view of rape as a "fate worse than death" has been replaced by the concept of rape as a brutal assault. Women have become much more willing to report sexual assault; they do not feel the shame that kept them quiet in the past. Sex is assuming a more mundane role, becoming another bodily function, as opposed to an ideal only occurring between two people united by the deity in a romantic embrace for all eternity.

The emphasis on relating to other people, as opposed to stage four dominating others depending on their position in the hierarchy, indicates a much stronger feminine aspect to stage five psychology. The masculine discriminates, the feminine relates. This is confirmed by the increasing power and authority of women in modern Western society. This does not mean that men will become feminine, any more than women became masculine during the past centuries of history dominated by males, but it does mean that traditional sex roles are dissolving.

Western hierarchy

Stage four psychology, with its hierarchical thinking, still dominates society's structure. For centuries, mythology of "royal blood" and Protestant values have led society to believe that some special people somehow merit being at the top of the social system, while those on the bottom do not. This has brought about the concentration of enormous amounts of wealth and power in the hands of a very few people at the top of the system. The problem is not only that some people are determined to get more power and money, but also that stage four psychology makes it easy for individuals to give up their personal power to those who seem to be higher in the social system. People on the top become inflated as to how important they are, and people on the bottom become negatively inflated as to how much less valuable they are. Democracy has shown repeatedly that people enter politics with new lofty ideals yet end up serving the old masters of power and wealth. Too frequently the person from the bottom of the system who rises to the top does not change the system but changes to fit into the new position. The problem is not with the system but with stage four psychology. Democracy has tried to solve the problem with laws controlling money in politics but it is like the ancient Hebrews making laws to prohibit the worship of graven images; neither restriction made much difference because the offending behavior is intrinsic to the group's psychology. The problem is stage four ego psychology and there is no true stage four solution. The answer will come as we develop into the new stage five psychology and the realization that we all are of equal value. Of course, we will then develop a new set of problems.

The ideal system for stage four and ego development is the hereditary monarchy. If the monarch was inadequate, he or she would eventually be replaced, hopefully with a better candidate. There was some sense of *noblesse oblige* toward the lower classes. The monarch identified with the nation, or as Louis XIV was alleged to have put it, "I am France," so that he or she felt some obligation to all the citizens of the nation. There were duties of one's social class, so that there was more to the concept of upper class than the modern idea of getting as much money as possible. A royal position was inherited, as opposed to being given to individuals particularly lustful for power.

With democracy, we have leaders, but exactly who gets those positions is a somewhat dicey proposition. Unfortunately, among those people one often sees less identification with the nation, more identification with specific groups they would like to favor, and most identification with their own ends. Too often there is little sense of obligation to those not capable of demanding representation through power or wealth. The drive to obtain the position is too frequently one of desire for personal power and aggrandizement, as opposed to service to one's fellows. It is for these reasons that I suspect that large-scale representational democracy is a transitional phase between the monarchy and the end of the dominance and primacy of the nation-state system of government, although only history will answer that question. Stage five people will not project great amounts of their personal power to national leaders, institutions, or the nation-state. The need to be identified with a nation-state, as compared with the city-state of the ancient world or the society of believers of the medieval world, is strictly a stage four phenomenon, as is the need for everyone to have a place in a social hierarchy.

The old authority, based solely on hierarchy, is gradually failing. It once was enough to be richer, lighter-skinned, older, manlier, or more elevated in society, to have authority. The only thing necessary to "pull rank" and assert authoritarian privilege over another human being was to somehow be seen as having elevated status in the social order. Under the old monarchy system, hierarchy and social status were parts of the myth that held the society together. Today, it is almost always a matter of money and power, and little else. There are virtually no other values to it and that is why it is failing. Very slowly, the social hierarchy is giving way to social equality. Authoritarianism is gradually being replaced by true authority and equality. The macho personality looks a little more silly with each passing year, and we all now know that it is an attitude based largely on underlying insecurity.

As the old psychology fades, it is regarded nostalgically by many. The John Wayne movie hero standing alone and defeating the shadow is a romantic look back at the dying myth. This level four romance is probably the greatest force behind gun sales in the United States. The Ayn Rand fantasy of the supposed great men of society as "Atlas" who "shrugged" and quit supporting the supposed lesser people is a romance of the inflated ego rebelling against a world of ever-increasing equality. If these stories seem adolescent, it is because they are; with each passing decade, level four psychology becomes more and more associated with the ego aggrandizement of adolescents and young adults, and less and less with mature adulthood.

Of all the change brought about by the new psychology, the greatest is the drive to reconcile the shadow. Instead of conquering or controlling it, future generations will focus more and more on integrating it and relating to former shadow carriers. This will produce a major shift in interpersonal relations. Think of all of the instances in our society in which one person controls or dominates another person, or one nation attempts to dominate another, and change that to people relating to one another, and you begin to see the massive psychological change that is involved. This change is so great that one can only say that it is a change in consciousness.

CHAPTER XVI

"...the centre cannot hold" (W. B. Yeats)

The material world

The previous chapter focused on the first of two sources of change for the West's stage four thinking: the idea of equality of all people as a beginning of stage five thinking. The second source comes from stage four's intrinsic strengths, rationalism and materialism. They contributed to its decline by bringing its underlying myth to a dead end.

Rational thinking and its emphasis on the material world were gradually strengthening in the Western mind as the medieval world drew to a close, but the pace increased dramatically during the Age of Enlightenment, roughly between the late 1600s and the late 1700s. Throughout the West there was a huge thirst for organized, rational knowledge of the material world. It was felt that a thorough exploration of God's creation on earth would lead to a greater knowledge of God, that is, confirm the myth. But it didn't quite work out that way.

While the power of reason and the breadth of human knowledge expanded explosively after 1700, faith remained relatively stagnant. Faith is, after all, confidence in the unseen and the immeasurable, and reason was rapidly moving in the opposite direction, to see and measure the material world. Reason became more and more powerful as laws of nature were discovered and principles of the sciences were established. It became possible to predict and control the material world as had never been possible in the past. But faith did not benefit from this surge in knowledge. Faith for the West was established in the 1500s and 1600s by such men as Martin Luther and it then remained static. Religions passed down the same doctrines while science advanced. It was as if religion was in a closed box, taken out every Sunday morning and acknowledged, and then put back in the box, century after century. Children were taught the religious stories, and the stories were acknowledged on Sundays. But their relevance to everyday life and morality gradually receded with the advance in materialism.

The advances in rationalism and materialism have brought the Western world to success unimaginable in 1500. We have lives of ease and health unknown even to kings of that time. We know the physical world as never before, we can stay warm in the winter, we have enough to eat, we have numerous labor-saving devices, we can bathe easily, our medicine has conquered many of the maladies which have plagued humanity, we have developed untold ways of entertaining ourselves, we have good transportation, and so on. We have learned to make fascinating, valuable, desirable objects. The physical world has never been so alluring.

The ideals of the 1600s and 1700s, that the exploration and explanation of the physical world would lead to a better understanding of God and his purpose, instead led to Charles Darwin. Faith remained unchanged, still late medieval, still in a world beginning in the Garden of Eden. The medieval stories gave comfort to the internal child, but did little to answer any rational questions of the ego.

As rationality and science strengthened, pressure was placed on faith. For some the solution has been to completely reject faith and elevate science and materialism to religious status; there is a scientific explanation for everything, and if something appears to be unexplained, science just hasn't gotten there yet. The scientist has worked to overcome the shadow of ignorance and expand our rational knowledge of the material world. But the Western myth is ultimately material, and science is unable to proceed beyond that limitation. It will not, for example, consider (much less explain) non-materialistic phenomena, such as extra-sensory perception or near-death experiences, so they are deemed impossible or just ignored. These ideas are seen as regressions to stage three faith and belief, and are rejected without any serious consideration, although the future may see them differently. Modern materialists denouncing reports of near-death experiences seem to be a curious echo of Pope Urban VIII and his cronies denouncing Galileo Galilei. Reports of near-death experiences are interesting in that they seem to be signaling the return of the concept of the soul to Western thinking; they occur more frequently now because of the lifesaving abilities of modern medicine. Perhaps this is only another fad, like the séance fad in the middle and late 1800s, and perhaps not.

Others realized religious scriptures to be parables attempting to express ideas which are almost inexpressible, and chose to hold to those ideas while rejecting the parables as physical truth. Another solution was a two-tiered one, with faith having its own compartment separate from scientific knowledge; that held up satisfactorily as long as conflict was avoided. Perhaps the most common solution has been to continue to pay lip service to traditional faith, and pursue material wealth and power with abandon. After all, the underlying myth has been one of God rewarding the believer with success in the material world, so why be halfway about it? Getting material goods means you are "blessed" according to the myth, and there is no need to concern yourself with how many "non-blessed" children starve to death every day.

What rationalism and materialism do not answer is what faith does; the need for faith has been there all along, just pushed to the back of the line. All of these wonders of science are great, but they don't help someone facing death. The only thing to fall back on is the old religion, right out of 1600. It has been in its box on the intellectual shelf, remaining static since Martin Luther. But the rational mind has developed for everyone in the West, and—admitted or not—it is hard to accept the old faith like people did in 1600.

Five centuries of stage four materialism have made us all into scientists, accepting rational thinking as absolute truth. It has brought us out of the medieval world of total faith, but at a cost. The material world and its wealth have almost totally displaced spiritual growth and values. Do we have a soul, or are we just a brain with chemical imbalances to be treated with medication? Is everything reducible to the laws of physics, or is there a soul in the body? Perhaps our rationality is now sufficiently strong that we can deal with the idea of the soul without slipping into medieval superstition.

I have heard a few dreams that seemed to suggest that they were messages from a deceased person the dreamer once knew. Generally speaking, the first consideration in interpreting such a dream is that the character in the dream is solely an image from the dreamer's unconscious; a dream of one's deceased mother would suggest input from one's mother complex. But occasionally some particularly uncanny dreams make one wonder. When I have suggested the possibility of a contact from a deceased person, it was not unusual that the idea was rejected as being impossible. Such a suggestion does not fit with the modern, materialistic, scientific Western mind.

Science cannot prove whether or not the soul survives after death. Science can only know what it can prove by repeated testing. Science has been an excellent way of seeing the world, because it has allowed us to understand and manipulate our reality better than any previous way of thinking. But it only knows what it can test and prove; you cannot have an experimental group and a control group for determining if there is life after death, a soul, or God. The problem with medieval thought was that it rejected everything that did not fit with faith as impossible. The problem with scientific thought is that it rejects everything it cannot prove as impossible. Is the medieval Catholic church's declaration that the earth could not rotate around the sun any more or less foolish than the modern rationalist who declares that there can be nothing after death?

The victory of materialism

The scientific awakening of the Enlightenment began as an intense effort to study the natural world with the aim of discovering the mysteries of God. But that deeper understanding of nature led to Darwin's observations and to his theories of natural selection and evolution. The publication of "On the Origin of Species"[185] in 1859 was the beginning of the split between modern knowing and believing, and that split was complete by the time of the Scopes Monkey Trial in Dayton, Tennessee in

1925. By that time the threat of the idea of a materialistic source of human existence was so great that laws had to be made against it (recall the Hebraic laws against graven images), and Mr. Scopes, a teacher, was arrested and tried for teaching those ideas, i.e., the theory of evolution. But in many respects that trial marked the triumph of materialism over spiritualism, even though Mr. Scopes was found guilty.

By the time of the Scopes trial, popular thinking was that evolution meant that we were descended from monkeys. That idea was contradictory to Genesis, which states that humans were created in God's "own image."[186] While medieval people may not have been keen on the idea that the human body was grand, that was not the case in 1925. The idea that the body was of God's image had become much more important than it ever was for medieval people. In fact, it was a time that the physical body was coming out from under layers and layers of clothing and taking center stage. It is not a coincidence that the Scopes trial was during an early sexual revolution, when the first vaguely modern bathing suits were appearing, when the new dances were "suggestive," and wearing makeup was becoming common for women. The human body was taking center stage.

The medieval concept was that the soul was the only important factor in each person, not the body or the conscious mind. The soul was seen as a higher self that would spend eternity in either heaven or hell. That was not the thinking of 1925. The body itself was the focus—the material part of creation, made in God's image—along with the conscious mind. The individual conscious "I," the ego, would go to heaven; the "I" had become the soul, and it was closely identified with the individual body. This was a complete shift in thinking from the medieval world, which had seen both the body and the conscious mind as temporary and dispensable, and only the soul as having any real value. The materialistic revolution had, in fact, succeeded entirely: it was the physical body and the conscious mind that were important and made in God's image, not the ethereal idea of a soul. Materialism had won a total victory. Belief that the material body and the conscious mind were "in God's image" made the individual a small copy of God and opened the door for inflation of the ego to become God's equal. Materialism was redeemed, in keeping with the Protestant ethic, as long as the specialness of human creation was maintained: in God's image and not from "the dust of the ground."[187] The medieval concept of the soul as a separate part of the individual was discarded. The soul had become the ego itself, a small copy of God, with a potential for hubris and inflation unthinkable in any earlier time in history. The tie between material success and perceived godliness, established by Protestantism, became even stronger.

The point that had been missed was that rationalism and materialism had won, while faith and spirituality had lost. Faith based on spirituality had been replaced by faith based on the literal Scriptures, a material thing that was claimed to be the Word of God. The medieval Catholic church had not allowed lay people to read the Bible for good reason; it is inconsistent and contradictory among other problems. What counted for the medieval person was the spirit of Christianity, the stories of the Scriptures, the faith in redemption of the soul.

When Protestants left the security of the Catholic church, the only thing they had for support was the Bible itself. The Bible assumed the leading role, as the newly independent Protestants felt they finally had access to what God supposedly said. This was their rock, a material truth in itself. The old spiritual truth as pieced together by the medieval Catholic church was replaced by the material facts of the Bible.

Protestants began analyzing the neglected but conflicting corners of the scriptures for God's truth, proof that the day of worship was or was not Sunday, that people were or were not predestined to salvation, and lately, that there would be a rapture, searching for absolute proofs among the contradictory ancient texts. Like the Shroud of Turin, the Bible had become a physical proof that was necessary for the new material age. Since the Bible was a physical reality, a thing, and not a spiritual reality, it was a thing to be taken at face value. When modern science made new findings, like the bones of dinosaurs that lived millions of years before humans, the dinosaurs had to be fitted into the materially real Bible stories of Eden and Noah's ark. "Intelligent Design" is another attempt to provide the physical evidence that the materialistic world demands in lieu of faith itself. (Relics like the Shroud of Turin were manifestations of faith for medieval people; they are evidence for modern believers.) This modern materialization of religion has made for absurd beliefs by the true believers (dinosaurs in Eden) or rejection of the whole thing by anyone who couldn't muster sufficient faith.

Modern religion could have easily dealt with Darwinism had it chosen to do so. Any thoughtful review of biology makes it clear that more complex organisms evolved from less complex ones; the question is how. Darwin said that this is because the fittest survive, and there is absolute proof this occurs in many circumstances: drug-resistant bacteria evolve to beat the medicines physicians prescribe, and skeletal records show gradual adaptation of animal species over time. But that does not mean that every change in the tree of life was due to survival of the fittest; that is strictly an assumption. It could just as easily be argued that the important changes occurred by God's will. The origins of modern humans are particularly curious; they are based on a very few fossils and a lot of assumptions. And survival of the fittest echoes the same Western myth that we use to explain almost everything else; the good guys beat the bad guys and get the girl, or the fittest outlast the less fit and get to reproduce. But religion stuck to Biblical infallibility with a creation in Eden. The religious establishment was as materialistic as the society it came from and needed the proof they thought the Bible to be, and kept religion securely in its box from 1600.

Churches became club-like organizations for people who shared the same materialistic beliefs: baptism of children versus baptism of infants, communion with wine versus grape juice, whether or not salvation was predestined. Each group had their own material key to the gates of heaven, gleaned from their material Bible. Spirituality was put in a closet, and was seen as dangerous when it slipped out. Heaven was a cloud-lined version of this world, with a separate-but-equal section for minorities.

Spiritual faith had lost, and material faith had won. Modern Catholics fared no better, as they had entered the modern material age along with everyone else and become another Protestant sect, psychologically speaking.

Pullback psychology

Protestant fundamentalism began in the mid-1800s as a reaction to the increasing impact of the modern world. It contributed to the major movement of Protestant evangelicalism beginning in the 1970s.[188] Fundamentalism could be considered to be a reaction to rationalism (as Charles Darwin) and materialism. Evangelicalism has more to do with white America's upset over social changes as women's rights and homosexual rights, but it also included a healthy dose of skepticism of science and rationality. The social changes all had to do with increasing equality issues: racial, sexual, and sexual identity, the very issues that the new psychology was ushering in. Scientific issues, as global climate change, disputed the notion that man has unlimited power to do as he wanted with the earth. Many people were not comfortable with these new ideas and began to feel nostalgic for the way things used to be.

The nostalgia for the past has grown in America, even as religious fundamentalism is declining. Racial and sexual equality are disputed. Scientific findings are being rejected as the long-established American anti-intellectualism has become more aggressive.[189] The authoritarianism of stage four is more evident than ever. This movement has appeared suddenly, historically speaking, and is a direct rejection of the psychological changes we are now undergoing. It represents a pullback to stage four thinking with all hints of stage five denied. It is a conscious suppression of the unacceptable results of change; the ideas are still there, they are just suppressed and they are not going away. This is why there is such hostility to any suggestion of these ideas or any person who might symbolize them, as people labeled liberal. A "liberal" is not just seen as the other side of the political spectrum but as a person out to destroy the world.

There was similar pullback thinking in the 1500s, when modern ego psychology was replacing medieval superego psychology. Catholics of the time denied science, specifically the concept of a sun-centered universe, and denied individual rights to belief in favor of church-dictated religion. In our time, people invested in pullback psychology deny science, specifically the concept of human-caused climate change, and deny individual rights, specifically the rights of minorities and women. The old way of thinking must be maintained at any cost. The religious claims are only a tool for the underlying psychology, and not vice versa.

Pullback thinking is a direct attempt to avoid the increasing influence of the new psychology. It is an attempt to return to an idealized past of absolute values, a past that never really was that has gone away forever. This involves a complete rejection of the shadow with a return of overt racial prejudice and denigration of the poor, plus hostility toward any equality of women and even toward women in general. It is accompanied by increased focus on attacking foreign enemies and keeping foreign people out, efforts to keep the focus of shadow psychology out of the country. The shadow is out there and does not need to be integrated; it should be attacked and controlled.

Stage four psychology sees life as a zero-sum game; there is only so much to go around and if I'm not getting it then someone else is. All is right when those higher in the hierarchy are getting more; that's how things should be. But when minorities and women start doing well, something is amiss, and stage four thinking wants to go back to the way things used to be.

Pullback thinking is a determined effort of the ego to maintain level four thinking: keep the shadow in projection, keep the people carrying that projection under control, keep the feminine suppressed, and keep women subordinate. It does not imply a lack of development, but a resistance to it; everyone in the West is dealing with the same developmental issues. Pullback thinking is an attempt to adapt by going back to an earlier time with no racial integration, no sexual equality, and with evil confined to the Soviet Union. It is only another way of trying to handle the changes of our time; it does not mean these people are any less developed than anyone else. These changes are frightening and upsetting, and everyone tries to adapt in their own way.

The Western mind is quite aware of the material that rational thinking has revealed. But some desperately want to cling to the security of the old stage four psychology, remaining as a child to the Great Father God, avoiding the passage into independent adulthood. They are frightened of their shadow and view it as a threat. They would rather deny reality than integrate the shadow and give up the old security. It is much easier to ignore Biblical contradictions and fabricate an irrational fantasy escape, such as the rapture, rather than deal with our time. But the rational cat is out of the bag and it is not going back.

Rationalism and materialism have severely damaged the old faith, causing some to reject rationalism and cling to the faith more than ever, while leading others to worship, covertly or overtly, the material world. Money and the power it symbolizes have reached a status previously unknown, another aspect of late stage four psychology. It has led to a materialistic world where the only value is price, a development the rationalists five centuries ago could never have foreseen. It has led to a world where there is no adult relationship to the soul. It has left us, as the poet T. S. Eliot put it, in "The Wasteland" (1922). It has left us ripe for new symbols and a new psychology.

Political and religious groups want to maintain stage four psychology, that of absolute ego dominance as well as the society built on that psychology. That was the world of 1800, but it is gone; too much of the shadow has entered our psychology. Shadow reconciliation and integration are well underway, both internally and externally. The feminine is moving toward parity with the masculine and it is not going back. The old authoritarian order is failing. A great deal has come out of the closet; closet doors don't hold very well anymore, and with each generation the doors open wider and become weaker. But the stage four ego still clings to its power and position, and some of us identify strongly with that. These people really want to maintain control and shut the doors again, and they're not going to give up easily. Expect more and more attempts at more and more social control in the near future.

By its nature the ego wants to maintain the system and keep the shadow suppressed and controlled; this is somewhat true of all of us. However, we are in the process of leaving the age of ego dominance. As old traditions of hierarchy, racial inequality, and sexual inequality fail, it is disturbing to the ego. The ground beneath our feet is shaking. There seems to be no respect for the old authority, either from younger people to adults, or from lesser nations to the greater ones. Women and minorities now have authority they never had before; it is no longer a given that a white male has the last word. It seems that the world is falling apart and it is frightening. We all feel this, and authority figures in general are attempting to increase their control to compensate for those feelings.

The impact of the West

Stage four shadow-conquering behavior has led to integrating the shadow and the feminine. The number of subjects of former European colonies now living as equal citizens in the former colony-holding European states is quite remarkable. In the United States, the descendants of former slave owners marry the descendants of former slaves. American business and military actions have forced or induced numerous Hispanics to emigrate to the United States, contributing further to integration.

This same ego-driven psychology has caused a great deal of traditional men's work to be exported to the non-Western world to increase profits, and many Western men have not adapted to this very well. Women have adapted better, leading to increasing power and importance of women and the feminine. More and more women are attending college and entering the professions, while their less flexible male counterparts seem to be at a loss.[190] Stage four conquering and controlling the shadow leads directly to stage five integration of the shadow and the feminine.

Many former colonies had Western stage four rationalism thrust on them at the point of a gun. Some of these societies are seemingly replacing rationalism with thinking associated with an earlier stage of development, medieval or even tribal, in an effort to rid themselves of Western influence; their religious background has become an identity at least as much as a belief. Other non-Western societies have adopted Western culture wholesale in an attempt to replace centuries-old traditional culture, to compete with the West. It is impossible to say how these experiments might turn out over the course of the coming centuries; the natural order of development has been upended throughout the world. The adoption of Western thinking may be deep or only superficial. Perhaps rational thought will prevail as we move into a one-world culture, but maybe traditional cultures will return to their old ways once the West has grown up enough to stop meddling with them. Only time will tell.

The modern field dealing with the issue is cross-cultural psychology; it holds various cultural characteristics strictly as equals with no hint of superiority. One such characteristic is thinking style, and one aspect of that is formal or analytic reasoning versus intuitive or holistic reasoning.[191] I suspect that these expressions are veiled ways of referring to Piaget's stages, that is, stage four formal operations versus thinking from earlier stages. Much of the modern non-Western world's thinking is some combination of the two, reflecting both the spread of Western logic and the persistence of the old ways.

The change in our time

All of this change is upsetting and frightening, even to the best of us. The old way is dying out, and the new way is not yet clearly formed. This brings us to our time, a period of divided psychology due to changing consciousness.

There were psychological differences between the two sides in the American Civil War. Those differences pale in comparison with current differences; they were only a foreshadowing of America's current division. The South was more hierarchical, more authoritarian, and more romantic than the North. Southern psychology was that of an earlier era, a time when the ego needed greater structure and control to prove itself. It needed women to be in a clear position, either on a pedestal or in the dirt, to keep the feminine under control. It needed the shadow to be under absolute control, so the thought of abolishing slavery was unthinkable.

Whenever one considers the American Civil War, one must keep in mind that only the wealthy could afford to own slaves in any significant number. Slaves were expensive commodities available mostly to the rich, less so to the middle class, and not to the poor. Yet great numbers of poor whites were willing to fight and die for the cause of the Confederacy. The issue of slavery was certainly behind the Civil War, but the underlying basis was two different value systems equally determined to define the future of America. The difference in psychology was the ultimate cause of the American Civil War. People may or may not vote for, fight for, or die for what is in their economic interest, but they definitely will do so for a cause that fits their psychology.

Southern psychology was fixated in a psychology from England before Oliver Cromwell, before the power of the royalty was checked in any way. It was romantic on top and brutal underneath. The North was just slightly more practical and pragmatic. Many in the North had begun to feel uncomfortable with the "peculiar institution" of slavery, that is, they had begun to have some vague realization of their own shadow side. Psychologically speaking, the North was perhaps one or two hundred years ahead of the South. However, both were still quite involved in stage four psychology. Once the rebellion was ended and slavery was abolished, both sides returned to the same attitudes toward African-Americans that they held before the war; in that respect nothing had changed.

The South attempted to secede from the Union and fought for the independent rights of individual states in opposition to a strong central government. It is reminiscent of civil war in France in the 1600s, when aristocratic nobles and lesser powers rebelled against a strong central government. But the development of the nation-state required that state and regional governments be subordinate to the central government. This assumption of power by the central government, forming the modern nation-state, reflected the growing power and strength of the ego in relation to the rest of the mind during the last few centuries, when the ego grew to be absolute master of its house. These processes in the external and internal worlds are typical of stage four development.

In contrast, the national division in our time is not over where one's development is in stage four, it is over the fact that we are leaving stage four and beginning stage five. This makes the psychological differences between people who accept these changes versus those who do not much greater than the differences at the time of the U.S. Civil War. I am thankful that we do not have an issue as galvanizing as slavery as we face our current differences.

A new world

Earlier I wrote that historians have paid little attention to psychological differences between the various civilizations of history. The most notable exception is Oswald Spengler and his great work, "The Decline of the West,"[192] first published in the early 1900s. He compared and contrasted the characteristics of the world's great civilizations, including their rise and fall, and used that as a basis for evaluating Western civilization. This led him to conclude that the West was in decline. At that time the signs of decline were subtle, although they aren't so subtle anymore. But what Spengler missed was the beginnings of the next great civilization rising even as the old one was declining.

Spengler saw each of the great civilizations of history as being separate entities in themselves, with no continuity from one to the next.[193] He was absolutely opposed to the idea that the ancient world grew into the medieval world which developed into the modern West, mostly because each was so different from the others.[194] He denied that there was any line of progress through history; for him progress is strictly a concept of the West. I agree with him that there are substantial differences between the great cultures of history, but I have found that there is a line of development linking the great civilizations that form our history. It is a line of psychological development and it indicates a purpose and direction in history. Consciousness has been developing and increasing in stages over the course of our history and there is every reason to believe that this process will continue to its own ends.

Like Spengler, it is easy to identify with the structure we have formed over the past few hundred years and see recent social and psychological change as only decline and destruction. It is a frightening end of a world. But it is also the birth of a new one. Spengler missed that entirely.

Some people will attempt to reject these changes completely and make every effort to maintain control and prevent change. Those people serve as the shadows for people who are more accepting of these changes, and vice versa. We have reached the point in our development that we are beginning to be strongly influenced by the new psychology. Part of each of us accepts it and part rejects it. Some people identify with one side and some with the other. Some of the rejecting group want to maintain control and maintain the old structure at any cost. And there is some of both sides in each of us; accepting that is a difficult task in itself.

CHAPTER XVII

A Myth of Our Time: Aliens and Flying Saucers

The Self in modern myth

The Self, the ultimate center of each individual human mind is always present throughout one's lifetime. It presents itself differently and is experienced differently during each stage of development; this is how it guides development. It is symbolized by the dominant parent in earlier stages of individual development. It is symbolized by the central figure of religion of each stage of history for the group. In one's personal past, it may have been projected to the mother or the father. In the historical past, it has been manifested by the God-images worshiped by our ancestors.

As a new manifestation of the Self begins to dominate consciousness, its symbols begin to appear in a culture's conscious awareness to guide that group in the development of a new psychology. In our time, new symbols of the Self have begun to make their appearances in myth and popular media.

This appearance takes two forms. The first is the overt appearance of symbols of the Self. Because the West is ending its group-centered childhood, the new symbols of the Self are no longer parent-child in nature. The new symbols are much more oriented toward the individual and individual experience. This chapter addresses these more overt experiences of the Self, something relatively rare in life, although not so rare in story and myth.

The second appearance is less overt but continually present on a daily basis. It is at the heart of the central problem of our time, the struggle to leave the old psychology and enter the new, to move from one symbol of the Self to the next. That struggle is the subject of the next chapter. This chapter lays the foundation for the next by first addressing the more overt experience of the Self.

The central figure of the West's myth, the basis of our old psychology, has been the conquering son of the Great Father. That form of the hero has been the carrier of the Self's image for the West for hundreds of years. Symbols associated with this myth include the knights, the "good guys in white hats," the "bad guys" to be captured, the king, the nation, and the ladylove, all of which have been introduced as some of the symbols of the old psychology. It is now time to consider symbols of the new psychology, and the best places for that are the fantasies of our time: novels and movies. These forms of media are where we bring our fantasies to life.

Each age has its hero stories. For the ancients, they were stories of their gods and goddesses, plus their mortal heroes as Odysseus and Heracles. In the medieval world, the heroes were the saints. Early Western people listened to troubadours sing songs of love and heroism, and they read stories about knights seeking the Holy Grail. In our time, we read novels and watch movies that expand the hero story. Novels have been the main method of storytelling in the West, more recently supplemented by motion pictures. Movies present a visual version of a story in combination with a background musical score that ties in the viewer's emotions with the plot development.

There was little variation in the stories of the gods of the ancient world or saints of the medieval world. The narrative would vary quite little, if any, over the course of generations. That changed with the novel. The novel relied on the individual imagination to produce a unique story. It allowed variances in the hero's actions that would have been unthinkable in the ancient or medieval world. The author can put the hero in any position and have the plot proceed in any direction. And if the reader does not like that story, another author and another plot may be chosen, giving the West more individuality in its mythology. In contrast, a person in the ancient world or medieval world could not alter the stories associated with Heracles or Saint Stephen.

There are any number of novels and movies with the traditional Western themes of the hero conquering the bad guy, or of lovers finding true love. We know those themes well as they are basic parts of the Western myth. But new symbols are appearing in our time, symbols associated with the new psychology.

I have selected a few modern stories that I feel give the best examples of the new symbols. Almost all of these are variations of the hero's story, which has been around for a very long time. The story of a society's hero gives that society a myth to live by, a way to deal with the issues of the era. The question is how do the hero stories of our time differ from the old ones? The new and different aspects of the hero's task give hints as to how we can deal with the issues of our time and issues in our lives. I noted in Chapter 3 that the heroes in the "Star Wars" trilogy and in "The Lord of the Rings" only succeed with the help of characters who would be considered their shadows. The hero's traditional task was to defeat the shadow; now he must have the help of his shadow to accomplish his task. That is a fairly new theme in fiction, and tells us something about us and who we are.

I chose the stories in these pages both because they have new symbols and also because they have been popular, some even immensely and enduringly popular. They have shown tremendous appeal to the imagination of many, many people. This popularity reflects the great appeal of these particular stories dealing with new symbols, and suggests that they resonate with the group's psychology. If the plots and the symbols were incorrect, the stories would not have attained the popularity they have.

The hero's story is an exceptionally old one, probably older than civilization. The hero faces a task, endures trials, takes risks, and emerges victorious. The specifics of the task and the difficulties have varied from age to age, and reflect the consciousness of the age. Stage two heroes were usually wily and sly, and used cleverness to avoid the gods and achieve their ends. Stage three heroes were typically saints who were often martyred while doing God's will. Stage four heroes conquered the shadow carriers, like the cowboys in white hats who rounded up the bad guys in black hats and sent them to jail. The hero's role is to handle the challenge presented in his time. The question is: how is the basic plot different and what is new in the stories of our time?

To answer this I will look at a few recent movie plots from a psychological perspective. Movies are made to be viewed as struggles in the outer world, like the rebellion against the empire in "Star Wars"; some characters are identified with the empire and some with the rebellion. But to view the story psychologically, take the hero or heroine as the dreamer and every other character represents some aspect of the dreamer's personality. Taking the story as a dream means that all the characters and their causes are different aspects of the dreamer's mind; the conflict is in the dreamer. The hero in the story represents the dreamer's ego, which must deal with the psychological factors symbolized in the dream.

A full analysis would go into great detail of all aspects of the dream. The analysis would begin with a review of the age-old hero's story, which is at the core of most of the movies considered here. The original "Star Wars," in particular, had numerous symbols and themes typical of the hero's story. There are many variations on the basic plot, but these are some typical themes: the hero receives a call to action, which he tries to avoid, but eventually heeds. He leaves home and crosses the threshold into a new world, beginning his adventure. He may be led by, or trained by, a wise old man figure. There may be a trip into the underworld. If he does not initially succeed, there may be a death and resurrection. Eventually he overcomes and succeeds in his quest. Even many variations on this story are somewhat standard. The best discussion of the hero and his quest is in Joseph Campbell's "The Hero with a Thousand Faces."[195]

You can think of novels and movies that are very popular as being dreams of the group, reflections of the group's mind. New themes and new symbols appearing in popular media indicate new psychological factors in the group's consciousness. I have mentioned the new theme of the hero requiring the help of his shadow to complete his task; this chapter is about another new motif.

Perhaps the most notable new theme in modern movies is the story of how the hero deals with aliens from outer space. The entire idea of unearthly humanoids from another world, not gods, angels, devils, or satanic agents, is new for us in our time.

Years ago, when I was in a midlife crisis, I dreamed I was in my bed and I found myself surrounded by invading aliens from outer space. There were any number in the room and more were coming in the windows. I woke in terror.

I was hardly Luke Skywalker or some other space hero. I felt terror in the dream and I continued to feel terror after I woke up.

Many movies have been based on this exact theme. Aliens from outer space invade, and what happens next? Movies have used this theme repeatedly, with all sorts of possible twists in the plot. It is archetypal, but it involves symbols activated in our time. Medieval people did not dream of invading aliens.

The first consideration in dream interpretation is whether the dream is about the dreamer's inner or outer world. I was pretty sure that if space aliens did show up on earth, the chances were quite slim that they would want to visit my bedroom, so the answer probably was to be found in my inner world. That is, it was about my psychology and not about my life in the outer world.

The setting was my bedroom. The motif of being in bed would suggest that the dreamer was somewhat "asleep at the switch," or unconscious of what was happening. I had not realized that my unconscious had anything to say to me.

The next consideration is content. People in the ancient world would have dreamed about their gods, people in the medieval world would have dreamed of angels, saints, or agents of Satan. It is only in our time that the idea of aliens from outer space has appeared. We have science fiction and we have sightings of unidentified flying objects. There is a long history of people reporting that they have seen strange objects in the sky, but never before at the intensity of the past seventy years or so. And it is no coincidence that science fiction literature has developed in about the same time frame as crime detective stories and modern psychology, all within the past 100 to 150 years.

There are numerous anecdotal stories about possible human-alien contacts, but they have never been proven with factual evidence. Despite a lack of physical evidence, a number of these eerie stories have never been satisfactorily explained. This area is neither absolute fact nor absolute fiction, and the lore that has grown up around it is best described as myth, a myth of our time.[196]

Space aliens are not angels, demons, gods, or spirits. They are humanoid, that is, more like us than not, but they are "advanced" enough so that they can travel from the far reaches of space to come to Earth. There is an implication of another intelligence other than what we know, and it is more advanced and powerful than our intelligence.

You don't hear many reports nowadays about sightings of Saint Peter or Saint Paul, witches or demons. There aren't many claims in the West that touching a holy relic has led to a miracle cure. But what we do have are sightings of flying saucers and aliens. No one claims to have been ridden by an incubus or a succubus in the previous night, or to have had their crops withered by witchcraft. But they do report alien abduction, crop circles, and cattle mutilation. There aren't many stories about people with the stigmata of the crucifixion, but you do hear about people who claim to have alien implants in their bodies. Martin Luther supposedly saw the devil and threw his inkwell at him; in contrast, Jimmy Carter, former president of the United States, saw an unidentified flying object. We have entered a new world. The magic and mystery have left saints and gone to saucers.

Saint Paul reported that he was on the road to Damascus almost 2,000 years ago when a light from heaven suddenly shined around him, and he heard a voice asking, "Saul, Saul, why persecutest thou me?"[197] After the experience, he was blind for three days, changed his name from Saul to Paul, and began to preach Christianity. Betty and Barney Hill reported that they were on the road in New Hampshire in September 1961 when they saw a light in the sky and were abducted and examined by aliens in a spacecraft.[198,199] We don't hear much about people seeing bright lights in the sky and converting to a new religion, but we do hear about lights in the sky and alien encounters. In fact, if you hear about someone seeing a bright light from the sky, the first thought is another flying saucer report, not another religious conversion.

It is fair to say that the lore surrounding aliens and unidentified flying objects is the only significant living myth of our time. Lip service is given to older myths, but they have lost their vitality. As each day passes, they are becoming more and more relics of our past.

Flying saucers are reported to easily out-fly powerful military aircraft. They appear and disappear at will. They are able to stop a motor vehicle. They can use a ray of light or energy to stun and even transport a human. The craft are usually described as round, that is, flying saucers. The aliens themselves are thought to be an ancient race (or races) and have been masters of space technology for thousands of years. They have vehicles that allow them to cross intergalactic space relatively easily, something that would take us many years traveling at the speed of light. They can abduct humans at will. They can communicate without speaking, including reading human thoughts. They are clearly much more intelligent and powerful than humans, yet they are humanoid. They appear to have an interest in us and occasionally want to examine some of us, but they do not seem to want to change our beliefs, contrary to Paul's experience on the road to Damascus.

The Bible indicates that Yahweh was frequently dissatisfied with the behavior of the ancient Hebrews, and often intervened into their affairs, usually punishing them. Similarly, Saint Paul said that a voice from the heavens told him to stop persecuting Christians. By contrast, Betty and Barney Hill reported that they were examined by aliens and released. The alien abduction stories frequently involve the examination motif; I can't recall reading one in which the abductee's beliefs were corrected or criticized.

John Mack, a psychiatrist, interviewed a number of individuals who reported that they had been abducted by aliens.[200] Of these, a few reported that the aliens had given them a message, usually vague, something along the lines that we should be taking better care of our environment. My impression is that the messages say more about the individuals' personal psychology than about aliens, but who knows. The most striking flying saucer reports that I have read, and I admit that I am not deeply involved with this issue, do not involve aliens giving earthlings a message or a warning. This theme does appear in the movie "The Day the Earth Stood Still"[201] (1951), in which the aliens want us to behave better. But to the best of my knowledge, the aliens don't have very much to say in the way of specific warnings about human behavior.

Imagine driving through the country on a deserted road late on a dark night, and your car breaks down. You decide to proceed on foot, hoping to reach a service station. Imagine, as you walk you see an eerie glow to the side of the road as you round a curve. Does it make you feel fear and chills? Imagine that you suddenly spot a being approaching from the direction of the glow. In your mind's eye, how would you imagine that being? My guess is that it would be some variation on the theme of an alien or extra-terrestrial. Five hundred years ago, the answer might have been Satan. But Satan is rapidly fading into the past; his time is almost over as a new myth is coming into being.

The eerie feeling of fright, curiosity, chills, the "magic," is the idea of the numinous. Aliens are psychologically exciting in our time, compared with earlier times when the saints and Satan had the magic. The saints aren't so exciting any more, but the idea of flying saucer people is. Whether or not the Vatican made Mother Teresa into a saint doesn't catch much attention. There is much more interest in whether the government retrieved bodies of aliens and a crashed spacecraft near Roswell, New Mexico, in 1947, or whether the government has other secret knowledge of flying saucers and aliens. The paradigm has shifted. The "magic" has changed. New symbols are numinous, and old symbols have lost their aura.

And before you pooh-pooh the idea, recall that virtually no Roman of the first or second century would have given any credence to the idea that a minor Jewish sect centered around an executed criminal would come to dominate the next 2,000 years of Western civilization. Never. We are now in the position of the Romans, at the end of one chapter in history and the beginning of a new one, so try to imagine. Real or not, it just may be that aliens and flying saucers are more important than one might think. Every civilization has its myths, and this is the only active one we've got.

In the medieval era, an extensive mythology developed around the supposed lives of the saints. I mentioned Mary Magdalene earlier; her entire story has almost no Biblical basis. But the medieval mind was able to produce stories about her because they matched the psychology of the times. Similarly, we have developed a body of ideas about aliens based on personal reports and anecdotes, with the details filled in by science fiction.

There is no absolute, undeniable proof that we have ever made contact with aliens. Without positive evidence, we can only assume that our flying saucer lore says more about our own psychology than reality, just as the stories about the saints reflected the medieval mind.

Maybe aliens exist, and maybe they don't; from a psychological perspective, it doesn't really matter. The evidence for Paul's experiences on the road to Damascus is about the same as the evidence for Betty and Barney Hill's experience on their trip. Paul's report came to be a dominant theme in Western thinking for almost 2,000 years. Now new themes are appearing in Western thought. We know the symbols behind the old stories. What is behind the new stories? Stories can only have psychological fascination if they involve symbols of active archetypes.

When Europeans began to encounter aboriginal people in the new world five centuries or so ago, they "saw" what they needed to see, that is, projections of their own symbols in the people they met. It took the Europeans centuries to begin to develop a more realistic appraisal of the non-white people they encountered. Another term for that process is overcoming racial prejudice, that is, withdrawing one's projections from another group so as to see them as individuals. Similarly, if aliens were to arrive on earth tomorrow our view of them would be strongly colored by our projections, and those projections are the basis for the alien myth. Until the presence or absence of aliens and flying saucers is definitively proven one way or the other they can only be analyzed as a myth, and even if their presence is proven the myth will still be dominant.

Flying saucers as symbols

Taken as symbols, flying saucers and aliens point to a "higher" intelligence in the inner world. It is of superior intellect, power, and wisdom, and its interventions can change the course of mundane life. It is usually unseen and has an occasional interest in our normal world, although not a controlling one. It appears only rarely. It is not from our world.

Through these pages, I have introduced the layers of older thinking that lie within each of us, and noted that they continue to affect our thinking. Each of these is at least vaguely familiar; we have the personal unconscious (the inner stone-age cave dweller), the inner child (Calvin or Susie), the superego or inner parent telling us to behave, and our ego, the center of modern consciousness. We know the knight and the lady as symbols of the ego, fighting to repress the shadow. But none of these characters is an alien.

The idea of the alien implies a being from another world, and from a psychological perspective that implies the world beyond the conscious mind and the personal unconscious. That world is the collective unconscious, the great unknown from which conscious awareness (including the personal unconscious) arose. Alien mythology implies another intelligent center outside of the conscious mind we know, a center in the collective unconscious. The alien stories suggest that it is an intelligence that is older and more powerful than the parts of the conscious mind that we know. The aliens are not gods, nor are they god-men as was Christ, but rather humanoids, although they are more advanced. While there are group sightings, the effects are usually individual, as opposed to the group involvement of traditional religions. And the aliens usually arrive in a round craft, often described as saucer-shaped.

Interpreting alien craft and aliens symbolically, there is only one part of the mind that even remotely fits the description, and that is the Self and its agents. The most typical representation of the Self is a circular form, the usual shape associated with alien spacecraft. The Self is definitely not from the human conscious mind, but rather an entity outside of human conscious thinking. It rarely makes any appearance in one's life or dreams, except perhaps during times of turmoil and change when it serves to re-center and stabilize the mind.

Of course, we live in times of turmoil and change, and it is worth noting that we have only had the term "flying saucer" since 1947. It is really one of the symbols of our time in history. There are numerous symbols of the Self; it can be represented in any number of ways in dreams. But flying saucers, the round objects in the skies, as symbols of the Self are a myth for our time.

The alien, a crew member from the unidentified flying object, is the representative or agent of the Self, as angels were God's messengers in the past. The alien-as-messenger connects us with the Self, the impact is made (ideally a reconciliation of the ego with the Self), and then the connection is broken. This typically happens only when the conscious mind is having difficult times, and once recovery has occurred, contact is ended. Only the insane may possibly have ongoing contact with the Self, and that is rare.

The negative side of Self experience

There are two ways the aliens are seen as arriving on earth, the negative and the positive. We begin with the negative, and an example is the movie "Independence Day,"[202] from 1996.

Essentially, the movie is about an alien invasion of the earth. Huge circular craft appear above a number of cities. The aliens begin to attack by destroying several cities. Air Force aircraft return the attack but fail. One alien and its craft are fortunately captured, and it is learned that the aliens travel from planet to planet, devastating life on each to steal the natural resources. The captured alien craft is used to visit the main alien craft and implant a computer virus, which leaves the aliens defenseless. They are then successfully attacked and destroyed, and the earth is saved.

At first glance, the threat of the aliens appears to be the ego's projection of its own undesirable qualities onto the saucer myth. The highly developed Western ego does have a track record of traveling from one place to another, destroying the aboriginal civilizations and stealing their natural resources. This image suggests aliens are like us but worse.

But a closer look reveals a little more substance. Recall the dream I reported earlier: I am in my bed and I find myself surrounded by invading aliens from outer space. There were any number in the room and more were coming in the windows. I woke in terror.

For all I knew as I was dreaming, the aliens were there to destroy me. I wasn't just afraid, I was terrified. I have repeatedly emphasized that we have a number of "parts" to our minds, from the caveman or cave-woman to Calvin or Susie to the internal parent. In its development, the ego comes to feel that it is ruler of all of these aspects of the mind, and indeed master of the entirety of the mind. Then the Self appears, something entirely new, something alien and powerful. The ego feels it is no longer master of its own house and feels threatened. The ego's feeling is exactly the same as the feelings the movie characters expressed when the aliens began to attack earth. All of the control and mastery the ego had developed over the years was being lost. The best way for the ego to feel secure is to imagine that it can destroy the invader and restore its former position of mastery. The movie provides that reassurance.

It is notable that the humans are only able to win against the vastly superior aliens by a trick. They infect the alien's computer with a computer virus, a pretty far-fetched idea. It is similar to the ending of H. G. Wells' "The War of the Worlds," in which the invading Martians are brought down by earth's bacteria.[203] In both cases, the humans win only by the slimmest of margins, as they are clearly no match for the aliens. This reflects how the ego regards the superiority of the Self. Probably because of this, "Independence Day" is not really a hero's story. There are heroic individuals, including fighter pilots, a president, and a computer programmer, and each contributes to the destruction of the aliens, but there is no true story of the hero dealing with the Self. It is not a story of a hero facing his or her own Self, but of heroes defending their system against attack. Although the Self is introduced, it is dealt with in stage four fashion of the good guys overcoming the bad guys. Perhaps the most heroic character is a fighter pilot who flies his plane into the heart of an alien craft, where he explodes an atomic weapon and destroys the alien craft; he sacrifices himself to defend the group.

When the Self first makes an appearance to the conscious mind, the ego may well react with fear, and "Independence Day" illustrates just what those fears are. The ego has built level four consciousness up through years of development to be the master of its realm. It is not a consciousness that submits to its faith, as did medieval consciousness. It is not a consciousness that is at the whim of the gods, as in the ancient world. It is a controlling and mastering process that demands to be master of its own house. It is identified with the conquering son of the Father God, and feels mastery of itself and the earth. But with the first realization of the Self, the ego feels the superiority of the new entity. It feels inferior and threatened, as it realizes there is something present which is alien and beyond control. The appearance of the Self or its agents (aliens) in a dream may be very threatening in that it is an omen that the ego may undergo a death and rebirth experience. As Jung put it, "the experience of the Self is always a defeat for the ego."[204] These feelings may be present no matter how much distress the ego is experiencing because of other problems. Hopefully, a threatening initial introduction will be followed by more positive dreams of the Self. It was in my case.

The positive side of Self experience

The positive vision of the Self and contact with it is presented in "E.T. the Extra-Terrestrial,"[205] a 1982 movie. In the opening scenes, earth-visiting aliens are collecting plant samples when government agents surprise them. The aliens quickly depart in their ship, accidentally leaving one crew member behind. He is befriended and sheltered by a boy, Elliot, who becomes emotionally attached to the alien, whom he dubs "E.T." The link between Elliot and E.T. becomes psychic, and Elliot begins to refer to himself as "we." E.T. learns to speak English, and indicates that he wants to "phone home," that is, make arrangements to return to his home planet. He then makes a device to contact his former crew members. Meanwhile, E.T and Elliot are becoming ill. E.T. is ferreted out by government agents, and both he and Elliot are captured and placed in a portable quarantine medical facility. E.T. appears to die, and Elliot is left alone with the seemingly dead alien. But the alien comes back to life, and Elliot escapes with him in a medical van. Elliot, with the help of his friends, avoids the authorities and manages to get E.T back to his ship, which has returned to pick him up. Elliot expresses sadness about E.T. leaving, and E.T. touches Elliot's forehead with a glowing finger and tells him, "I'll be right here." E.T. enters the spacecraft and departs.

"E.T. the Extra-Terrestrial" is a hero story, and the hero is Elliot. He heeds the call to adventure and meets the alien. He enters into a new world in his contact with E.T. He defies conventional authority to carry out his quest. He is changed psychologically in the process and becomes a new person. So how does this hero story differ from older ones?

In the first scenes the aliens have landed on earth in their Self-symbol ship, more or less a sphere. That is, the Self has made contact with the conscious mind; it has landed on earth, conscious reality. But authority intervenes; we watch as government agents move in, apparently in an attempt to capture the aliens. It is easy to say that the government is, in fact, attempting to capture the aliens, or keep the aliens from us, or has secret information about them. That may or may not be, and I certainly don't know. But if it is your dream, it is your authority, the part that is invested in the system that we have, and that is the ego. We can interpret the authorities in this case as the individual's own ego that may feel threatened by invaders, as in "Independence Day," or as the group's shared values, which do not accept weird ideas coming from unknown sources. Thus the idea that the government is hiding crashed flying saucers or has made secret contact with aliens is part of the myth. Something alien is entering conscious awareness, and it is perceived as a threat by the ego, and—at least at first—the ego moves to protect itself. But does the government really have hidden aliens and flying saucers? Who knows?

One of the agents wears a prominent set of keys, keys not for unlocking but keys for locking and controlling. They are a badge of control and authority. There is no sense of the alternative associations one might link with keys: unlocking, freeing, or exposing secrets. Those keys do not unlock; they only lock.

In "Independence Day," the authorities were the "good guys" who fought off the invading aliens. In "E.T. the Extra-Terrestrial," the authorities are the "bad guys" who attempt to suppress contact with the Self and even control the Self. Authority has not changed from the last movie to this, but its role has changed, as the viewer's perception of the Self has changed. Authority is there to protect the established order, both in the inner world and in the outer one. It should be noted that the menace of authority was toned down in the 20th anniversary edition of "E.T. the Extra-Terrestrial"; the weapons of the authorities were obvious and threatening in the original version, much less so in the later edition.

"Independence Day" is about a group effort, not an individual one; it calls for self-sacrifice to save the group and avoid the Self as a threat. It does not lead to further individuality. In contrast, "E.T. the Extra-Terrestrial" is the story of one person's contact with the Self. It is about an individual effort on the part of one person, Elliot, who goes against the group's rules to find himself. This individual contact with the Self is the basis for the process of becoming a true individual. It is not a group effort.

Elliot, the hero of "E.T. the Extra-Terrestrial," is a child, not an adult. For this story, the Self makes its contact through the child part of the personality; that is not always the case. The ego—the adult in charge—may not like the idea of an alien presence it cannot control. Usually authorities are symbolic of the group's rules, society's collective values, and those rules do not include personal contact with the Self.

Early scenes in the movie suggest that Elliot has more than a few problems. He is living relatively well in a nice suburban house, but there is no father present. We learn that the father recently left the family, leaving an open wound. Elliot seems to be his older brother's servant. He appears to be lonely, socially inept, perhaps living in his older brother's shadow. Other children treat him with scorn. The movie does not emphasize his pain and discomfort, but it is there. Elliot's life before meeting E.T. is hardly in its best phase. Contact with the Self usually only occurs during times of distress and change, when dreams featuring the Self may help conscious awareness reorient itself. The Self contact serves to assist the individual to become who he or she really is, to find and fulfill individual potentiality. By the end of the story, Elliot will be a changed young man.

Elliot hides E.T. in his room. By the next day, Elliot has become attached to E.T. to the point that he develops a psychic connection with the alien. E.T. drinks beer he finds in the refrigerator, and Elliot, at school, becomes drunk and begins freeing frogs scheduled for dissection in the biology lab. E.T. views a kissing scene in a television movie, and Elliot kisses a girl in his class. Through his contact with E.T., in becoming one with

E.T., he changes from a passive, downtrodden person with low self-esteem to a heroic character, taking action in life, living his life more fully. Changes such as these are typical for the hero story; what is not typical is that they develop after contact with an alien.

Elliot cuts his finger, and E.T. is able to almost immediately heal the wound. This is an allegory for the healing that Self contact has for Elliot's mind.

E.T. makes a device to contact his former crew members to be rescued and taken "home." Meanwhile, he is becoming ill, and because of the psychic connection between the two, Elliot is also becoming ill. I assume that E.T. becomes ill because he is only an agent or messenger from the Self, and not the Self, and as such his time away from the center is limited. Perhaps he caught an earth virus, like the aliens in "The War of the Worlds." Whatever the cause of the alien's illness, Elliot is also becoming ill because his contact with the Self, E.T., is weakening, as E.T. fades. If an individual going through such a process loses the connection with the Self prematurely, the results are potentially disastrous. The movie shows this by having Elliot weaken as E.T. weakens.

It is at this point that the authorities discover E.T. He and Elliot are placed in a mobile medical quarantine unit. The medics discover that E.T. has DNA, that is, he is a humanoid, like us. It then appears that E.T. dies; the Self does not do well under the intense scrutiny of science.

E.T. and Elliot are left alone in the medical unit. E.T. comes back to life, and Elliot's illness resolves. The death and rebirth theme is not unusual in hero stories. The first instance of this was hardly in the story of Christ; it was already an old motif by that time in history. It may mark the culmination of the change process in the hero, as he is reborn into a new life.

Elliot then heroically escapes with E.T. in a medical van. They avoid authorities and continue their escape by bicycle with the help of Elliot's friends. By this time Elliot is a leader of his peers, a huge change from the first of the movie. They get E.T. back to the alien craft, where he bids Elliot farewell. Elliot is sad to lose E.T., but it is not as devastating as it would have been had the loss occurred earlier. E.T. places a glowing finger on Elliot's forehead, and tells him, "I'll be right here." The effects of the contact with the Self will remain with Elliot throughout his life. He knows the Self, the greater consciousness, exists, "right here." He knows who he is. He has moved from the mire in which he had become entrapped, back into the mainstream of life, on an individual pathway.

"Starman"[206] (1984) has many of the same themes as "E.T. the Extra-Terrestrial," with one more: the alien leaves the heroine pregnant. Symbolically, one could say that she was pregnant with new consciousness created by her contact with the Self.

The ego and the Self

These movies provide some basic themes that appear when the ego encounters the Self. It may at first be sensed as a threatening experience. One's ego may reject the experience. It primarily occurs during times of turmoil and change. The personality may reorganize and follow a new path after the experience. The individual is left with a new sense of purpose. And once the experience ends, it ends, even though the effects may last a lifetime.

These exact same remarks could be made about any vision of the Self in any of its previous forms as God-images. But the new version of the experience of the Self is strictly an individual one. It does not have a specific group effect. It does not involve a parental archetype. It comes with a direct message of healing and individuation for only one person.

There is an indirect group message of others' experiences of the Self, that the Self may make contact in time of distress and provide comfort and growth. It only tells the group that this could happen to any individual and what the results may be. It does not indicate that they have been redeemed by the incident, but they have become aware of its redeeming powers.

Flying saucers and aliens are a myth of the West, possibly based on reality and possibly not. It may seem doubtful that flying saucers or aliens could be featured in any religion of the future, but a professor of religion has suggested that the UFO phenomenon is a new religion in the making.[207] Whatever the case, they serve as a medium to carry the myth of the Self in our time. As a living myth, they represent the fact that the Self is coming into the conscious thinking of Westerners as a part of the new psychology.

Jung said that flying saucers symbolize the "wholeness of the Self" that "anticipate" the resolution of the opposites, that is, the combined opposite halves of the Self in Christian lore: Christ and Satan, good and evil.[208]

Although this is a myth of the group, it portrays an individual experience of the Self. As such, it may serve as a transition between group myths of the past—group religions—and an individual relationship to the Self in the future. UFO stories spread the myth, and even though only a few people actually have had these experiences of the Self, many more have been touched by the myth and what it symbolizes. The myth then helps shape core values of the new psychology in those it has reached. Relatively few people ever met Christ, but many were moved by his story; each person does not need to have a flying saucer experience to make this a powerful motif.

The observing, or examining, aspect of flying saucers represents the observing aspect of the Self, and is the same theme as the eye of God symbol, which may be seen on the reverse of the Seal of the United States, shown on the back of an American one dollar bill. It updates the theme that God is watching one's every movement, that perhaps the Self is recording for some future reconciliation. It is not the image of God the mother or father, watching over us and correcting our behavior. It is the image of something humanoid yet superior to humans. It is an image of the Self.

There are many ways the Self can be symbolized in a dream or in art. Previously, I noted that a circle or the sun may serve as such a symbol. In a dream, a new solar array had been installed on the roof to collect energy from the sun, that is, a link with the Self had been established. In another dream, a huge engine was discovered; it was made of an impossible combination of parts. The Self is often symbolized by a combination of opposites, as fire and water, and as in the engine dream, where the motion of the engine parts formed such an opposition. A ring may serve as a Self symbol, as will be discussed in the next chapter. The Self might be dreamed of as some annoyance or something unacceptable that has attached itself to you; it is not quite the threat seen in "Independence Day," but it is not something that you initially want to accept as a part of yourself. These are individual experiences of individual symbols, and they vary greatly from person to person.

But of all the various symbols for the Self, the flying saucer myth is the only collective form active in our time. It is the only living myth of our time. As a myth, it suggests that something alien has landed and made contact, but that contact is only with the individual. After I had the dream of aliens entering my bedroom, I never had a similar dream again, although I did have a number of dreams with references to the Self. One alien invasion is enough for anyone, I suppose.

But what are UFO's? James Kirsch, a physician and Jungian analyst who was in analysis with Jung both before and after World War II, reported that he had seen an unidentified flying object. This apparently occurred in 1954. Kirsch wrote Jung a letter detailing the experience; the letter is lost, but Jung's replies to Kirsch mentioning the event survived.[209] Jung found it curious that Kirsch did not photograph the object despite having a camera.[210] I discussed the incident with Dr. Kirsch years ago, and this is what I can recall of our conversation. Kirsch was on a visit to his family's home in Guatemala when the maids sighted a flying saucer. Kirsch said that he and others could see it initially. The sighting continued for an hour and fifteen minutes. During that time, Kirsch went to his room and began a letter to Jung to report the event. He returned to the viewing area, where others continued to see the flying saucer, but he was no longer able to see it, apparently because he had considered the psychological basis for the flying saucer phenomena while writing the letter to Jung.

It was John Mack's impression that something beyond our usual laws of physics was occurring in the reported alien abductions, perhaps interactions with beings from another planet or another dimension. He was struck by the passion of the people reporting the experiences, the similar descriptions of the abductions, and the lack of explanation from classical psychiatry; he noted that the people involved did not have mental illnesses. But Dr. Mack was apparently unaware of Jung's idea of flying saucers as symbols of the Self, and Self psychology.

On the other hand, there are certainly a number of reports of UFO sightings which defy psychological explanation.[211] The most fascinating reports are of U.S. Air Force crewmen whose nuclear warhead missiles were temporarily deactivated as unidentified flying objects hovered directly above their launch facilities.[212] These events involve trained observers, radar confirmation, and significant manipulation of highly controlled weapons systems. I find these reports difficult to dismiss, but I suppose they could be the result of some unknown physical or psychological effect; but again, who knows?

I don't think that Jung ever made a final decision on the "reality" of flying saucers, and I have no idea. Maybe some of the stories are "real" and others are based on Self psychology. It could be that the appearance of aliens is synchronous with the appearance of Self psychology in our time. Just because a person from the northern hemisphere dreams of an aboriginal Australian does not mean that such people do or do not exist; the dream person is only another symbol in the mind, and that is what is important.

The impact of Self psychology on the individual will be a gradual erosion of the importance of public opinion and what others think in the outer world, and a similar erosion of the ego's sense of importance in the inner world, with an increasing desire to find one's own unique individuality and meaning in life. Its appearance marks the beginning of the end of ego dominance in the inner world, and of nationalism and identifying with the nation-state in the outer world. Not everyone need have a direct experience of the Self, but Self psychology will come to permeate society. This will give each individual a respectful relationship with their own Self and their own myth, and a respectful awareness of others and their myth.

The appearance of this as a new myth of our time marks a page turning in history. While only a few people experience it, many people are aware of the motif, as the Self begins forming the new psychology. The myth of flying saucers and aliens coming to earth means that the Self is coming into human conscious awareness, and a new consciousness is taking shape.

CHAPTER XVIII

The Task of Luke Skywalker and Frodo Baggins

Modern hero stories

When I first saw "Star Wars"[213] in 1977, It struck me that it was the best science fiction movie I had seen. It had references to myth and the hero's story, to earlier science fiction, and it was just a good movie overall. It was a sensation at the time as nothing like that had been done before. Now it looks dated, but "Star Wars" opened the door and set the standard for much that came later.

What is most striking about the "Star Wars" trilogy is the strong presence it has maintained in Western culture since its initial release. More recent episodes, "The Force Awakens,"[214] and "The Last Jedi,"[215] contain almost identical themes as the first three movies of the series; both were well received and were not considered repetitive. I think that is because the underlying themes remain important.

When I first saw "Star Wars," every aspect of the story seemed to fit together, but I wondered why the only round object in the movie, the Death Star, was evil and had to be destroyed. (The Death Star is a huge, big as a moon, spherical space station and war machine, capable of destroying planets.) That same theme was present again in the third movie of the series, "Return of the Jedi." In the meantime, I had read "The Lord of the Rings" trilogy, and the same basic ideas were present there; the entire plot involves destroying another round object, a ring. "The Lord of the Rings" books were subsequently made into a trio of movies, which were also quite popular, almost as popular as the "Star Wars" movies. The main theme of both the "Star Wars" trilogy and "The Lord of the Rings" trilogy is an epic struggle with a few individuals fighting against an overwhelming force concerned only with control and power over the world. And central to both plots was the destruction of a round object. Because of the immense popularity of these stories (continuing to the present), I knew that they must say something about the psychology of our time, and I resolved to unravel the mystery.

Both the "Star Wars" trilogy and "The Lord of the Rings" trilogy tell the age-old hero's story, but with important modern modifications: the hero is only able to accomplish his task with the help of a character who is his shadow, and the only significant round objects in the plot must be destroyed. Integrating one's shadow is an important aspect of the new psychology, so it is not at all surprising that the theme of shadow integration would appear in a movie reflecting the epic struggle of our time. The hero needs the help of his shadow in order to accomplish his task; this is directly opposed to the traditional Western myth, in which the hero must overcome his shadow to achieve victory. But why would the round objects be dangerous? The round objects appear to be Self symbols in both stories, but they are not invading flying saucers; in both stories the round objects are under human control. And both stories involve a great war; what is that about?

Both trilogies are based on the theme of a hero and a few individuals resisting and overthrowing an overwhelming force of control. In the "Star Wars" movies, the Empire has already taken over and a small group has begun a rebellion. In "The Lord of the Rings" story, a similar force of control is attempting to take over the known world and a few resist. In both cases the hero and his companions are in a struggle with the world hanging in the balance. The audience wants the hero to win; somehow we are invested in this fight; in some way the battle is a part of us and our psychology. Both stories make it clear that the struggle is of epic proportions with the potential for dire consequences if the battle is lost.

It is no accident that the theme of rebellion against an overwhelming force of control appears in these extremely popular stories. It is a major theme of our time and our lives. It is a reflection of the struggle between the old and the new psychologies, and it is central to who we are and our time in history. The old psychology seems to be an all-powerful, controlling force, and the new seems to be in rebellion against that force. Consciously or unconsciously we want to know how to deal with the problem, and it is for that reason that the modern hero's tale is so satisfying: it suggests that one can successfully meet the challenge. The way the heroes of our stories handle those conflicts gives us hints as to how we might handle our own issues, and reassures us that it is possible to do so satisfactorily. This specific struggle, the revolt or resistance against a mighty controlling force, is the conflict of our time and it is a conflict within each one of us. Once that struggle is accomplished these stories will lose their magic and their psychological allure, and new stories will be produced. But the magic of these stories remains for us because they reflect the struggles of our time.

Again, I am taking these stories as dreams, so that each character represents some aspect of the dreamer's mind, and not "us versus them" in the outer world.

The story of Luke Skywalker

"Star Wars" opens with a scene in which a spaceship of the Empire, commanded by Darth Vader, overtakes and captures another ship carrying Princess Leia. The princess has stolen plans of the Empire's greatest weapon, the Death Star, a massive spherical war machine capable of destroying planets, to be passed to the Rebel Alliance. Before she is captured, the princess gives the plans and a message to two robots, who then escape to the planet below. The robots are obtained by Luke Skywalker's uncle, Luke's adoptive parent. While cleaning the robots, Luke sees part of the message from the princess. Luke helps the robots find the person the message was addressed to, an aging Jedi Knight, Ben Kenobi(Obi-Wan Kenobi), living as a hermit in the desert. Ben tells Luke about having served as a Jedi Knight, that Luke's father was also a knight who had been killed, and suggests Luke accompany him to deliver the plans. Luke declines, but when he returns home, he finds that his aunt and uncle have been murdered by the Empire in their search for the robots and the plans, so he goes with Ben. They hire a smuggler, Han Solo, to take them to the rebels. During the trip, Ben begins training Luke to be a knight, and explains the Force, an energy that flows throughout the galaxy. When they arrive where the rebel planet should be, they only find rubble; the planet has been destroyed by the Death Star. Their ship is then captured by the Death Star's tractor beam and pulled aboard. Through stealth, Luke and Han rescue Princess Leia while Ben disables the tractor beam. Ben and Darth Vader meet and begin to duel, allowing the others to get back to their ship. Ben is killed, or dematerializes, and the others escape. Using the stolen plans the rebels are able to form an attack on the Death Star. As the rebel pilots, including Luke, attack the Death Star, Darth Vader and other Empire pilots attempt to stop them. Luke hears the guiding voice of Ben, who tells him to use the Force to guide his mission. Luke is able to fire a missile into a vulnerable port on the Death Star, causing it to explode; Vader escapes. Luke, Han, and company are rewarded by the Rebel Alliance.

"Star Wars" is a good example of the hero's journey, and contains a number of typical motifs. Luke meets Ben Kenobi, the wise old man in the desert. He initially refuses the call to adventure when Ben suggests he help deliver the Death Star plans. There is a massacre of the innocents, when Luke's adoptive parents, his aunt and uncle, are murdered. (The hero is often an orphan, like Luke.) Luke then answers the call and goes with Ben. He learns about the Force, and begins training as a Jedi Knight; in doing so he crosses the threshold into a new reality. When Ben dematerializes, the master is lost, and Luke must go on alone. He uses what he has been taught to accomplish the hero's task. Those themes are timeless parts of the story of the hero. In almost every aspect, Luke's story could have been a hero's story in the Western tradition, with the hero beating the bad guys. Only two themes did not fit. One is the shape of the Death Star. No other craft, in any of the Star Wars movies, is spherical, and no other craft is as destructive. The other is the rebellion itself, a drive to completely overturn the entire government, not just to get the "bad guys" or "clean up" that government; this is not supporting and defending the system typical of stage four.

The second movie of the trilogy, "The Empire Strikes Back,"[216] is probably the best of the three. The plot is quite involved and is only briefly summarized here. Although the Death Star was destroyed, the Empire's forces have regrouped and driven the rebels into hiding. Luke learns, from Ben's voice, that he is to seek out another Jedi Knight, Yoda, for further training. The rebel base is attacked, and the rebels are scattered. Luke begins training with Yoda, a small green humanoid. Meanwhile, Leia and Han are captured by Darth Vader. Luke senses this and breaks off his training to attempt a rescue. Han is given to a bounty hunter. Leia escapes. Luke is confronted by Vader and they engage in a desperate battle with light-sabers. Vader tells Luke that he is Luke's father and asks him to join him and rule the galaxy using the dark side of the Force. Luke declines and loses the fight after his hand is amputated; he falls into a massive air shaft and almost plummets to the planet below. He is saved by falling onto an antenna, where he hangs. He uses the Force to contact Leia, who returns to rescue him. They go to a rebel ship, where Luke receives an artificial hand. Luke's companions leave to search for Han.

"The Empire Strikes Back" makes it clear that one rebel victory does not mean the war is won. Luke develops his Jedi skills further under his new teacher, Yoda, but he is not ready for his confrontation with Darth Vader. The face-off between Luke and Darth Vader confirms that Darth is Luke's shadow. Luke is defeated and disheartened by Vader, and is almost killed. It is interesting that he falls until he manages to be caught on a cross-shaped antenna, where he hangs until Leia rescues him. Christ was hung on a cross, and Odin hung himself on the World Tree in an act of self-sacrifice; this is another hero motif. The movie carries the feeling of the disappointment of grave defeat by the overwhelming strength of the Empire and Darth Vader; it is tempered only by our knowledge that the hero will eventually prevail. It is a reminder of the strength and resilience of the established psychology of our consciousness and the difficulty of changing it.

A notable scene occurs during Luke's training. In an imaginary scenario, Luke confronts Darth Vader and cuts off his head. Luke then removes Vader's helmet-mask and discovers his own face. It is a pointed reminder that the shadow is a projected part of oneself, and an attack against the person carrying one's shadow projection is actually an attack against oneself.

The third movie, "Return of the Jedi,"[217] begins with Luke freeing Leia and Han. Luke returns to Yoda for further training, but finds that Yoda is dying. Yoda confirms that Darth Vader is Luke's father and tells him that he must face Vader to become a knight. The rebels learn that a second Death Star is being constructed, more powerful than the first, and plan an attack on it. Han is to lead a party to destroy the Death Star's temporary shield generator on the planet below; that will allow rebel craft to fly into the Death Star and destroy it from within. When the attack begins, Luke senses Vader's presence, and feels he must confront Vader, as he is still redeemable. Both Luke and Vader enter the Death Star and meet the Emperor, the ultimate head of the Empire. The Emperor explains that the rebels are walking into a trap. The rebel ground party is captured, so the rebel craft are unable to penetrate the Death Star's shields. A duel begins between Luke and Vader, with Vader again tempting Luke to join him and turn to the dark side of the force. Luke is infuriated and attacks Vader with great anger, and cuts off his hand. This enrages the Emperor, who begins to kill Luke with the energy of the dark side of the Force. When Vader sees his son suffering, he turns on the Emperor, and destroys him. Before dying, the Emperor mortally wounds Vader. As Vader dies, he and Luke reconcile. The ground team is then able to destroy the shield generator, allowing the rebel craft to destroy the Death Star.

The most important motifs of the third movie are the destruction of the second spherical Death Star and the need for the hero to have the help of his shadow to accomplish his task. Luke actually fails because of his anger; why should he be angry with Vader for suggesting he join him and the Dark Side of the Force if he were not tempted? As angry as he becomes he must be quite tempted. He fails and is being killed by the Emperor when Darth Vader destroys the Emperor so that Luke's task may be accomplished. Were it not for Vader, Luke and the rebellion would have failed.

The Emperor is not portrayed as a human being, but rather as a ghoul, a nonhuman fiend. The prequel movies, made afterward, demonstrate that the Emperor was a real person who was seduced into evil.

But in the original trilogy of movies he is not human, but something monstrous. He is a symbol of everything the Empire and Darth Vader have been fighting to promote, a symbol, not really human.

The Emperor in "Star Wars" is parallel to Sauron in "The Lord of the Rings." Both stories hinge on these two nonhuman characters. The Emperor and Darth Vader (prior to his redemption) are identified with the "Dark side of the Force." The Emperor is a focus of this energy, a personification of it. This is similar to Sauron, another personification of an energy repeatedly referred to as evil, dark, and controlling.

It is worth noting that the "Star Wars" movies illustrate the collective struggle that is taking place at the same time that the hero is locked in his individual battle. There is the group's war with the rebels attacking the Empire, but ultimately victory depends on the success of the hero in his individual struggle. It is not about many heroes upholding the existing order. This is saying that the group's battle is won by the individual making his or her effort in a personal battle. The pathway to the next psychology lies in each individual facing an individual conflict, and not in a group effort. The group effect is then aided by the individual struggle, but the individual comes first.

The motif of shadow reconciliation in "Star Wars" is clear. But why is the only Self symbol, the Death Star, a deadly device that must be destroyed?

The story of Frodo Baggins

Many of these same themes are found in *The Lord of the Rings* trilogy. Again, it is the hero's journey that takes place against the backdrop of a great battle for control. The hero's task is critical for winning the war, and the hero is only able to complete his task with the help of his shadow. The destruction of a round object is again the main theme. But this time the round object is a ring carried by the hero, as opposed to the Death Star operated by the Empire.

The Lord of the Rings is a trilogy consisting of three novels, later made into movies, *The Fellowship of the Ring*,[218,219] *The Two Towers*,[220,221] and *The Return of the King*.[222,223] The movie versions follow the plot of the novels by the same names closely enough for our purposes. However, the story of *The Lord of the Rings* actually begins in a prequel novel, *The Hobbit*,[224] and the movies of that story (in three parts[225,226,227]) deviate significantly from the novel. The movie versions of "The Hobbit" are fundamentally different from the book, and those differences are important for understanding our time.

The book form of *The Hobbit* is a naive children's story written in the 1930s. The hero of the story, Bilbo Baggins, goes on a trek with a group of bumbling dwarves. As the story progresses, the dwarves rely more and more on Bilbo to pull them out of scrapes caused by their own bungling. They do not become brave warriors until almost the end of the story, after Bilbo has won their treasure back for them and they decide to defend it. There are certainly evil characters in the story, trolls, goblins, and a dragon, but they are traditional figures that could be taken from any number of fairy tales. The story is an adventure with its dangers, but it is more in the nature of "Little Red Riding Hood" or "Snow White." This is not the case with the movie version of the story.

The dwarves in "The Hobbit" movies appear to be more short Special Forces warriors than the clueless bumblers in the novel. Most of all, the movies are "dark" with a great fearful foreboding from the start, most unlike the book. The difficulty is that "The Hobbit" movies were made after the movie versions of "The Lord of the Rings," so that "The Hobbit" movies have the same dark and threatening feel as "The Lord of the Rings" movies. But in fact, *The Lord of the Rings* books were the sequel to *The Hobbit* book. *The Hobbit* book was the foundation on which *The Lord of the Rings* was built, and not vice versa. This is a problem.

The Hobbit book was first published in 1937, before World War II, before Nazis and the Holocaust, before the Iron Curtain, and before nuclear weapons and the threat of nuclear war. Most importantly, it was written before the great drama of good and evil enacted in *The Lord of the Rings* was formed in the mind of the author. The book is as naive as the world was naive in the 1930s. No one had any idea of just how evil that evil could be; the world had much to learn. It was out of that mind-set that the author had Bilbo take the ring, a harmless prize in *The Hobbit*, and it was the author's evolving vision that led to the realization of the horror of the ring and the need to get rid of it in *The Lord of the Rings*. The transition from naively facing traditional fairy-tale evil in *The Hobbit* to facing terrifying, horrible, total evil in *The Lord of the Rings* is lost in the movie version. It is an important marker of change in our time, and for that reason, I am sticking with the book version of *The Hobbit*.

The Hobbit begins with an explanation of what hobbits are. In that the book is a story for children, hobbits are pictured as a race of small people, vaguely like leprechauns. They live in holes in the ground, but the holes are well-appointed dwellings with doors, rooms, pantries, and other amenities. They are a child-sized fantasy people made for children to identify with. This contrasts with *The Lord of the Rings*, an adult story in which the hobbits are still small people physically, but the connotation of small is more in the sense of ordinary people who are not the great lords of the land. The hobbits have become transformed into ordinary people who must face a great struggle. The hero is the proverbial "little guy"; their actual stature is irrelevant, although they are certainly short compared to humans.

But *The Hobbit* is a story for children, and the hero of the story is Bilbo Baggins, a hobbit. The local wizard, Gandalf, chooses him to serve as "burglar" for a band of dwarves. A dragon has taken over the dwarves treasure and former home inside a mountain, and they are determined to get both back, with the help of Gandalf. Neither Bilbo nor the dwarves are happy with Gandalf's selection of Bilbo as the burglar, but all finally agree, and Bilbo sets out with them on the adventure. They overcome many obstacles in a lengthy trek, and Bilbo becomes more and more capable as events unfold.

Midway through the trek, deep inside tunnels beneath mountains, Bilbo becomes separated from the others and lost. He finds a ring and absentmindedly slips it into his pocket. He then comes upon Gollum, a creature living in a pool at the base of the mountains; Gollum had lost the ring. Gollum wants to eat Bilbo, who escapes. Bilbo learns that the ring is magical and makes the wearer invisible. With the ring, his capabilities as a burglar increase substantially. As the journey continues, Bilbo becomes more and more competent. The dwarves increasingly rely on him to reach their goals.

Bilbo and the dwarves arrive at the mountain containing the former home of the dwarves, now occupied by a dragon. Bilbo discovers the vulnerability of the dragon, so that a local archer is able to slay it. Then the local people want a share of the dragon's treasure because they helped the dwarves and because their town was destroyed in the process of killing the dragon. The dwarves refuse to share, and both sides prepare for war. Before war breaks out, a larger army of goblins attack, and the dwarves and men must join together to fight the goblins. The goblins are defeated in a close battle, and the treasure is then divided between the dwarves and the local people. Bilbo rejects his full share of the wealth, but he does bring a small portion home.

Most of all, *The Hobbit* is a children's story. By identifying with the small person, children can imagine going out into the world, establishing an identity, overcoming obstacles, and succeeding in making their fortune. An important motif is overcoming greed, including the greed of the dragon, the greed of the dwarves, and even the greed of a trio of trolls. All of this is woven into the hero's quest.

Neither the ring nor Gollum is particularly emphasized in the story. Gollum loses the ring, Bilbo finds it, and Bilbo escapes Gollum. The entire episode is presented as just one more event in the story, with no special emphasis. The ring is only presented as a magical device that makes the wearer invisible, and nothing more.

There are three Self symbols in *The Hobbit*. When Bilbo first scouts the dragon's treasure, he finds the most wondrously beautiful jewel in a sea of jewels, the Arkenstone. It is a Self symbol, and probably symbolizes the culmination of his journey and discovering his individuality. Another Self symbol is the wizard Gandalf, as Ben Kenobi and Yoda were in "Star Wars." They also could be considered agents of the Self, there to lead the individual to further development.

But the most important Self symbol is the ring that Bilbo finds. In the story, finding the ring is at first a trivial matter, as if he had found a coin. Bilbo soon figures out the ring's powers and uses them to become a very skilled burglar. The finding of the ring marks Bilbo's change from being frightened and unsure to having confidence, ability, skill, and power. In that the ring is a Self symbol, this suggests that the Self has given Bilbo the fate and the events in his life so he can develop new skills as well as confidence, ability, and power in life.

Another point to note is that the ring had belonged to Gollum, a shadow creature. Bilbo found the ring, but it was property of Gollum. Of course, if Gollum had not lost the ring, or if Bilbo had given it back, Gollum would have eaten Bilbo. Nevertheless, it was Gollum's ring and while Bilbo did not, strictly speaking, steal it, that is what he really did. Bilbo took power from his shadow, just as the ego takes power from the personal unconscious, just as the West has taken power and wealth (slaves and oil, as examples) from the less developed people of the world. It is behavior typical of developmental stage four, the stage we are leaving. It is only because we are leaving that stage and beginning the next, that the behavior of the ego and the West in general have become an issue. It is only in our time that the concept of "ripping off" of nature and the "third world" has become a major point of concern. It is the theme of the 2009 movie "Avatar."[228] This sympathy for the "noble savage," the primitive, and all that has been lost with civilization, has been a growing theme in the West since Christopher Columbus made his reports on the new world he had found. It is the same psychology as awareness of the shadow; primitivism is the shadow of civilization.

The importance of the ring and its acquisition by theft are not emphasized in *The Hobbit*. In the story, Bilbo even denies the truth of how he obtained the ring. *The Hobbit* is for children, and children grow up by developing an ego that strengthens by repressing its shadow and gaining energy by doing so. It is not ready to deal with the truth of the machinations it finds necessary to grow and become a functioning adult. That realization is an adult story.

It is as if the author was aware of these issues, and brooded on them after publishing *The Hobbit*, because when *The Lord of the Rings* opens, it is clear that the danger of the ring has been realized. The tone of the story has shifted completely. It is an adult tale of bravery in the face of terror, all in an effort to get rid of the ring that had been so easily obtained. The ring is seen as an item of great evil, which is capable, in the right hands, of enslaving the world. Yet it is the same ring that was so helpful to Bilbo.

The Hobbit is a children's story in which the hero must find the ring to achieve success. *The Lord of the Rings* is an adult story in which the hero must get rid of the ring to achieve success. The stories are two halves of the same process.

Jung might say that the first story is for the first half of life, while the second is for the second half of life.[229] The first half of life is marked by an expansion out into the world. The individual strives to make money, propagate, achieve socially, and become useful and capable. The second half of life calls for a different principle based on a turning away from striving and achievement. The tasks of the first half of life are clear, but those of the second half less so. This becomes a particular issue for us in our time, in that the civilization of the West has emphasized the goals of the first half of life more than any other culture that has ever existed. We have a culture based on striving, overcoming, using, achieving, conquering, and so forth, and it is winding down. The new psychology we are developing has much more of a second-half-of-life nature, with its emphasis on reconciling with the shadow rather than conquering it.

The psychology we are entering is based on principles that demote the ego from its position of being the absolute center of conscious awareness, with the introduction of the shadow, the unconscious, the anima or animus, and especially, the Self. The ego does not give up that position willingly. No one likes to acknowledge shadow qualities. It is hard to accept the idea that the anima or animus is in the inner world, as opposed to a lover to be pursued in the outer world. And as to the Self, remember my dream of invading aliens and the movie "Independence Day"; the ego does not like company it can't control. This is not an easy transition, and there are reasons that "Star Wars" and *Lord of the Rings* portray a struggle of epic proportions. This struggle takes place in both the inner and outer worlds; it is a theme central to our time.

A notable deviation that "The Lord of the Rings" movies made from the novels is that the hero of the story, Frodo Baggins, is a young adult, but in the books he has reached 50, middle-age even for the long-lived hobbits. His task is really a mid-life task, but I suppose younger heroes sell more movie tickets, so there is a younger Frodo in the movies.

Frodo is the nephew of Bilbo Baggins, the hero of *The Hobbit*. As Bilbo aged, he adopted Frodo, his orphaned nephew. Note that Luke Skywalker and Frodo Baggins, as well as a number of other heroes, are orphans. When Bilbo reached a ripe old age, he retired to live with the elves and write poetry. He left everything, including the ring, to Frodo, the hero of *The Lord of the Rings*.

Centuries before the story begins, Sauron, referred to as the "Dark Lord," made the ring. He is a presence throughout the story as the source of evil, always in the background. He is not human, but an archetypal presence as was the Emperor in "Star Wars." He made the ring as an implement to control the world, but lost it in a battle. Years later it was found and then taken by Gollum through murder. Gollum crawled into the cave where he lived for years before he lost the ring to Bilbo.

The ring is repeatedly associated with evil, greed, lust for power, and lust for the ring itself. Early in *The Lord of the Rings*, the wizard Gandalf warns Frodo not to wear the ring. As the story progresses, Frodo becomes more and more dominated by the ring, more jealous of possessing it, more suspicious that others may be trying to take it. It becomes a burden of increasing weight. The ring is not only a malignant object, but it is also tied to its evil creator, Sauron, so that anyone possessing the ring becomes drawn to him. Additionally, it has the potential of seductively inflating one's sense of importance, so that the individual wearing it has delusions of great power.

Here is the basic plot of the three books and movies that make up *The Lord of the Rings*: Gandalf visits Frodo, warns him of the evil powers of the ring, and tells him that he must take the ring and leave the Shire, the hobbits' home. Frodo, his gardener Sam, and two friends set out, barely escaping the Ringwraiths, horrific agents of Sauron who are seeking the ring. Frodo and company make a difficult trek to the east and manage to find temporary refuge with elves. There a council is held and it is determined that the only way to safely deal with the ring is to destroy it by returning it to the volcano from which it was forged. The volcano is in Mordor, Sauron's land far to the south. If Sauron captures the ring his power will be increased immensely and his armies are already on the march. A band is chosen to go with Frodo toward Mordor. The trek continues until one of the group falls under the sway of the ring and attempts to take it from Frodo; the group then splits up. Frodo and Sam continue the journey to Mordor; meanwhile, their companions become involved in the wars unleashed by Sauron and his followers. On their trek to Mordor, Frodo and Sam capture Gollum, who has been drawn by the allure of the ring. Gollum agrees to help them and tells of a secret tunnel into Mordor. But Gollum betrays them in the tunnel by leading them into the lair of a giant spider; Frodo is stung and rendered unconscious. Frodo initially seems dead, but recovers; he and Sam escape and continue their journey into Mordor. The last leg is a desperate trek across a desert and up the side of the volcano, with Gollum following. Frodo reaches the spot where the ring can be thrown into the volcano, but at the last minute he refuses to part with the ring and puts it on his finger. At that moment Gollum attacks Frodo, bites off his ring finger to get the ring, and plummets with the ring into the volcano. When that occurs the ring is destroyed, the armies of Sauron fail, and Sauron, as a black shadow, is blown away by the wind.

This condensed version of the plot makes it easy to see the many parallels with the "Star Wars" trilogy. The hero in both tales is involved in an epic struggle. He is reluctant about beginning his task, and is aided by a wise old man figure. The group fights the evil forces as the hero struggles, and the group is not able to achieve victory until the hero succeeds. Both heroes suffer amputations; Frodo loses a finger and Luke a hand (amputation is another hero motif). The good wise old men or wizards, Ben, Yoda, and Gandalf, are balanced by their evil counterparts, the Emperor and Sauron, and the hero's actions tip the balance to the good. When the struggle ends, both the Emperor and Sauron dematerialize; but more importantly, when the story ends, all of the super-human characters are gone, including Ben, Yoda, Gandalf, the Emperor, and Sauron. Both Luke and Frodo are only able to complete their tasks with the help of their shadows, Darth Vader and Gollum. And in both tales the round object of great power is destroyed. At heart, "Star Wars" and *The Lord of the Rings* are the same fundamental story but with a different cast of characters in a different time and place.

In both "Star Wars" and *The Lord of the Rings*, the heroes are guided by, and in conflict with, agents of absolute good and absolute evil. Ben Kenobi, Yoda, and Gandalf guide Luke and Frodo only for the good. The Emperor and Sauron represent only evil. When the struggles of Luke and Frodo end, all of these super-human agents of good and evil are gone, leaving the humans and hobbits to fend for themselves. These super-human beings are Self symbols, standing for the positive and negative sides of the Self. They represent the Self divided into its dark and light aspects, as is true of our world today. We are likewise leaving the age of good and evil, and as we accomplish our struggle, our need for good and evil icons will also end.

For centuries, there had been no king of Middle Earth, the setting of *The Lord of the Rings*, and the struggle ends with the restoration of the king. The man who becomes king at the end of the story had lived as a ranger and wanderer, always present but not recognized as royal. The image of the king is a major symbol of the Self. The theme of the restoration of the king means a returning awareness of the presence of the Self, although the Self had been present all along, but unrecognized. The Self is returned to its rightful place at the center of the psychological kingdom, the inner world. This could only happen when the ring was destroyed. Middle Earth then had its king and harmony was restored to the world.

The ring and the Death Star as symbols

This brings us back to the meaning of the round objects in these stories. Both tales are classic hero journeys with the additions of the shadow helping the hero destroy round objects. Both the Death Star and the ring are Self symbols, but they are Self symbols in service of humans, specifically the human ego. The Death Star is a machine of great power, a tool operated by humans. The ring on the finger is a tool of the human hand, giving invisibility and power. The hand is where the person grasps reality, where the human will exerts itself. This imagery suggests that the person who wears the ring or commands the Death Star thinks that the Self is his tool, his servant. These stories indicate this thinking is immensely dangerous and threatening, and a great struggle is required to overcome the problem.

The symbolism of the ring and the Death Star is the ego identified with the Self. That is not a problem for a young person; a degree of it is a normal part of stage four ego building. But an ego identified with the Self cannot continue development into stage five. "Star Wars" and *The Lord of the Rings* are stories about escaping the trap of the ego identified with the Self, and show that it is only possible via the shadow.

In *The Hobbit* Bilbo finds the ring and casually uses it to become a competent burglar. He keeps the ring secret and pretends that he became an excellent burglar through his own resources; he even comes to believe it himself. This is a young person's view, that they made their success entirely on their own. As they find their way in life, they build skills, confidence, and ego strength.

It is only later, in *The Lord of the Rings*, that Frodo realizes that the ring is actually a frightful master. It is the ego identified with the Self that prevents further development and keeps the individual in late level four.

Identifying with the Self means the ego feels that it is making its own fate rather than living the fate that the Self gave. It means forgetting everything that was once attributed to fate, luck, or the deity, and assuming those powers for oneself. It means forgetting the luck of being born into a better or worse family, of being born a certain color or sex, of having better or worse schooling, or getting breaks or not, of making the right decisions or not, of having a more or less attractive face and body, and a million other things that life gave the individual, as opposed to what the individual did. This thinking is the norm for the first half of life (as in *The Hobbit*), but it is dangerous in the second half (as in *The Lord of the Rings*).

It is worth noting that the typical symbol for atomic energy, an image of an atom consisting of a nucleus surrounded by six revolving electrons, is a Self symbol. Humanity's underlying unease with atomic energy lies in the idea of this force in human hands, parallel to the Death Star and Frodo's ring.

We live in a crossover time between an old ethic and a new one, when the old God-image is weakened and the new one has not become strong. The old image is given lip service but not true allegiance; this creates a power vacuum for something to worship, some God-substitute. The ego slips into that role, becoming inflated, as if it were "God almighty" itself. The old God-image is gone and the ego does not want to give up its power to a new one. The new God-image, the Self, is in each person as opposed to God in heaven, and the ego can easily identify with that archetype. From a psychological point of view, the ego has identified with the Self, the archetype behind the God-image. It becomes inflated. Thus our era of many self-important people.

For an ego identified with the Self, the Self seems to be the ego's tool, the ring one wears. The ego has gotten the idea that it produced what the Self gave; it thinks that it is godlike and has made its fate. This causes an exaggerated sense of one's importance that is not based on reality, and allows one to be susceptible to the lure of evil deeds in that one is "special." In terms of *The Lord of the Rings*, if you put on the ring you start to think that you are an important person and begin to fall under the rule of Sauron.

When Sam, Frodo's companion and gardener, put on the ring, he immediately felt the lure of conquering the world and making it into a great garden; he resisted the ring's seduction when he wisely realized that he would be much happier tending his own small garden. The Death Star likewise seduced with the temptation of great planet-destroying power under the control of its commander. Both represent the illusion that the Self is the servant of the ego, that the powers given by the Self are the ego's powers. This is only the inflated ego's delusion. The ego wants desperately to hold on to that fantasy; hence the great struggle dramatized in "Star Wars" and *The Lord of the Rings*.

In the medieval world each person believed that the entire world was a fated test set up by God, and one's task in life was to live out one's fate according to religious doctrine. Kings were kings and paupers were paupers, but both felt that they would be held in equal judgment in the afterlife. Pride of personal accomplishment was seen as sin. One's fate in this life was only a test to determine whether one's soul was fit to enter heaven. One's fate or one's lot in life was not something one made, but rather, was something given by God, and it was of minor importance compared with life after death. A medieval person would say that wearing the ring means that the individual thinks that they alone created their fate in life, and that they are usurping the place of God.

The modern West began with the idea that one should copy Christ and face life heroically, and strive for success on the earthly, material plane. Despite Christ's teaching that his kingdom was not of this world,[230] he became the West's role model for heroic action in the material world. The idea gradually developed that people who did well in life were more Christ-like, and hence better people; the poor were obviously at the other end of the spectrum. This has gradually and insidiously continued to develop, more so as Christianity has weakened. People who do well in life easily feel that they are particularly blessed by God and hence special. Gone is the idea that having wealth and success is just another test; rather, it is a marker of specialness. The ego easily becomes inflated and puffed up. If one is blessed and special, then one can do as one chooses, and that can easily include evil.

This was held in check by the monarchy and the system of heredity royalty, and by traditional Christianity. The inflation of egos was not completely stopped, but it was restricted and curbed. That has failed as the old religion has faded to become a badge to be worn rather than a belief to be held.

Medieval Catholicism was a city-centered religion with Rome as its focus, as the Eastern Orthodox Church was focused on Constantinople, Judaism on Jerusalem, and Islam on Mecca, continuing the tradition of the city-states of the ancient world. A religious center city, as Rome, Jerusalem, or Mecca, is a Self symbol. With the Reformation, protestant northern

Europe lost Rome as a Self symbol; while the nation-state picked up some of that power, it was not as numinous as had been the holy city. That extra power went to kings, who became even more powerful after 1500. As kings have since lost their luster, it has mostly come to the egos of modern people, contributing to the inflation of our time.

Mass culture and democracy are particularly prone to producing inflation. If one is chosen by one's peers as a leader, then it is easy to think that one is special and somehow superior to those doing the choosing, and the personality easily becomes inflated. Likewise, if one is a celebrity of some sort, then one is obviously a superior person. Providing employment for the masses or handling the money for the masses is proof-positive that one is superior. This dynamic attracts more narcissistic personalities who, by their personality shortcomings, believe that they are superior people. But even the less narcissistic are easily seduced by the feeling of specialness that a position of prominence in mass society engenders; the choice of the crowd becomes the choice of God. Inflation of the personality easily comes with the selection, and the chosen one, who is just another human being, comes to believe that he or she is superior and special, and is immune to the laws that lesser human beings are held to.

I have used the example of people who have achieved more than average success in life thinking that they are somehow better than their peers; that is not completely accurate. The ego will grasp at any straw to feel that it is somehow superior to others—be it lighter skin, a bigger truck, a faster car, a costlier handbag, or some other imagined asset. Having a gun in your hand may be sufficient. That is the way the ego thinks; it is not capable of seeing other people as true equals. Christianity and the royalty system controlled it somewhat, but those controls are gone. Inflation has become a major problem of the age.

The solution is individuation, becoming an individual in a relationship with the new God-image, the Self. This involves shadow reconciliation, anima or animus integration, and realizing the Self as a transcendent and superior center of the mind.

Narcissism and inflation

Narcissism is an extreme focus on oneself as compensation for a wounded or inadequate sense of self-value. It develops when a child feels unloved and undervalued, and learns to compensate for that by feelings of superiority. It leads to an individual who needs to feel superior to his or her fellows to compensate for a repressed sense of inadequacy. Negative narcissism has the same roots, but the feelings of inferiority are not denied, so the individual feels inferior to others. We are all a little bit narcissistic, negative or positive, in that parenting is never perfect. In the extreme, the problem is pathological narcissism.

Inflation is an exaggerated and false sense of oneself because of identification with an archetype. On a grand scale, there are those identified with Christ or Napoleon. On a lesser scale are mothers who identify with the Great Mother, supporting the whole family, and ending up exhausted, or preachers who identify with the savior archetype, ending up needing to be saved. Identification with an archetype frequently ends in some form of disaster when reality finally hits home.

There have been narcissistic and inflated people throughout history. What is new in our time is an epidemic of inflation based on identity with the Self.

Evil and the dark side

In the past century or so, the traditional Christianity that had carried the image of the positive side of the Self for two millennia has weakened, allowing its repressed dark side to emerge. Initially, the ego was to copy Christ by overcoming in the material world and pleasing God the Father; psychologically, this built ego strength, as the ego succeeded in learning to manage the physical world. But with the passage of time, the ego has grown so strong that the guiding myth has been gradually set aside. It has been eroded by the ego's growing materialism. Now people claim they know what God wants, which is really what they want, or they ignore God completely; the myth is spent. But the dark side of the Christian myth is no longer repressed by the positive side, and it will not be as long as the old psychology remains active. It is stronger than ever, as it has grown while the light side has weakened; a medieval person would say that Satan has finally won. It gives the ego more and more power, but at a great cost, the exact pattern established by Sauron and by the Emperor. The only way out of the situation is a new myth, a myth with the whole Self separate from the ego; I have described this as the new psychology.

After centuries of control, the old psychology is not going to go easily, as the great wars in the stories of Luke Skywalker and Frodo Baggins attest. This means that the problem of inflation in our time is compounded by the fact that the dark side of the Self has grown powerful as the light side has weakened, adding the potential for great evil to the problem of great inflation. Identification with the Self easily becomes identification with the dark side of the Self because of the ego's demand for power.

The ultimate evil masters in both stories, Sauron in *The Lord of the Rings*, and the Emperor in "Star Wars," are both phantoms and not real people. They are both symbols of the dark side of the Self and pure evil, and both stories point to the ultimate controlling factors of the ego identified with the Self as evil. They indicate that ultimately the outlook for an individual whose ego is identified with the Self is not a good one; seduction by evil and ultimate disaster are predicted.

Both "Star Wars" and *The Lord of the Rings* tell the story of the hero as he is aided by positive wizards, Ben Kenobi, Yoda, and Gandalf, as he fights the negative wizards, the Emperor and Sauron. At the end of the stories, all the wizards are gone, and the individuals are left to carry on with their lives. The wizards are personifications of the light side and the dark side of the Self. Both stories could have easily featured Christ and the Antichrist in a great battle at the end of the age as described in the book of Revelation in the Christian scriptures, with Christ as the positive side of the Self and the Antichrist corresponding to the dark side.[231] Recall that we are living at the end of an age, and recall that when these stories end, all of the wizards are gone. These are stories for the end of the Christian epoch and the end of the old psychology. In *The Lord of the Rings*, the new Self symbol appears in the last scenes as the king in his rightful place as ruler of the land, while the lives of the little people go on as ever, without the ring. The image of the true, whole Self is revitalized, while the positive and negative representations are no longer present.

In the developmental sequence of stages one through four, the Self is seen as the Great Mother Goddess, then her children as gods and goddesses, then the Great Father God, and then the son of the Great Father. This needs a slight correction. The combined positive and negative aspects of the Self appear in the symbols of the first two stages. The Great Mother had a terrible side, and a loving side, and there was equal variation among the gods and goddesses of the ancient world. (Likewise, the Hebrew vision of the deity before the Babylonian captivity was both negative and positive.) But the medieval God the Father and his son are only symbolized as the positive side of the Self. The negative side was carried by Satan and repressed into the unconscious. For consciousness in stages three and four the Self is only present in its positive aspect, at least until the end of stage four, our time

That leads to the problem of our time. As the old psychology and its age end, there is a resurgence of the dark side of the Self as it is no longer held in repression. In fact, the Self is neither good nor evil; but the medieval myth and the Western myth have seen the Self as divided into good and evil aspects. The dark side of the Self, known as Satan in Christian thought, becomes more manifest and overt, as suggested by the stories discussed in this chapter. For late stage four, the Self image becomes the sons of the Great Father God, Christ and Satan. At the very end of the stage, it is possible that Christ may recede as Satan ascends in power.

Think of Luke Skywalker in his duels with Darth Vader; Luke loses both. During the first, in "The Empire Strikes Back," his hand is cut off and he only barely survives. They duel again late in "Return of the Jedi." In both contests Luke fights furiously, and I have suggested that he must have been very tempted by Vader's offers to join him and rule the world to evoke such fury. We see Luke as torn between two great forces, the dark side and the light side of the force essentially torn between the light and dark sides of the Self. In a similar fashion, Frodo was torn between keeping the ring and serving Sauron, versus disposing of the ring and serving Gandalf. Jung refers to this as a "crucifixion of the ego," its "agonizing suspension between irreconcilable opposites."[232] Both heroes required their shadow to handle this impasse; that is, one must integrate the shadow to deal with the divided Self. This is the third way, the alternative path between the opposites, that leads to a realization of the undivided Self. Level three and level four psychology dictate dark and light sides to the Self, seen as the good deity and evil Satan. Level five psychology includes a united Self, neither dark nor light.

I have mentioned various opposites in the course of these pages, such as consciousness versus unconsciousness, the ego versus the shadow, and thinking versus feeling. People are often emotionally torn between opposites. The answer is almost always a third way, usually a path between the opposites. The ultimate resolution of the conflict of opposites is the realization of the undivided Self. This requires integration of the shadow. With shadow integration, the united Self may be realized; with shadow projection, the Self slips into its light and dark aspects, and the temptation of the dark side grows.

With the new psychology appearing in our time a new Self image appears, a personal, whole image that contains all possibilities, positive and negative. The Self of the new psychology is beyond separation, including that of good and evil. I have wondered if society's emphasis on good during the past 2,000 years might have surreptitiously heightened evil as strongly as it emphasized the good. Perhaps every saint has been counterbalanced by a murderer?

Jung saw a change in the group's vision of the Self beginning in the book of Job, in which Job brought Yahweh to realize he had some pretty bad qualities.[233] This led to a split in the God-image, a split between the good God and the repressed evil Satan. That split is ending in our time, as the Christian myth draws to a close in the West. That is to say, from the developmental point of view, stages three and four of development require identification with the positive side of the Self in order to develop the superego and the ego, and we are now leaving stage four. Whatever model you choose, history, religious history, psychological history, or developmental psychology, ultimately the process is the same. The path is to get through the end of stage four without identifying with the Self and becoming inflated, integrate the shadow and anima or animus, and come to realize the Self as the separate and superior center of one's own being.

The key to beginning the process is acknowledgment of one's shadow and at least beginning to integrate it. Shadow awareness deflates the inflated ego and allows individuation.[234] You can't think that you're godlike and special when you admit your shadow.

The great battle scenes in both "Star Wars" and *The Lord of the Rings*, as well as the struggles of Luke and Frodo, all emphasize the fact that moving away from the great "I will" of ego psychology is no easy step. It is more intense and demanding than the medieval move away from impulse-oriented psychology of the ancient world; the only way that was possible was through the constricting demands of the medieval church. The development for our time does not rely on an external structure, but rather on the psychology of each individual. It requires each person to develop an awareness of the Self, and recognize that the ego is not the totality of one's being, but rather only a spokesperson for a complex group, a group that includes the unconscious and the shadow, the inner child, the superego, and the Self, a higher center of conscious awareness that is always watching.

We are living in the time of the ending of the Christian myth and the beginning of a new psychology based on the myth of the personal Self. The Christian myth has been the guide for the development of the Western superego and ego. The ego used that myth to develop and now wants to continue with that myth to maintain its sense of power. As the Christian myth has weakened, the previously repressed dark side of the myth has become prominent. The dark side of the myth gives the ego a great drive to power and possession, and an inflated sense of self-importance, at a probable cost of subservience to evil. As long as the ego feels the need to identify with the old myth, it is subject to being dominated by its dark side, as that side is now the strongest. The only way out is a new myth, the myth of the undivided Self. Through individuation, especially integrating the shadow, the power of the negative side may be overcome.

CHAPTER XIX

Harry Potter and the Problem at Hogwarts

The story of Harry Potter

The Harry Potter series of books and movies has been another phenomenon worthy of attention because of its great appeal, its psychological underpinnings, and because it is almost a textbook of some of Jung's ideas. The seven books and their corresponding movies tell a story of a boy who is chosen to go to Hogwarts School of Witchcraft and Wizardry, with each book relating the events of one of his seven years at the school. It is really one long novel in seven parts.

The story of Harry Potter is essentially the basic hero story of the West. It is not based on the new psychology and is included here as contrast with the previous chapter. At its heart is the quintessential theme of Western psychology: the hero beats the bad guy and gets the girl. Harry fights and overcomes Lord Voldemort, the evil wizard who killed his parents and many other people as well. Originally Voldemort was also a student wizard at Hogwarts like Harry, but unlike Harry, he was a nasty character from the beginning. Voldemort used his years at Hogwarts to develop his evil skills and subvert many of his classmates into following him.

Of course, Harry beats Voldemort in a final showdown in the last book, and saves the day just like Roy Rogers. But we have to ask ourselves, how did this situation arise at all? How could Hogwarts let something like this develop? The question is unanswered in the narrative, and the evidence indicates that it could easily happen again. All it takes is another bad guy signing up at Hogwarts to learn to be a wizard. The unanswered question in the Harry Potter series is the problem at Hogwarts that allowed the

253

situation to develop in the first place. After seven years of Harry Potter heroics, Hogwarts remains as vulnerable as ever.

The Harry Potter story is unique in that it follows the traditional Western theme of the hero overcoming his shadow, and at the same time sets up a question, the problem of evil at Hogwarts, which can only be answered with the new psychology.

Unlike "Star Wars" and *The Lord of the Rings*, the Harry Potter story is very much in the Western tradition, so it provides an opportunity to contrast the West's traditional way of handling evil with that of the new psychology. It shows why the West's method of dealing with evil is problematic, and why integrating the shadow has become necessary. It shows how shadow integration is a better method of dealing with evil. And it illustrates why a seemingly minor aspect of Jung's psychology, the psychological functions, is important.

The story begins before Harry is born, with Voldemort's descent into greater and greater evil. He learns of a prophecy that says a child is to be born on a certain date and only that child or Voldemort will live. He interprets the prophecy to mean that he must kill the child, Harry Potter, or be killed, and so he attempts to kill the infant Harry. He kills both Harry's parents, but when he tries to kill Harry, the magic spell from his wand rebounds and seemingly kills Voldemort instead; we learn later that his soul actually survived. It is at this point that the first book opens. The newly orphaned Harry is left on his aunt and uncle's doorstep. They become his adoptive parents and treat him shabbily while doting on their natural son. At age eleven Harry is invited to attend Hogwarts, and he begins his first year there.

Harry Potter and the Philosopher's (or Sorcerer's) Stone[235,236] is the account of Harry's first year at Hogwarts. Harry and his friends realize that someone is attempting to steal the philosopher's stone. They learn that the culprit is an instructor who is possessed by Voldemort's soul, and the stone is to be used to return Voldemort's soul to life. Harry saves the day and Voldemort is thwarted.

Year two is presented in *Harry Potter and the Chamber of Secrets*.[237,238] Hogwarts students are being magically petrified. Harry and his friends determine that the cause is a basilisk that has ascended from a chamber beneath Hogwarts. It has been evoked by Voldemort's diary from the years he was at Hogwarts. Harry manages to kill the monster and save his girlfriend-to-be in the process.

Harry Potter and the Prisoner of Azkaban[239,240] is about Harry's third year at Hogwarts. He rescues his godfather, who had been accused of helping Voldemort murder Harry's parents, and proves his godfather to be innocent.

Harry Potter and the Goblet of Fire[241,242] is the story of an elaborate kidnapping plot by Voldemort that takes place in Harry's fourth year. A tournament is held between schools of magic, and Harry's name is mysteriously entered, even though he is underage and should be ineligible. Harry wins the competition, and as he grasps the winner's trophy, he is magically transported to Voldemort's lieutenant, who uses some of Harry's blood in a potion to regenerate Voldemort's body. Voldemort gets a new body, but is unable to kill Harry, who escapes.

Harry's fifth year is the subject of *Harry Potter and the Order of the Phoenix*.[243,244] Harry says that Voldemort has returned but this is not believed by the public. Voldemort and his associates, the Death Eaters, attack the Ministry of Magic to get the original prophecy, which indicated that Voldemort had to kill Harry or vice versa. Harry and friends drive them off, and Harry is vindicated when Voldemort is seen in the attack.

Harry Potter and the Half-Blood Prince[245,246] is the narrative of Harry's sixth year. It tells of Harry and the Hogwarts headmaster, Albus Dumbledore, as they unravel Voldemort's secrets. They learn that Voldemort has hidden parts of his soul in magical objects, making it extremely difficult to kill him. The school year ends as Dumbledore is killed in an attack on Hogwarts.

The seventh and last installment in the series is *Harry Potter and the Deathly Hallows*.[247] (The movie version was in two parts.[248,249]) Harry drops out of school to prepare to face Voldemort. He and friends find and destroy the objects in which Voldemort has hidden sections of his soul. Harry then defeats Voldemort in a final battle, and the series ends.

Harry Potter as a traditional hero of the West

More than anything else, Harry is a hero, an excellent representative of the hero archetype. He has extraordinary powers even as an infant, when he seemed to kill Voldemort. This is parallel to Heracles, a hero of the Greek Myths; two snakes were sent to kill him as an infant, and he throttled a snake in each hand. Harry is an orphan, as is Frodo Baggins and Luke Skywalker. There is a massacre of the innocents; Harry's parents were murdered, Luke Skywalker's adoptive parents were murdered, and King Herod had infants murdered when he heard Christ was born.[250] Harry did not try to avoid the call to action, that is, his invitation to Hogwarts, but his uncle certainly did it for him by avoiding the invitations to the school. When Harry left home, he crossed the threshold into another world, the world of magic and wizards. The wise old man of the Harry Potter saga is Albus Dumbledore, a parallel to Gandalf, Ben Kenobi, and Yoda. Harry is killed by Voldemort and comes back to life, as does Osiris and Christ; Frodo seemed to be dead after he was bitten by a huge spider and he came back to life, and E.T. also went through death and rebirth. And most of all, Harry behaved heroically and accomplished his tasks.

Early in the series it becomes clear that Harry must face, and hopefully defeat, Voldemort. By the end of the series, Harry has carried this out, finally achieving victory. It is the Western hero story of the protagonist defeating his shadow. As such, there are important differences when the Harry Potter story is compared with "Star Wars" and *The Lord of the Rings*, because those two stories vary from the Western tradition. The Harry Potter character is similar to Luke Skywalker and Frodo Baggins, just younger. The positive wizard in the Harry Potter story is Albus Dumbledore, and he is somewhat similar to Gandalf of *The Lord of the Rings*, and Ben Kenobi and Yoda in "Star Wars." The greatest differences are in the "bad guys," the symbols of evil.

Voldemort is certainly a nasty character, a psychopathic killer, more or less on a par with Darth Vader or Gollum in that respect. But there are important differences. Vader carries out the Emperor's wishes and plans, but does so without prejudice. He kills if he must but it is only to accomplish his ends. Gollum kills to eat, and would kill to get the ring, but again, it is without prejudice.

But Lord Voldemort is a man obsessed with proving himself, proving that pure-blood wizards are better than those from non-magical (muggle) families, and proving that he can best Harry Potter. He kills to impress. His entire agenda is proving himself; it is the basis of his drive for power. Anyone with such a drastic need to prove himself is ultimately an individual with extremely low self-esteem. Voldemort's entire agenda is to prove that he, and to a lesser degree his followers, are superior. He needs to show the world, to impress the world. At heart, he is a wounded boy spending tremendous amounts of energy to compensate for a low opinion of himself by impressing others. He cares deeply about what others think; by contrast, neither Vader nor Gollum care at all.

Darth Vader does evil to serve the evil Emperor. Gollum does evil to serve the ring, and by extension, Sauron. Voldemort does evil to serve his grandiose ego, an ego using grandiosity to compensate for low self-esteem. The Harry Potter story has no equivalent to the Emperor of "Star Wars," or Sauron of *Lord of the Rings*. The Emperor and Sauron are symbols of the dark side of the Self, absolute evil in contrast to almost two millennia of Christian good, and that is not present in Harry's tale.

Voldemort is portrayed as coming from a malicious family and having a wicked character. Nevertheless, he is just another one of many students who go through Hogwarts, just like Harry Potter. While he does evil, he never is portrayed as a servant of pure evil, only a servant of his own pride. Ultimately, he is only another "bad guy" of Western myth.

Voldemort is not equal to the Emperor of "Star Wars" or Sauron of *The Lord of the Rings*. Both are portrayed as pure evil incarnate and not human. Voldemort is somewhat like Darth Vader, but he serves the evil inside of himself, rather than the external evil figure of the Emperor. An important point of "Star Wars" and *The Lord of the Rings* is that both stories make absolute evil into a character in the plot. The deaths of the Emperor and Sauron mark the end of the good and evil problem as the old psychology ends. The Harry Potter series does not do that; it leaves the principles of good and evil intact, so the traditional myth continues.

Voldemort's opposite is Albus Dumbledore, headmaster of Hogwarts. He is somewhat parallel to Gandalf, but not quite. He has many of Gandalf's qualities, but he is much more human than Gandalf. Gandalf makes an occasional mistake, but there is never any doubt that he is solely a representative of good. On the other hand, as a young man, Dumbledore had thoughts of ruling the non-magical world, and he discusses that and some of his other shortcomings in his final conversations with Harry. Dumbledore is a skilled wizard, but also very human. Gandalf was not human, in that he always represented the positive side of the Self. He made mistakes, but he was never tempted to the negative side because he was a symbol of, an avatar of, the positive.

When Harry Potter is about to begin his first year at Hogwarts, he meets another young wizard-to-be, Draco Malfoy, and it appears that Draco is Harry's shadow, in that Voldemort is supposedly dead. To a degree, Draco does fill that role. Throughout much of the story Draco is in league with Voldemort, aiding and abetting him at every turn, until Voldemort's demands finally become even too much for Draco and his family to endure. For a while it seems that the defeat of Voldemort will require that Harry combine forces with Draco, but that does not happen. Ultimately Draco and his family are pushed to the sidelines in Harry's final confrontation with Voldemort. Draco and his family are shamed and shunted aside but they are not redeemed. The story closes with indications that an unresolved split remains between Harry and Draco. Absolute evil is not overcome, as it was in "Star Wars" and *The Lord of the Rings*. Rather, while one evil person is overcome, the situation remains ripe for the next bad guy to enroll at Hogwarts.

There is no shadow reconciliation in the Harry Potter story. Harry does not require the assistance of his shadow to accomplish his task, as Luke required Darth Vader's help in overcoming the Emperor, or Frodo required Gollum to finally dispose of the ring. The Harry Potter story ends with Harry and his friends at one end of the famous "Platform Nine and Three-Quarters" and Draco at the other. Opposites are not united; the shadow remains in projection.

Overcoming evil is central to the Western myth, and living the myth means that a hero is repeatedly battling evil, that is, continually repressing his shadow. The problem of good and evil is central to the Western myth, and the only way to get past the problem is to get past the myth, as Frodo Baggins and Luke Skywalker did. Harry Potter did not.

The mythology of the West is based on the separation of the Self, the God-image, into positive and negative sides, and maintaining the positive side means that agents of the bad side must repeatedly be defeated. It means identifying with good and overcoming bad guys, over and over. This happens because the underlying structure of the mind, developed through the Western myth, requires it. It happens because the shadow remains in projection and cannot be assimilated, so it must be conquered and reconquered. The conquering behavior repeats again and again, battle after battle because the Western myth is unable to resolve the good versus evil conflict.

A particularly fascinating aspect of the Harry Potter story is how well the elements of this problem are laid out. These are twofold: Harry does not assimilate his shadow, and more importantly, Hogwarts remains divided. As Harry's story ends, the structure necessary to nurture and develop another Voldemort is still in place at Hogwarts, ready and waiting for the next bad guy to enroll. This is exactly the traditional psychology of the West. The only thing needed is another bad seed to fall into the fertile ground. This structure at Hogwarts reflects the traditional psychological structure of the West, and the Harry Potter story makes this easy to grasp.

The four houses and the four functions

When Harry Potter arrives at Hogwarts School of Witchcraft and Wizardry, he learns that the school is divided into four houses. The new students are sorted into one of the houses almost immediately by the Sorting Hat, a magical hat that determines which house is most appropriate for each student. Newcomers are assigned to one of the houses according to his or her character, and they room with that group for their seven years at Hogwarts. The four houses are Gryffindor, Slytherin, Ravenclaw, and

Hufflepuff, each named for one of the four founders of Hogwarts. Students assigned to Gryffindor are described as brave and daring, those to Slytherin are ambitious and cunning, those to Ravenclaw are intelligent, and those to Hufflepuff are hard workers.

The four-fold pattern of the Hogwarts houses is parallel to Jung's concept of the four functions of conscious awareness, that is, four ways in which one can perceive reality.[251] They are sensation, thinking, feeling, and intuition. Essentially, you sense reality, you think about what it is, you value it and have feelings about it, and you intuit what its origins are and where it is going.[252] The theory is more complicated, but that is the gist of it.

The only direct identification of a house with a function is that Ravenclaw is closely identified with wit and wisdom, that is, the thinking function. My guess is that Gryffindor is analogous to intuition, Hufflepuff to sensation, and Slytherin to feeling. The head of Hufflepuff is Professor Sprout, the herbology instructor, a down-to-earth, practical gardener, reflecting basic sensation. And as for Slytherin, their entire agenda, like Voldemort's, is proving that they are superior, compensating for tremendous feelings of inferiority; feelings dominate. The identity between houses and functions is approximate and not perfect, but it is sufficient to lay out the problem, making Hogwarts and its four houses analogous to an individual with four functions.

Everyone thinks, feels, senses, and intuits. (Intuition is the basic sensing of what the possibilities of a situation are, putting two plus two together and grasping what that infers or points to; it is not extrasensory perception.) The issue is what functions are emphasized and best developed. Modern adults typically have one very well developed function, two fairly well developed functions, and one poorly developed function. The best developed function is referred to as the superior function. The next two, less well developed, are the auxiliary functions, and the fourth is the inferior function. The functions consist of two paired opposites, thinking and feeling on the one hand, and sensation and intuition on the other. The opposite of the superior function is always the inferior function. That is, if the superior function is thinking, then the inferior function is feeling, and vice versa. If the superior is intuition, then the inferior is sensation, and vice versa.

The infant, in developmental stage one, has no developed function of conscious awareness; all four functions are potentially able to be developed. Young children and primitive people have developed only one function. The development of the first function probably begins in developmental stage two, as conscious awareness forms itself into an individual entity separate from the mother. Jung reported that primitive people had only one developed function, citing Egyptian and early Christian mandalas indicating only one conscious function.[253] He associated the development of the first function with the beginning of civilization.[254] With stages three and four, auxiliary functions are developed, with the fourth remaining the weakest. In that conscious awareness always develops out of the unconscious, the less developed functions always remain less conscious than the superior function. The inferior function remains largely, if not completely, unconscious. As such, it can never be equal to the other three functions; that is the price of consciousness development.

The caricature of the absent-minded professor illustrates a well-developed intuition and poorly developed sensation. The professor is so engrossed in his theories that he loses track of the real world and, for example, can't find the glasses that are on his own nose. In contrast, a person with a strong sensation function might be so involved in the basic facts of their world that they miss intuitions that someone might be enamored of them, or that someone might be laying a trap for them.

The problem of the four functions would appear to be only a minor footnote in psychology, but it is actually central to development of the new psychology in a roundabout way. That development involves integrating the fourth function, the inferior function, into the conscious personality. Thus the therapeutic emphasis on the thinking person getting in touch with feelings, or the feeling person thinking through a problem before reacting emotionally. I don't think that it is necessary to have a personal agenda of integrating the inferior function, but it is worth attention, especially if one is in psychotherapy. I suspect it comes as a natural part of the process of developing the new psychology, stage five consciousness. (I also don't recommend any fancy testing; it is a better subject for meditation and reflection.)

The fourth function is always tied to the unconscious and is always inferior in development compared to the other functions. It can be integrated somewhat but never developed like the other functions. For example, a feeling person may work to develop their thinking function, but it will always be somewhat primitive, and it will never be as able and refined as the feeling function.

The fourth function is the weaker function, the place of weakness in the individual, the ground of the shadow. Integrating the inferior function is analogous to integrating the shadow; both processes are aspects of the new psychology. The Harry Potter story shows how the inferior function is tied to the shadow, and how integrating the shadow and integrating the inferior function are closely related.

The students of Slytherin house are shown as being the most ambitious and power-hungry of all the Hogwarts students, suggesting an underlying feeling of a lack of power and need to compensate. There is a repeated emphasis on Slytherin students trying to be superior to the other students by emphasizing their pure-blood status, belittling non-magical (muggle) people, and belittling students from non-magical families. Like the inferior function, Slytherin is the school sore spot, infantile and demanding, frequently despised by members of the other houses. And when someone evil, that is, Voldemort, shows up and promises power they are ready to follow. All of this indicates an orientation felt to be inferior, with a tremendous need to compensate. The inferiority centers around feelings, and because of the inadequacy felt, the feelings are all negative.

The character that is Harry Potter's primary shadow is Voldemort, who was in Slytherin house when he was at Hogwarts. A secondary shadow character is Draco Malfoy, who is in Slytherin during Harry's time at Hogwarts. The shadow is not the inferior function, but they are associated; the shadow typically comes through the inferior function.

The Slytherin house represents the angry inferior feeling function of Hogwarts. It is not developed feeling, as an interior decorator might have for room arrangement, or a virtuoso musician for music. It is basic, even primitive, hate, and it is easy to see that it is entirely based on a tremendous reservoir of denied feelings of inadequacy. This is not developed feeling, but feeling of the inferior function, and it means that feeling is the inferior function of Hogwarts.

The most developed function has the most skill and talent, and the opposite is true of the least developed function. A thinking person can have some simple-minded, almost dopey feelings. In contrast, a feeling person's thinking processes can be amazingly irrational and illogical. The inferior function is always the least developed function. As such, the inferior function is always connected to the unconscious, so that it becomes an access to the unconscious.

If we take Hogwarts as an individual, then the inferior function would be the Slytherin house. Not only is the Slytherin common area located underground, it is beneath the Hogwarts lake. A body of water is typically a symbol of the unconscious, and the Slytherin dormitory is under the lake. By contrast, the Gryffindor dormitory and common area are located in a tower, and the Ravenclaw facilities are in another tower. These two houses represent the superior function and the best-developed auxiliary function. In that the inferior function is feeling, that would indicate that the superior function is thinking. So we have the thinking Ravenclaw in a tower, representing the best-developed function. Thinking is the primary function of a school; perhaps the Ravenclaw tower is the highest. It is followed by the Gryffindor house in another tower, representing the second function, intuition. The Hufflepuff house is in the basement, that is, just below ground level, suggesting a less developed sensation function. And deepest of all, below the Hogwarts lake and thus connected to the unconscious, is the Slytherin house, representative of the inferior feeling function.

Different people have different superior and inferior functions, and the Harry Potter story could have featured any of the houses as superior and inferior. The problem group could have been the Gryffindor house who were always trying to win with heroics rather than hard work, because they were from old wizard families, for example. The fact that the feeling function and Slytherin house are inferior at Hogwarts is strictly a characteristic of Hogwarts; it is not a universal principle. But the basic structure of one superior function, two auxiliary functions, and one inferior function is pretty much universal for Western adults.

The Western myth of the hero defeating his shadow is based on the relationship of the superior function and the inferior one. The superior function must strengthen and excel at the expense of the inferior function, as the ego must strengthen at the expense of the shadow.

For most Western people, our psychology has developed a superior function and one auxiliary function extremely well. A third function may be developed somewhat. But the fourth function has been left behind, barely developed, closely tied to the unconscious. That lop-sided process is necessary for consciousness development, a process that involves splitting conscious awareness from its shadow, or to put it another way, splitting conscious functions from the inferior one. The ego identifies with the more capable functions and builds its strength as those functions strengthen; meanwhile, the rejected inferior function is the area the shadow comes from. The purpose in the split in Western consciousness has been to develop a certain aspect of conscious thinking—the superior function—to a height of perfection. This strengthening of conscious thinking and strengthening the ego has led to the dominance of the West. It has come at the cost of being cut off from the inferior side of one's own mind.

I have discussed how Christianity has reflected and supported the split in the Western mind, consciousness from the unconscious, consciousness from shadow. One of the central icons of Christianity, the cross of Christ's crucifixion, has symbolized that dynamic in accordance with the four functions. The cross is a mandala, but a distorted one; the lower extension of the cross is usually pictured as significantly longer than the upper three. The upper three projections (for the head and two arms of the crucified Christ) are of equal proportion. But the lower extension, grounded in the soil of Golgotha, represents the extra distance the three conscious functions of the developing ego need to maintain from the fourth function, the inferior and unconscious one. As a mandala, its emphasis is not totally on centering, as is a true mandala; rather, its emphasis is on centering away from that which it is not, the unconscious and the inferior fourth function. The focus was on the trinity of functions, as Father, Son, and Holy Ghost, or superior, first auxiliary, and second auxiliary, functions, away from Satan or the inferior function. This has served the West well in its task of development of a strong ego with three capable functions.

We are now at the point that further improvement of the superior aspects of conscious mind is not possible in mature adults, in that the process is complete. Further development of the personality now calls for integrating the fourth, the inferior, function. The ego is now sufficiently strong that the weaker aspects of the mind can be integrated into conscious awareness without fear of being overwhelmed by their primitive contents. This is the next stage in consciousness development. It has become time to assimilate the inferior function, the location of the shadow, the aspect of the mind that has been held separate for thousands of years. All good has been assigned to the superior function, and all evil was associated with the inferior function. As the fourth function and the shadow are gradually assimilated, the problem of good and evil gradually becomes an issue of the past. The new hero seeks to reconcile with the shadow, not suppress it. That is the psychology we are entering.

The hero, the shadow, and the inferior function

The Harry Potter story stays firmly in the Western tradition. The Slytherin house, representing the inferior function, remains unassimilated and remains a continual source of trouble for future generations. When the next bad guy (shadow figure) enrolls at Hogwarts, another hero will arise and do battle to maintain the superiority of the "good" houses over the inferiority of the "bad" house, Slytherin.

The Harry Potter story illustrates the relationship of the shadow (Voldemort) to the ego (Harry), and how the shadow is related to the inferior function. If you look at the entire story as one person's dream, so that all parts belong to the mind of the dreamer, this becomes clearer. The projection that the shadow person carries is usually colored by the values of one's own inferior function. For example, a person whose superior function is thinking would be more likely to have shadow material associated with feelings.

The theme of the integration of the inferior function is present in both *The Lord of the Rings* and "Star Wars." In the last scene of the original "Star Wars," there is a quartet of Luke Skywalker, Han Solo, Princess Leia, and Chewbacca (Han's sidekick), as they are given awards for saving the rebellion. Chewbacca is a humanoid and quite intelligent, but he is also a great hairy beast, a symbol of the primitive inferior function. In *The Lord of the Rings*, prophesy emphasizes the importance of the "Halfling," a reference to the Hobbits. They are the diminutive members of the quaternity of heroes, humans (especially Aragon), elves (as Legolas), dwarves (as Gimli) and the Hobbits, particularly Frodo and Sam. The Hobbits are repeatedly referred to as being the least in size, but of great importance, a reference to the fourth and inferior function and its importance in achieving wholeness.

That integration does not occur in the Harry Potter story. The fourth function is not assimilated, nor is the hero's shadow. In that many members of the Slytherin house were associates of Voldemort, and hence losers in the story, their resentment can only increase with the passage of time. The situation will only continue to fester, as it is a central part of the myth that fostered the story.

In Harry's fifth year, as told in *Harry Potter and the Order of the Phoenix*, the Sorting Hat's song goes beyond telling about its usual purpose of dividing the students into four houses, and discloses its fears. It says that splitting the students into houses may be wrong and may bring the end of Hogwarts. The school is in danger from outside, and those within must unite or crumble.[255]

It is most remarkable that the Sorting Hat's fears are never resolved in the Harry Potter story.

It doesn't take knowledge of Jungian psychology to realize that the Sorting Hat's fears are accurate and something must be done at Hogwarts. Obviously the houses need to be integrated, with better mixing of the pure-blood students with those from non-magical families, or perhaps the houses could be eliminated entirely. But if we take Hogwarts as a model of the typical Western mind, one realizes that this is much easier said than done. The houses, that is the four functions, are in place in each of us, and the only way out of the problem is to assimilate the inferior function. We are back to the exercises of the thinking person getting in touch with feelings, and the feeling person attempting to work out some rational thinking, and so on. The superior functions must lose some of their status to the inferior, to allow the inferior to speak. For example, the thinker can give a million explanations, all good ones, to avoid the distasteful task of dealing with feelings. But the competent thinking function must stand aside some of the time and allow feelings, no matter how ill-defined, how difficult to verbalize, or how primitive, to be expressed. This goes hand in hand with shadow integration.

If this principle were applied to Hogwarts, at the least it would mean that Slytherin would not be shown any negative bias: at the end of Harry's first year, house cup points are rather arbitrarily awarded to the "good guys" in Gryffindor house, to the detriment of Slytherin, who had been leading the competition up to that point, so that Gryffindor wins the house cup for the year. No wonder Slytherin is resentful. Slytherin could be given some modest additional recognition or voice: there could be a course in old wizard families, for example. But Hogwarts is firmly in the Western tradition, with one inferior function, so these changes will not take place.

If the Slytherin house was slightly better assimilated, so that the feelings of resentment and inferiority were assuaged even a little, the Slytherin students would feel just slightly more attached to the student body as a whole rather than solely to their house and Voldemort would not have gotten the foothold that he did. If Harry had been able to forge any type of amicable relationship with Draco, then Voldemort could have been thwarted much more easily. In other words, assimilating the shadow and the inferior function greatly lowers the probability that evil will be able to develop and be acted out. An evil student entering Hogwarts is like an evil idea entering into one's mind; the question is whether or not it will find fertile ground and grow. That fertile ground is usually the unassimilated inferior function and the shadow. The Western myth is based on the need for separation from the inferior function and the shadow, so that fertile ground is always available as long as the myth is dominant.

There is one other aspect of the Harry Potter story that should be considered, and it really is a consideration of the entire Western myth as opposed to Harry's story in particular. It is acceptable for us to dislike spoiled, snobby rich kids, and that is the short description of the Slytherins. It is easy for them to be the "bad guys," and although it is an acceptable prejudice, a prejudice it is. If this story had been written in 1500s France, Slytherin would have been populated by rich Protestants; in 1600s England it would have been arrogant Catholics; in 1800s America, angry African-Americans; in 1930s Germany, cunning Jewish people; and in 2000 it might be dangerous Muslims. With the Western myth, there's always a bad guy to hate. Hate simply means that there is an unintegrated part of the mind that is rejected and found in projection, and the people who carry the shadow projection are rejected and despised.

To put it in terms of *The Lord of the Rings*, there is always some reason why one can feel special and superior to other people, that is, to wear the ring. Slytherin's point of view is that they are superior because they are from long-established families in the magical world, and not from non-magical (muggle) families. It is equally easy for the reader to think that he or she is not like that, to look down on the Slytherin students as wicked, and to feel superior because the reader is not feeling snobbish and superior like Slytherin; yet that is just another way to put on the ring. Young adults will continue to need this as they go through stage four psychology and strengthen their egos, but adulthood in our society is moving away from such thinking.

The truth is we all have a shadow and an inferior function. It is easy to project either, or both, to would-be bad guys, and it is hard to realize that both are really projections of parts of one's own mind. The next stage of consciousness development involves understanding that conflict and dealing with it.

CHAPTER XX

"Democracy is coming to the U.S.A." (Leonard Cohen)

The nature of change for the United States

The United States declared its independence in 1776 with ideals of liberty and equality. They were grand ideas, but the reality was slavery, dominance by an upper class, and inferior rights for women. Over the intervening years the United States has gradually moved from the realities of 1776 toward the ideals of 1776. Slavery was abolished and women have increased rights, yet great problems remain. I have noted that the lack of complete success in these endeavors is not due to a lack of trying, but due to the huge psychological difference between the reality of 1776 and the ideals. Meeting those ideals requires a new psychology, and in moving toward those ideals we are ushering in that psychology. Just as it took centuries for the pagan world to end and the medieval world to become fully established, these changes do not happen overnight.

American psychology is strongly rooted in an over-idealization of the past and a desire to maintain a status quo based on those ideals. Yet that status quo has been repeatedly upended by sudden crises causing painful changes that have forced a reluctant America to gradually move toward new thinking. These sudden, hard-fought crises of American history must also be considered as a part of its psychology. These characteristics combine to make a psychology so resistant to change that change only comes in sudden lightning bolts, almost out of the blue.

Despite the apparent causes of the crises of American history, their ultimate impact has been to move the United States further into level five psychology. For example, the purpose of the American Civil War was secession from, and restoration of, the Union, but the unintended consequence was the abolition of slavery. Each great crisis of American history has brought the United States nearer to level five psychology. Thus the great psychological dynamic of American history is entrenched level four psychology being dismantled and replaced step by step, crisis by crisis, with level five psychology.

The movement of America away from a solid level four society in the hierarchy of the king of England toward an egalitarian level five society suggests that the United States has a particular role in history. It is a transition between level four and level five psychology. That transition occurs in cyclic steps, each step involving a crisis.

Generational and crisis cycles - Strauss and Howe

There are two cycles in United States history, the one a generational cycle of approximately twenty years and the second a crisis cycle of about eighty years. Over the course of its existence, these two cycles have gradually moved the United States along the developmental road from the level four realities of 1776 toward the level five ideals of 1776. These patterns were discovered by William Strauss and Neil Howe and are outlined in their books, *Generations*[256] and *The Fourth Turning*[257]. Strauss and Howe present American history as a succession of repeating patterns of generations, punctuated by a series of major crises. The authors relate the crises to the generational sequence, usually with four generations of about twenty years each between the major events. The major crises include the American Revolution, the U.S. Civil War, and the combination of the Great Depression and World War II.

Psychic life cycle - Edward Edinger

Strauss and Howe demonstrate four basic types of generations recurring throughout American history. The four generational types, Civic, Adaptive, Idealist, and Reactive, have an archetypal basis. The four types form a generational cycle that is roughly parallel to the archetypal sequence of stages in the Psychic Life Cycle originated by Edward Edinger and set out in *Ego and Archetype*.[258] Dr. Edinger was a Jungian analyst practicing in Los Angeles.

Edinger's cycle is somewhat complex but has four major parts. The cycle begins with an ego aligned and identified with the Self. Because the aligned ego identifies with the Self, it becomes inflated and rejects the Self, step two. Third, the inflated ego having rejected the Self becomes alienated. Fourth, the alienated ego repents and begins to realign with the Self. The ego then reconnects with the Self, back to step one, and the cycle repeats. The four positions of the cycle are ego aligned with the Self, ego inflation, ego alienated from the Self, alienated ego repenting and realigning with the Self. These same four positions are echoed in the sequence of four generational types proposed by Strauss and Howe, indicating that the historical sequence is archetypal.

The cycles of American history

The generational cycle begins with a Civic generation establishing, or reestablishing, the American ideal in a crisis, as when the Revolutionary War established independence, the Civil War destroyed the Southern rebellion and ended slavery, or World War II ended with the defeat of the Axis countries. The mastering of each crisis seems like an outstanding success, proving that the United States, through trial-by-fire experience, had established, or reestablished, alignment with the basic American ideals.

Success seems grand following each crisis; the country feels that it is on the right track. But that leads to inflation; being on the right track turns into feeling that the country is special and has the God-given right to do as it will. The excesses of U.S. military and covert intervention since World War II are excellent examples of the inflation. After the Revolutionary War, the United States was held to have a "Manifest Destiny," an inflated idea of specialness that allowed repeated mistreatment of Native Americans and stealing land from Mexico.

An Adaptive generation follows the Civic generation. A good example is the generation between those who fought World War II and the baby-boom generation. The Adaptives initially honor the Civic generation for their bravery and dedication in bringing the country through the crisis, but in doing so they contribute to the inflation the Civic generation has begun to build. Later, after the Idealist generation becomes alienated from their Civic leaders (next paragraph), the Adaptive generation tries to see both sides of the issue and mediate between the two.

The Adaptive generation is followed by an Idealist generation. The best example is the baby-boom generation born after World War II. They realized that the great success of the World War II generation was inherently flawed, as it was, after all, only a small step in the long-term transition from stage four hierarchy to stage five equality. The baby-boom generation saw rampant inequality and racism in the United States, hardly American ideals. They were aware of the inflated American foreign policy in Vietnam and in the nuclear arms race. The baby-boom Idealist generation realized the failure to meet the ideal and rejected the country and its values, leading to alienation.

A Reactive generation, born during the following twenty years, senses the alienation and the lack of an ego-ideal connection in society, and reacts with elevated crime, alcoholism, and suicide rates, but eventually make a tough adaptation in their adulthood. The current example of this group is referred to as Generation X.

The Reactive generation is then followed by the new Civic generation, and they are the primary handlers of the American crises. Each crisis is caused in no small part by the lack of maintaining the ideals established in the previous crisis, and also because each of us has strong ties to the older psychology. In each new crisis, the elder Idealists rally the younger Civic generation to establish a new alignment with the American ideal, and the cycle starts again; the primary difference is that the newer psychology has grown stronger and the older is now weaker due to the complete upset of the system occurring during the crisis. After each crisis America is more in line with the American ideals of 1776 than it was before. The crisis cycle will continue at least until the new psychology is fully established and the old psychology is replaced by the new.

Each of the major crises has shaken the United States to its core, and each has completely rearranged society and moved it closer to the American ideal. Following each crisis, there has been a slow drift backwards in a reactionary direction, but that drift has never taken the country back to the status it was before the crisis.

The continuing American revolution

Each crisis has been a continuation of the American Revolution. This includes both the external social structure and the internal psychology. Jung once said that "revolutions are always symptoms of a great mental transformation."[259] The continuing American revolution is a change away from the hierarchy system based on the old psychology to a new world of equality based on the new psychology. It is ongoing and has not ended. The movement from hierarchy to equality continues to date, crisis after crisis.

The United States is a great transition from royalty to equality, from level four psychology to level five. The old myth that royalty and ego psychology were based on, the myth of the conquering son of the Great Father God, is virtually finished. The old myth began to falter when the ideal of equality was introduced and royalty was rejected. The speed of the deterioration of the old myth has increased since and it is failing even more rapidly in our time. Meanwhile, a new myth is beginning to dominate Western consciousness. It is the role of the United States to continue in this process and serve as the mechanism of transformation of the old psychology to the new.

After each crisis, the old psychology attempts to reestablish control. It encourages the maintenance of the social hierarchy, with some people being held as better than others and not all people being equal. In that it is based on the myth of the conquering hero, it always needs a hierarchy and people to conquer and repress. But with the passage of time the myth has become weaker so that the foundation of the hierarchy is weaker. People do not feel as invested in the system as they once did and the hierarchy is not as supported as it has been in the past. As time passes, those who identify with the hierarchy, who would still consider themselves to be in a superior class, attempt to reassert their power, but without the support of the myth they are only pretenders to power. Then another crisis occurs and the old psychology is weakened further as the strength of the new psychology gradually increases.

A mirror of this process occurs in the inner world, as the ego gradually loses its central, dominant position in the mind, and as it slowly learns to be aware of the other parts of the mind, including the shadow, the unconscious, and the Self. The inner world endures the crises as does the outer, as the process of developmental change occurs. In the inner world, the ego is gradually being removed from its inflated position of complete dominance and control; in the outer world, those positions symbolizing complete ego control are gradually being eroded to less and less power.

The first great American crisis was the declaration of independence from England and the Revolutionary War. For the average American, little changed; the social order remained the same, as wealthy families continued to rule the new nation as they had in the past. But the country's ties to the old myth of a royal hierarchy were permanently severed. This was the first concrete step away from the old myth and the royal system, the first step away from the myth of the monarch as earthly Self symbol for the system. The president, as first citizen, could never be as strong a symbol of the Self as the monarch had been. The process of transferring the symbol of the Self from the group symbol of the monarch to the individual had begun. With this step the old system was irretrievably lost and attempts to reinstate it by an ersatz royal class composed of rich Americans would fail in time. The old myth was fatally wounded.

The second great American crisis was the Civil War. In this crisis the most blatant inequality in the system was removed. Inadvertently, slaves were entirely freed, suggesting that the shadow was no longer totally repressed as it had been. At the outset of the war, no one had any thoughts of freeing a huge population of uneducated slaves, people who had been deliberately kept in an uneducated and primitive state by their owners, and allowing them to mix with white Americans. The war was not fought to end slavery, and emancipation was only a war strategy, not an end in itself. Few whites in the North or South felt these people were suitable to be free citizens; yet that is what happened. It set the stage for real integration, which would begin a century later.

The importance of the emancipation of slaves, and later the integration of their descendants, cannot be underestimated. For centuries, African-American people have carried most of the burden of the shadow of white people in the United States. This mixing-in of a people who have been held in utter contempt because they embodied the shadow of the white populace could only mean that both groups would eventually have to face and integrate their personal shadow. The two groups could either destroy one another or learn to accept each other, and the only way to accept the other was to learn to accept themselves and their own shadow. This great process, so terribly painful and hardly complete, has contributed hugely to the psychological developmental process occurring in America, and will continue to do so for centuries.

It helps to put this in the proper light to recall that Alexis de Tocqueville, the French author of *Democracy in America* who toured the United States in the 1830s, thought that slavery would end in a race war.[260] I cannot overstate the greatness of the gulf between the races that existed by 1860, the incredible size of the problem of racism, and despite how far we have to go, how far the United States has come with it. Although extremely significant racial problems remain, the United States of today has performed what would have been termed an integration miracle in 1830. When the psychological underpinnings of this are considered, it marks a sea change in the course of Western humanity and an example for the world. It is certainly far from finished but it definitely has begun. Racial integration and its parallel psychological integration do not come easily for the ego. We will continue to fight this battle for generations.

The third great American crisis was the Great Depression and World War II. I am inclined to think of the crisis as the Great Depression, and the cure was World War II. The Depression started as a financial crisis and was solved by employment provided by war industries, by war taxes on the wealthy, and by the resulting leveling of wealth that occurred during the war.

World War II created great opportunity for women and African-Americans to improve their independence and status by working in war-related industries. Because of the financial leveling that occurred during the War, post-war America enjoyed one of its greatest periods of prosperity with a huge growth in the American middle class. The crisis demonstrated that democracy could maintain its course between extremes of the left and the right, Communism and fascism.

But it may be that the greatest benefit of the crisis of the Great Depression and World War II was the effect of the economic leveling that occurred as a result. This was partially due to the financial losses caused by the stock market crash of 1929 and the depression that followed, and also by the strongly progressive taxes levied by the U. S. Government during World War II. The result was the extremely prosperous post-war period of 1950 to 1980. I noted that perhaps the greatest long-term impact of the Civil War crisis was not the war's direct objective of ending the rebellion, but rather the ending of slavery. I suspect one of the greatest long-term impacts of the Great Depression and World War II is the revelation of the beneficial effects of the economic policies of the time, policies which curtailed great accumulation of wealth. Those policies brought about the prosperity of the 1950 to 1980 time period, contrasting vividly with current economic policies and the current depressed economy.

The next crisis

There were four generations, approximately eight decades, between the Revolutionary War and the Civil War, and also between the Civil War and the Great Depression and World War II. There have been about eight more decades since the beginning of the Great Depression, suggesting that America is again nearing a time of major crisis.

The root cause of the Great Depression was the fact that the very wealthy had accumulated most of the money.[261,262] On the one hand, money is a marker of influence in a society, and the more you have the more powerful you are. On the other hand, money is the medium of exchange of a society, and if it is hoarded and not exchanged society shuts down, that is, it enters a depression. That is what happened in America's last great crisis, and it is happening again now; a very few people have the bulk of the money. The problem then was temporarily solved by our entry into World War II; but the temporary solution no longer works and we have to face the issue again.

For the individual, depression is an emotional symptom which occurs when personal libido is dammed up and ceases to flow; no energy (libido) for life is available. There is a parallel in group psychology. Money is the libido, or energy, of the group; money may symbolize libido in a dream. Our money is fiat currency, created money, money only having value because we all agree that it has value. Modern money is a group process, a collective function. It is not a commodity like gold or silver, but rather the group's psychological energy, its libido. Depression for the group occurs when monetary libido is dammed up and ceases to flow, the same as for an individual.

One way or another, some people end up with more money than others. Some people are born with it. Others are just good at making money, just like some people are really good at painting portraits, cooking, or doing total knee replacement surgeries. So if there's money, there will be some people with more than others; that's not the problem. The problem is super wealth and the special status that seems to come with it.

There are two complications with vast accumulations of money. One is that when the ego feels it needs something, like more money, more sexual partners, bigger houses, faster cars, or more power, it can never get enough. Typically that is because the thing sought is a compensation for inadequacies the ego feels, and because the inadequacy is never met by the thing pursued the need continues and even grows. The pursuit of more proceeds relentlessly.

The second complication is money's tie to the old psychology, ego psychology, that those who are successful are somehow superior people. In the old royalty system wealth confirmed one's position in the class structure, but that is no longer the case as the myth behind that system is pretty much dead. Now great wealth only serves to give inflated egos the illusion that they are somehow special people, even royalty, and that somehow the old royalty system is still intact.

Extreme accumulation of money by a few people means that there is less money for the rest of us to circulate, causing a depression. Adding to this is the idea that because one has obtained money or power, one is therefore special, somehow elevated above one's fellow human beings and therefore level four royalty. Somehow one is a part of the old upper class, the royal class of the last centuries, a step above the rest. It is at that point, as Frodo would put it, that one puts on the ring, or as Jung would put it, the ego becomes inflated.[263] It is then extremely easy to think that one is a special person, and because of being special, one has a right to special privileges. It is easy to rise above what is fair and legal for ordinary mortals. Governments may be bought and sold, and those of lesser status fleeced to support the would-be royal class. The accumulation of money and power then accelerates to catastrophic proportions.

I initially thought that the problem was mostly the buying of government, but I realized that there is more involved. It isn't the money as much as it is would-be princes helping other would-be princes, the members of the self-appointed royal class doing one another favors. Legislative princes help industrial princes who help banking princes. How can someone who fancies himself a noble turn down the plea of another noble and worry about what becomes of the masses?

Which brings us back to the Great Depression and our current financial problems. It isn't just that a few people have gathered a lot of money, but also that they have used the influence it buys to manipulate the system in their favor so as to accumulate even more money to the point that there isn't enough left for the non-rich in the system to use as a medium of exchange, and the system starts to shut down. It is the ego identified with the Self, convinced of its own superiority, demanding more and more power, until a collapse comes. The inflated ego thinks it is special and above the group and not a part of it. In its specialness it forgets that it is actually a part of the human race which has been developing by interacting with one another for at least 200,000 years. It forgets that for millennia all members of the group have assumed the roles necessary for development in the stages; suddenly they are not a part of the group and have no role in it, except to soar above and withdraw increasing sums.

This problem is compounded by the psychology of our time. People who are strongly identified with the old psychology see these would-be princes as superior people who are rightfully elevated in the national hierarchy. Because they see sexual and racial equality movements as destroying their world, they look to the princes to protect them from these forces. Thus they are easily manipulated by any promise that change will be stopped, despite the fact that the princes typically work to ensure that financial benefits only go to their fellow princes, and not to the commoners who elected them.

Ultimately, the problem is inflated egos, those who feel that they are special and deserve much more than their peers. It is supported by ordinary people who strongly identify with stage four psychology, who feel that the inflated few are truly the elite of society and should have special privileges. It may produce a failure of the system and another of the major crises of American history. Each crisis has brought America another major step away from hierarchy and closer to equality, and the next should be no different.

I don't want to overlook inflated egos based on military power. They too could cause a crisis if a military adventure goes badly wrong; I suspect the world is tiring of the West's need for domination. I wonder how much longer what is left of the middle class can pay for military domination of the world; the super-rich certainly do not expect to pay for it. Whatever happens, the next crisis is likely to come from inflated egos pushing things to the point they break.

The old European royalty system had built-in controls over the ego's drive for power and money. Under the old system with its hereditary hierarchy, no ego could become more important than its place in the system. No one could consider themselves more important than their class role, preventing ego inflation beyond a certain predefined point. The ruling class and the monarch identified with the country, and to some degree wanted the country to prosper, as opposed to claiming a status above and beyond the nation-state. Christianity also dictated limits on behavior; people really believed that they were under God, and not a replacement for

God. All of this put some brakes and restrictions on egos and ego desires; the myth held the world together. Everyone, from the top of the system to the bottom, believed it. Everyone was thoroughly involved in the myth.

The dominant myth of a society is the glue that holds the society together, the belief that people are willing to die for. Today the Western myth is dead. What is left of it is self-important people out for ego aggrandizement, convinced that they are special, the West's royalty, all at the expense of their peers. I think it involves many of us to some degree, but some are certainly much better at it than others. It is a choice to wear Frodo's ring and serve the dark side.

This is why "Star Wars" and *The Lord of the Rings* have resonated so strongly with the public, if only on an unconscious level. They point to a way out, a solution, a possible answer, a hope, for a society dominated by the extremely materialistic end-phase of stage four thinking. The stories portray great forces controlling the world and our psychology. In our external world, corporations have become agents in their own right, being served rather than serving, and government has become an agent for them. We have unlimited war with unlimited funding. Religion has become a support system for it all. Those trusted with control have become corrupt. In a parallel fashion, the internal world is dominated by inflated egos demanding control and material rewards.

This psychology has produced a great push toward a United States composed of the rich and the poor, the winners and the losers, with no middle class. The rich commit the crimes and the poor go to jail.[264] It is an attempt to return to the old European class system based on the old psychology and the old myth, with the monarch as Self symbol at the head of a hierarchy of royalty over commoners. It was once sincerely believed that this was God's order on earth, not some random arrangement. The problem is that no one believes this anymore. The myth that held all this together is dead. There is no sense that there is an upper class that is rightly elevated above the commoners; there is only a sense that someone has managed to get more power and money than their peers. The only value is price.

Capitalism is part of the problem: Piketty demonstrated that capital accumulates more rapidly than the economy grows so that capitalism inherently increases inequality.[265] Capitalism has fit well with the level four ego. It worked reasonably well as long as the old myth lasted, as there was some sense of limits. The difficulty now is that any sense of limitation has been lost with the myth, leaving predatory economics dominated by inflated egos. In *The Hobbit*, Bilbo took power (the ring) from his shadow Gollum, just as the ego takes power from the personal unconscious and as the West has taken power and wealth from shadow people. The level four personality feels it has the right to take what it will from people carrying its shadow, be they lower status citizens or third world people, and capitalism has been the tool used to do this. It is highly unlikely that unfettered capitalism will be the West's future economic system.

In our time, fewer and fewer people have more and more wealth and power as our society becomes less democratic, and people identified with the old psychology find security in this. At the same time more and more people are identifying with the new psychology and its emphasis on democracy and equality. These two principles are on a collision course which will produce a major crisis in the not too distant future.

Chapter XXI

Civilization in Transition

The middle way

The modern middle class has its roots in the guild system of medieval Europe, but it really began to develop at about the time of the Enlightenment. It is not a coincidence that the beginnings of the changes we are well into now also started at that time. The world at the dawn of the West was mostly one of extremes, the rich and the poor, the nobility and the commoners. The solution to the two extremes is the third way, a way between the opposites, and the middle way of the opposites of rich and poor is the middle class. The middle class rose as the ideas of equality and democracy rose; this is not an accident.

The Whig and Tory political factions, the forerunners of modern liberal and conservative political parties, have their beginnings in the same time period. These parties stood for change and resistance to change; their appearance meant that the gradual change from hierarchy to equality had begun.

The idea of a middle class is only superficially a monetary one. From a psychological point of view, it symbolizes a life that is neither inflated positively nor negatively. It is a life of equality without hierarchy. People will continue to pursue excellence, but for themselves and not from a need to feel superior to their peers.

The dictatorships of Europe that caused World War II were fundamentally attempts to solve the problem of the opposites of nobility versus commoner as the old system of kings, tsars, and kaisers broke down during World War I. Fascists identified with the establishment and industry, and saw themselves as nobility. Communists identified with the workers and commoners, and saw themselves as nobility. Other than some theoretical differences, the fascists and the Communists were about the same. They solved the problem of the opposites by identifying with one side and repressing the other, that is, murdering millions of people who were deemed to be carrying the group's shadow.

Communist leaders became just another privileged class raised above everyone else, exactly what they claimed they were destroying. Communists are especially prone to disparaging the middle class but it is just an underhanded attack on the only real solution to the class problem. Rather, they identified with the working class to achieve power, then made themselves the ruling class, perpetuating the problem.

Fascism and Communism placed the state over the individual; all individuality was sacrificed for the state. Obviously this is contrary to individual development, and it is also contrary to the flow of history, which has been to develop the individual. Both movements are historical dead ends, taken only in our crossover times.

In practice, both fascism and Communism murdered millions, that is, both systems attempted destruction of the projected shadow, an impossible task. The shadow is a part of every mind, and murdering people who carry the projected shadow does not get rid of it; the problem only goes underground, into the unconscious. Time passes and the shadow problem returns because the underlying psychology remains the same. The solution is not in executing the rich, starving the masses, reestablishing the nobility, revitalizing religion, fascism, or Communism, but in psychological development.

In the short run, any government policy can be imposed by means of arms, but given time the psychology of the population will eventually assert itself. Francisco Franco, dictator of Spain from 1935 to 1975, was able to execute enough of his opponents to force the country to accept his point of view for a while. Now, despite all the dead, Spain seems to me to be politically pretty much the same as it was before Franco's time in power. The psychology remains much the same with the opposites in the Spanish collective largely unresolved, as was nicely illustrated by the 2006 movie

"Pan's Labyrinth."[266] Executing, or otherwise denying, one part of consciousness never resolves a conflict; it only perpetuates it. Time passes and the same issues rise again. The American Civil War ended slavery and states' right to secede, but did little to change the underlying American psychology as evidenced by attitudes toward African-Americans. The psychology remained the same for decades afterward, and only began to change because of painful encounters between the races, painful realizations of personal attitudes, and psychological growth over time. The use of force can change the group's laws but its psychology only changes with work, time, and development.

We are now torn between the endings of the old psychology and the beginnings of a new one, which I have described as the change from developmental stage four to stage five. Ego psychology wants to return to 1800 and a solid stage four class structure. This is an attempt to go back to authority and the old way, to reestablish a ruling class to control the rest of society, and to return women and minorities to traditional roles. The psychological need for this is so great that some people will deny their own best economic interests and deny scientifically demonstrated reality to hold on to the old myth. But the myth that society was based on in 1800 no longer functions; it has lost its hold and the underlying psychology is changing. The current would-be ruling class is based only on money and power, and nothing else. Without a group consensus determined by a shared myth, rule based only on power or money will not last. Development dictates that a new myth and a new consensus will form.

The elite and the masses

Each great age of the past was led in its formation, growth, and maturity by an elite group of individuals. The ancient world was led by warrior kings who founded and expanded city-states and empires, from Babylon and Assyria to Egypt to Greece and Rome. Each of those great civilizations was led by an elite group, often hereditary, and usually warriors. These people were frequently held to be gods by the people of their empires. The medieval world was led by the great minds of faith who provided the framework of dogma on which the medieval church, and by extension, the medieval world, were constructed. These people were held to be saints. The West was built by an elite of kings and nobility arising out of the medieval age to forge nation-states of great power; the nobility set society's standards by courage in battle and by courtly manners. In each great age, an elite few led the masses. The foremost leader of this elite few, as a pope or king, served as the earthly manifestation of the Self, God's representative on earth.

For the West, the end of the idea of leadership by the elite began with the American Revolution and gradually developed. Then World War I dealt the old authority in Europe a death-blow. Suddenly the world was ruled by the non-elite: elected presidents and prime ministers, and fascist and Communist dictators. The leadership of the old ruling elite was history. With their end, authority in general began a death spiral; now every person of the masses is an expert and knows the "truth" despite what science or statistics demonstrate. Everybody knows what should be done to straighten out the world. Modern politicians come from this.

José Ortega y Gasset in *The Revolt of the Masses*[267] (1930) described this as the masses revolting against the old elite. He observed that politics in the twentieth century involved the replacement of the nobility from the elite classes with elected leaders and dictators from the non-nobility. I don't think the masses so much revolted as much as they realized that the old elite were not especially competent and their time in history had ended. As the old myth failed, the old elite began to appear as mere rich people with no better, and possibly a worse, sense of world direction than any other citizen. But because the West continues to feel the pull of level four psychology, and because there is a desire for the leadership of a true elite, a void remains. As a result, charismatic personalities, celebrities, powerful people, rich people, movie stars, and society icons slip into the role of nobility and exert a strong pull over the masses. This has led to the current popular culture, notoriously superficial and with few real values.

Authorities are frequently held in contempt, sometimes rightly because they have little to support their ideas, and frequently wrongly because "everybody knows" what the truth is. Once it was only the king or the pope who knew, now every person in the street can tell you the answer, although too frequently it is based on manipulated information. The problem of our age is not a return to medieval superstition but the ease which the mass ego can be manipulated by its shadow fears and prejudices; the only solution is shadow integration and individuation.

The fact is that we are all in the masses now. Some like to believe that their position in life has made them into nobility above the masses, as if the old hierarchy was still alive; that probably only means ego identification with the Self and inflation. The only true solution is to find one's own individuality. The rise of mass culture is really a first step toward individuation on a large scale.

Our time in history is a time of the masses with no true elite, no underlying philosophy of society, no fundamental moral code; it is an interregnum between the old and the new. This is the cause of the general alienation, insecurity, nihilism, and anxiety of our time. A new elite will form, a core group to lead in the new epoch we are entering. It will shape a new ethic and a new moral standard based on the new psychology. It may be that the new elite has begun to form, and that some people who will be considered key individuals by future generations have already made their contribution, and maybe not. It is impossible to say at our point in history. For about 300 years, Christianity was only another religion in the ancient world, with a number of dogmas and sects, and it did not begin to take solid form until the First Council of Nicea in 325 C.E. We are now in a time similar to that of early Christianity.

What is certain is that the new elite will reflect stage five psychology. It will not be an advocate of the nation-state, military power, corporate power, masculine dominance, segregation, or any other manifestation of level four psychology. The new era will be based on an ethic of the individual and true democracy, not of leaders and the led. The new elite may only be the leading thinkers in individuation psychology, not directors of others; the next era is one of equal individuals, not followers or leaders.

Modern leaders fancy themselves as being elite because they have reached positions of power over the masses, but they have actually only managed to manipulate the masses sufficiently to be elected. They are elite only in the sense that they have gained power; in fact they are still members of the masses, just as mass-minded as anyone else. There is no true aristocracy or elite in our era because there is no guiding ethic, as we are in a transition between two great cultural epochs. Because forming a cultural ethic takes years, the impression arises that modern mass culture is a true culture with true leaders. But current leaders are only other mass people trying to ride the mass dragon by controlling and manipulating; they are hardly a source of values, ethics, or morality for a new culture. There is no sense of maintaining a moral stance. They are easily seduced and inflated by the huge amount of money and power available to them, leading to identity with the dark side of the Self and evil.

The problem is that would-be leaders are often seeking a position because of their own conscious or unconscious needs (or should I say their own mental problems), as opposed to actually wanting to serve their fellows. The psychological need to lead other people frequently grows out of an insecure, wounded internal child that goads the ego to gain control to assuage the wound. That wound may drive the ego to gain control and power to compensate for abuse or a felt lack of security and stability in childhood, or to gain fame to compensate for feelings of inferiority as a neglected child, among other possibilities. There may be an inflated ego identified with the dark side of the Self. Thus the ease with which leaders, especially national leaders, use violence and inflict deadly force on others, behavior that most people would never do to another human being. It is unfortunate that the strength of a person's will to power is not an indication of the person's capabilities as a leader; we are only learning this as the age of leaders draws to a close.

The idea of leaders and hierarchy began late in the prehistoric era and has continued to our time when it is finally beginning to end. The hierarchy served a very important purpose in developing consciousness: leaders and those higher in the system served as role models, both for themselves and those below them. Nobles were supposed to behave in a noble fashion so that everyone could learn proper behavior. They also served as models for forming parts of the mind; kings ruling the realm were ideals of how the developing ego should rule the inner world. That work is nearing completion for most people in the West and the time of leaders and hierarchy is ending.

As each historical stage ends, those holding power attempt to extend power and maintain the past ethic by trying to eliminate the new. Pagan Romans executed Christians, medieval Catholics used the Inquisition to suppress individual independent thought and Protestantism, and the modern West is following suit. In such times, the old ethic is no longer guiding development, but those who strongly identify with it work to maintain the old forms and suppress new ones. There has been a vast increase in the power of the state during the past 100 years, and this power has become more oriented toward controlling the citizens, as those identifying with the state feel the threat of the ebbing of nationalism and national control. People with strong ego psychology who demand control are drawn to these positions. Law and law enforcement has become increasingly a matter of supporting the powers-that-be rather than administering justice. People of power feel they have the right to suppress others and deprive them of their rights so as to maintain the status quo. They believe that history has ended, further change is only deterioration, and the only remaining job is to maintain the status of the very successful few against the many. There has been a consistent history of violent abuse of people advocating equality in society, including suffragettes, unionists, socialists, hippies, civil rights advocates, and any people who have felt the pull of the new developmental ethic of equality. As I have outlined, as the old morality fails, there is a huge potential for ego inflation and evil among these would-be leaders as they attempt to hold on to the past and thwart the future.

While the cause of the U.S. Civil War was the secession of eleven states, the actual push for action came from Southern aristocrats. The political culture of the South was composed of paternalistic and anti-democracy aristocrats who held slaves, and less affluent Andrew Jackson democrats who felt that all white males were equal and who owned few, if any slaves. The former rejected democracy, demanded succession, and started the war. The latter, who typically did not like African-Americans or Northerners, fell in to support their fellow Southerners and did much of the actual fighting.[268] But it was those who considered themselves the American elite who started the war; they were not democratic in any form and did all they could to maintain an old hierarchy vaguely based on European royalty.

Maintenance of the status quo, an artificial ruling class of would-be elitists, and control of the rest of the population are all directly opposed to the flow of both American and Western history and they will not succeed. Growth is intrinsic to life; all life either grows or dies and our time is not an exception. A new ethic is arising from the collective unconscious of Westerners; it will not come from the ego or the intellect. It will develop as it will, not as we want, guiding formation of the next culture. A primitive person would say it comes from the gods; a modern person would say that it is from the collective unconscious. It comes to us; we don't make it up.

Imagine Roman citizens of 2,000 years ago worrying about what seemed to be important events in their politics and their future. Would the Praetorian Guard replace the emperor? Did they assassinate the last one? But what was really important was that a new ethic based on the Christian religion was very gradually gaining strength, almost unnoticed. I wonder if there is a parallel in our time.

Power and control in America

As the old myth dies, a new myth is born and a great page of history turns. In this process we change. With each passing generation, old values are outgrown and new values emerge as we are pulled toward future development. We are now changing away from hierarchy and dominant masculinity, and toward relating to others as equals. The old group myth is being replaced by individual myths with a strong sense of individual equality. In the individual, what seemed to be neurosis may open the door to individual identity.

As a part of this process, the United States is now facing another crisis because the ego and those who identify with it want to maintain control and even extend their power. Those who have power, authority, and great wealth, and those who identify with those people, will attempt to return to the social order of the past. As this happens, the need to increase control will increase. This is because there is no myth to regulate behavior, only frightened, insecure egos attempting to compensate by controlling others with as much force as necessary. The lack of a guiding myth dictates that the controllers will grow more and more insecure and need more and more control, and they will become more corrupt in this process. Eventually the system will collapse in a new crisis. Until that time, expect more social control rather than less. The inflated ego does not understand boundaries, constraints (for itself), morality, or conscience, but it does understand control of others. The inflated ego and its symbols will continue to press for total control. It is difficult to conceive of the enormous size of this monster without the help of science fiction; hence we have "Star Wars" and *The Lord of the Rings* with portrayals of the mighty force of the Empire or the vast armies of Sauron. Now these forces are on the march. They will bring the United States to its next great crisis, and who knows, maybe others after that as well.

There may be hints about our current developmental change, from level four to level five, by considering the West's last major change, from level three to level four. In the late 1400s, individuals were becoming more and more aware that the medieval church was falling far short of its ideals, producing conflict in individuals such as Martin Luther and leading to the Protestant Reformation. Trust in the level three power structure headed by the medieval church was lost, and trust in the individual and in the nation-state began to take its place. Developmentally speaking, much of the push for the change from level three to level four was increased awareness that the group ideals were not being met. This produced internal conflict which led to development into stage four. There are parallels to this in our time when the shortcomings of the nation-state are patently obvious, with power that should benefit the nation as a whole used for the benefit of the few. This will encourage movement toward level five psychology.

It is possible that the next American crisis may be somewhat different than the earlier ones because of how much Americans have changed since the Civil War. People are now more psychologically aware with some shadow awareness. There is a fairly well established sense that it is wrong to be prejudiced against other ethnic and racial groups. Women's status has advanced tremendously in recent years. Homosexual people have become accepted. This suggests that a degree of stage five psychology has already entered Western thinking; perhaps the crisis may be handled with more psychological and less physical confrontation. In America's previous crises, stage four psychology was pushed slightly toward stage five thinking, but it remained firmly in stage four. It just may be that the next crisis will leave us with stage five psychology slightly dominant, or maybe it will be the crisis after the next one. Only time will tell. Ultimately the crises will lead to a truly democratic United States.

Of course, there are any number of people strongly identified with stage four psychology who will resist the transition.

Can the developmental process be stopped? For a while, maybe, but not for long, because the new psychology is in both the people who would stop it as well as those who identify with it. Nero and other Roman emperors attempted to destroy Christianity, but their efforts made little difference. Ancient world philosophy held many of the ideals of Christianity, centuries before Christianity arrived; the tendency to develop a Christian psychology was already present and growing before Christianity began. Protestantism developed in a similar manner, emerging despite military and political resistance in northern Europe. There is every reason to believe that the next developmental level will arrive on schedule.

It is striking how many of the cherished values of history are merely developmental milestones: masculine dominance, love of the city-state, the society of believers, devotion to the nation, excessive property rights, social hierarchy, and specific forms of the deity, as examples. They each play their part in the great developmental sequence and then make their exit; the only thing permanent is change.

I suspect that the United States does have a Manifest Destiny, that there is a special and exceptional quality to America. But that is not in any level four sense of power to dominate others; that is a cheap interpretation of a great truth. Rather, it is an exceptional destiny to transition from the old psychology of hierarchy to the new psychology of equality. That is where America's great destiny lies.

There is no liberal or conservative solution for our future. Massive efforts to stop change, as by General Franco, and to make change, as by Chairman Lenin, have only ended in great bloodshed. The conservative cannot avoid the new epoch, and the liberal cannot know what specific form it will take. From the perspective of developmental psychology there is no plan for action except to live each day morally with personal shadow awareness; our descendants will work out the details over the next few centuries. We only know that it will involve stage five psychology.

The United States is gradually building up to another crisis. It will be another in a series of events that are slowly moving the United States from stage four psychology, based on royalty and hierarchy, to stage five psychology, based on individuality and equality. I strongly suspect that it is the destiny of the United States to lead the world in this transition, no matter how hard it attempts to avoid it. It is a difficult transition for anyone. But those who are particularly identified with the system, those who have managed to achieve significant status, wealth, and power are extremely susceptible to ego inflation in the process, feeling that they are special people, greater than their peers, and exempt from the laws of their fellows, may find it most difficult. Their demands will bring the United States to its next crisis, moving it further into stage five psychology.

CHAPTER XXII

C.G. Jung and the Destiny of the West

The work of C.G. Jung

The work of Jung could be summarized by saying that he realized the modern West had lost its guiding myth and sought a replacement. He was the first to grasp that the underlying myth of Western Civilization, the myth of the conquering heroic Son of God, was ending and a replacement was not in sight. These realizations came to him at approximately the time of the outbreak of World War I, when the old order began to fall apart; royals were executed, kingdoms fell, and millions were massacred. When the myth changes, the world changes.

At the beginning of the twentieth century, the myth that had held the West together was entering an ending phase. The symbol of the conquering son of the Father God had set the tone for centuries of Western civilization. It continued the masculine dominance that had already been in place for thousands of years, and the dominance of the Great Father God that had been present since the Hebrew Babylonian captivity and the beginnings of Christianity. Jung realized it was failing in its role of providing the central guiding symbol for our civilization, and as a result the West was entering a period of chaos.

For Jung, beginning to investigate the problem a century ago, the signs were far from obvious as the problem was just beginning to appear. Jung saw subtle indications in his patients and in his own dreams. In contrast we now see obvious signs in our daily lives. It is not just that Christianity's hold over Western people is fading. Religion is the primary manifestation of the myth of a society, but not the only one. The myth is the underlying order and arrangement that provides the structure for society and meaning for individuals and their lives. It is the omnipresent glue that holds everything together, so deeply ingrained into the mind that it is almost invisible. As the myth fades, structure and order are lost for society and meaning of life is lost for the individual.

Jung's search for a new myth began with the realization that the West did not have a myth to live by.[269] This led to years of analyzing his own dreams and fantasies, as well as those of his patients. He came to the conclusion that a new myth was being born, the myth of the Self, the God-image in each of us. Rather than a group God-image, the Self in each individual would serve as the organizing principle for a new myth in each person. Jung termed the process individuation. Individuation typically begins when one becomes aware of their shadow.[270]

Individuation is a specific part of the greater developmental process. It is the part most important to us, as it describes the dominant psychological changes beginning in our time. It is the individual's path from the psychology of the old myth to that of their own myth, from stage four to stage five. It is the process of becoming a true individual.

Jung's discovery of the Self marked the first time that a Western person became aware of an aspect of the God-image as a part of the mind, the archetype of the Self, rather than an external group God-image, as religions had done previously. God remains unchanged, but the God-image, a human perception, is no longer a group process.

The relationship with the Self is an individual one, without the group approach that traditional religions have provided for millenniums. It is absolutely individual and hence more freeing than any previous religious orientation, and yet it is also much more burdensome, because all that religion provided in the past must now come from the individual. The moral demands are much higher; after all, slavery was once considered both lawful and Christian. Just because something is accepted by law or religion does not make it right, particularly for the individual. Forgiveness for one's personal shortcomings can only come from reconciliation with the Self; it can never come from another human being, be it shaman, pope, or pastor.

Jung's concepts of Self, shadow, anima, and animus have not found general acceptance in contemporary psychology for two main reasons. First, Jung's work has been largely ignored by contemporary psychology because it seems alien. Second, Jung has repeatedly been accused of being a mystic as opposed to a psychologist.

The first cause of these difficulties is that Jung was concerned with what I have called the new psychology, the way of thinking we are moving into and not the psychology we are leaving. Earlier I pointed out the difficulty of understanding that we as a people have a psychology, and that there is a psychology of the West, and it is not the same as medieval thinking. I compared the problem with a fish living in water understanding a bird living in air. It is even more difficult to grasp the idea that we are transitioning into a new way of thinking with new rules; those rules are foreign. New ideas are filtering into our thinking but they have not been defined in contemporary psychology. For example, although most psychologists would admit that each of us has a shadow or "dark side" that concept has not entered mainstream psychology even though Jung began emphasizing shadow integration decades ago.

The second cause is the accusation that Jung was a mystic. I think this is because a great deal of his material is quite difficult to understand, and because it deals with "mystical" subjects such as alchemy and Gnosticism. But Jung was dealing with a difficult situation: he was a person of the old psychology facing the question of a new myth for the West, a completely alien situation. In contrast, I have Jung's ideas, and I can contrast them with Piaget's, and I can compare those with changes in historical trends occurring in the past century—changes which were just beginning when Jung wrote. Jung had none of those advantages.

Jung had a series of fantasies beginning in 1913, immediately before World War I, the time when the old psychology first began to seriously unravel. He carefully recorded those and numerous other "active imagination" fantasies in journals over a period of about 16 years. The exact nature of this material has only recently been made public, with the publication of *The Red Book*,[271] the final form of the material from his journals. It is almost entirely the product of his unconscious. He then spent much of the rest of his life interpreting it. That material is difficult and convoluted. The only parallels he found were from "mystical" texts such as alchemy and Gnosticism. It appears to me that the reason Jung focused so heavily on Gnosticism and alchemy is that is where he found the closest matches to the images in his fantasies. He had to go into those sources in depth to make some sense of the material arising from his unconscious.

Jung's position at the time was that he realized the myth of Western civilization, the heroic son of the Father God, had lost its hold and that as a result we did not have a myth to live by. He realized the answer could not come from the outer world and took the material from his unconscious as a valid source for answers. His published writings tend to focus on explaining this material, making his work difficult to understand.

The result is a body of work that is obtuse and seemingly mystical, with references to personality structures, such as the shadow, not recognized by mainstream psychology. It is oriented toward thinking in a way different from Western tradition. It is no wonder that Jung has remained at the edge of contemporary psychology. Rather than attempt to seriously deal with Jung, his critics have been content to accuse him of mysticism and attack his personal foibles. But Jung laid out the basics of what I have called the new psychology, the psychology we are developing into. He developed treatment that moves the patient toward that psychology.

It was Jung's idea that a neurosis may be an individual's key to beginning individuation[272]; Jung's contemporaries considered it something to be cured. It was Jung's idea that the unconscious was like a 2,000,000-year-old man inside who is available for advice, as opposed to a cellar for undesirable thoughts repressed from the conscious mind.

The psychology he pioneered opened doors to great vistas we never had before. This is not because of the psychology of C.G. Jung's personality, but rather, because of the psychological thinking that he introduced. Jung's personal psychology is irrelevant: he was changing throughout his life. The Jung before his split with Freud was not the same Jung after their split, and he was not the same Jung after an almost fatal heart attack and near-death experience in 1944 at age 68. In a sense, his entire life was a development of his stance in psychology. It is possible that after the heart attack he was the first person to begin to adapt stage five consciousness— perhaps.

But that consideration is too much of a focus on Jung's personal psychology and too little on the psychology that Jung started. For instance, I would not want to debate on whether or not Jung was a feminist or for women's equality, and it is irrelevant. What is relevant is a psychology that says archetypal feminine is equal to archetypal masculine and hence women as symbols of the feminine are equal to men as symbols of the masculine. I don't recall reading that Jung said that, but his psychology does. Jung was more of an introvert, but analytical psychology makes introversion exactly equal to extroversion, favoring neither. All the world may be viewed symbolically, with feminine equal to masculine, introvert equal to extrovert, feeling equal to thinking, and so forth. Jung only opened the doors of analytical psychology; it is not something he made up based on his personality, but rather it is something he discovered or uncovered. I am much more interested in what Jung discovered, analytical psychology and the consciousness we are developing, as opposed to Jung the man.

Jung's psychology gives us the archetypes, so that I can present developmental history as an archetypal process. It allows modern images from dreams and art to be compared with images from past millenniums to reveal the archetypes continuing to manifest through the years of human experience. It encourages a view of the world as symbols, with the dynamics of life appearing as interaction between the archetypes those symbols represent. It gives a relatively straightforward view of the mind. It presents problematic (neurotic) thinking as a key to discovering one's own individuality, not something to be eliminated to be able to better fit into society. It places a focus on becoming an individual and finding one's individual myth rather than probing the past for the "cause" of one's problems to be corrected to be normal. It contains the synchronicity principle as an alternative to the cause and effect principle, the dominant rule of Western thought. Jung's psychology includes the collective unconscious and indications that it may extend beyond the barriers of space and time. And his psychology does all this in a context that is, at its core, religious—yet religious only in the context of the experiencing individual, even an atheist. Did Jung say all that? Maybe and maybe not, but his psychology does.

It never hurts to remember that Jung was only another human being exactly like the rest of us, even though he did produce an amazing set of breakthrough ideas. He opened the door to analytical psychology and made a good foundation for many of its basics. But Jung was a pioneer and analytical psychology will grow beyond him. The future may see him as a founder of the new elite of the new age, but again, it may not; that is for the future to decide. Our job is to consider the psychology he uncovered, and for each individual to determine their own future according to their own Self. The era of the savior for the group is over; Jung's answers were ultimately only for him alone. We have entered the time for each person to work out their own answers.

Jung's psychology is difficult to grasp because the only way to truly make the connection is to develop, to move into the next stage of consciousness. Otherwise it is only a collection of ideas—shadow, Self, persona, and so on—that the ego doesn't make much sense of. And what the ego understands, it doesn't like as it all points to putting the ego in second place. That development is not an easy task but rather something the ego will go out of its way to avoid; it may be that it even took Jung most of his life to get there.

Jung's findings in the internal world have been paralleled by events in the outer world, specifically the rise in status of women and the integration of minorities. Women have moved from a second-class position to almost-equality with males in just over a century. The integration of women as equals into what was a male-dominated society in the outer world is parallel to the integration of a man's anima (his feminine side), or a woman's animus (her masculine side), into conscious awareness in the inner world. The integration of minorities, who have carried the shadow of Western civilization, parallels the integration of the shadow in the inner world.

The events in the outer world confirm Jung's assessment of events in the inner world, and show that both are part of a greater developmental process. Jung did not pick anima, animus, and shadow integration arbitrarily; he intuited them as parts of the next step in our development. The movements toward equality of the sexes and integration of minorities are not coincidences; they are the next developmental steps.

It was not a coincidence that the fantasies that set Jung on his road of discovery occurred on the eve of the outbreak of World War I. The opening of that conflict was a marker of the beginning of the end of the old world order, and the beginning of an apocalyptic century. The centuries-old psychological split in the Western mind, the ego against the projected shadow, was made manifest in the physical world beginning in 1914 when trench lines were cut across northeast France, intensifying with the Iron Curtain and Berlin Wall, and lasting almost continuously until 1989. It involved World War I and II, plus the Cold War with threatened nuclear war and annihilation of civilization. Those 75 years, 1914 to 1989, were an apocalyptic time in history, a time of some of the greatest horrors Western humanity has ever inflicted on itself, a time of sacrifice of millions and millions of human beings. It reached a climax in 1962 in the Cuban Missile Crisis when nuclear war was narrowly avoided. With the fall of the Soviet Union and the Iron Curtain in 1989, the West was left with a world that did not have a manifest and concrete division of the conscious mind and the shadow, a world in which the shadow was no longer firmly placed on the other side of the trench or wall. We entered a world in which the shadow was with us on a grand scale. Thus we live in a post-apocalyptic world; movies such as "Mad Max"[273] serve to make the symbolic devastation of order and morality in the inner world visible as a devastated outer world.

That split is healing, as the drive to integrate the shadow gains momentum. Many in the West are trying to resurrect the great division and the great enemy on the other side by trying to force Muslims into the role once held by Nazis and Stalinist Communists. But the Muslims just don't fit the bill; they really just want the same equality and individual rights that the rest of us want. Both the Nazis and the Stalinist Soviets were hostile and aggressive; the Muslims as a whole are aggressive only in the same sense that bulls become aggressive enough for a bullfight after they have been repeatedly stabbed by barbed sticks. Unfortunately the Muslims have oil, and the West's greed for it provides further motivation to perpetuate the idea of Muslims as shadow figures. But the resurrection attempt won't work; the great division has ended; the shadow is no longer contained. The West has become security crazed in a desperate attempt to capture the shadow, no longer conveniently on the other side of the Berlin Wall and certainly not confined to Muslim lands. It is here among us, in the heart of each one of us, and it will not be contained by our security measures no matter how obsessive or invasive. This is an attempt to go back to the divided world of us versus the shadow, controlled by leaders thriving on power projected to them by fearful people needing to be led; it is an attempt to return to the past and not an answer for the future.

Jung's answer was the individuation process, becoming aware of the shadow, the anima or animus, and the Self. Jung was only slightly ahead of the rest of us; we are following right behind, going through the same developmental changes. From that perspective his work was not about the vague and esoteric but about the stuff of our daily lives. He saw his patients were reluctant to accept their shadow; Westerners have likewise had difficulty accepting minorities as equals, as it meant that all the odious qualities once projected to them had to be owned as personal, a part of one's own shadow. The parallels are similar with the gradual move to equality women have made in a once masculine society. This is not coincidental; it is our developmental pattern. The realization of the Self is next, and we know it has already made its appearance in our stories, movies, and myth. It has arrived and its influence will grow.

CHAPTER XXIII

Development and Religion

Consciousness development and religion

Historically speaking, the changes of our time have been almost instantaneous. The only parallels in history are the rapid changes that occurred when the ancient world became Christian, and when the medieval world became modern. From a historical standpoint, those changes occurred rapidly and they led to entirely new worldviews, new psychologies, new thinking, and new structures of society. We are in a similar period of great change.

We face these changes at the time of the triumph of materialism and rationalism. Traditional religion holds little answer for the educated person; now it is often a tool used to manipulate people attempting to cling to the past. It offers a shopworn theology which requires childlike naivety to deal with its inconsistencies. Materialism itself holds no basis for faith or belief, only presenting a world made of atoms and nothing else, no soul, no God, no magic in the system. There is no ultimate purpose in life in general, much less in one's personal life; it is all a matter of survival of the fittest and grab as much stuff as you can.

Science's seventeenth century search for evidence of God in the physical world led to Darwin and the idea that life evolved out of matter; the material world became God. Materialism as a belief system is confirmed by the zeal that some people identifying with science display when attacking such non-material ideas as near-death experiences, the soul, reincarnation, and so forth. This makes science into a doctrine of faith rather than a tool for gaining knowledge. Theirs is not a call for a scientific examination of the issue but an attack on any suggestion of something non-material in the world. Ironically, this tendency demonstrates our inborn need to find God one way or another. We are intrinsically religious beings; it is a part of human nature.

We had religion before we had civilization; it is many millenniums old. We have probably been religious since we have been human, and we will continue to be so, but the forms change. The problem is that all of the experience of religion comes down to a few numinous episodes that only a few experience. If you are very lucky you might experience something that suggests there is more to this world than material reality. You might have a near-death experience. You might experience a dream of a deceased loved one, leaving the feeling that they somehow continue to exist. You might experience some other uncanny event or odd coincidence that suggests there is more to the world than its material components. Most people don't, but they like to know it is possible.

These numinous incidents combined with awe of life and death are the real core of religion. All the creeds and sermons and scriptures are mythological forms used to express that core in the psychological values of the time. We can thank rationalism for stripping away the mythological facade, leaving the individual to discovering belief on a personal basis. We are returning to a time of spirituality and of life having meaning beyond the material, on an individual basis consistent with reason.

The development of consciousness through the stages of development not only suggests that we have more stages of development ahead of us, but that the process has some intrinsic design or plan with a possible goal or end. It is a process based on archetypes, which have been in place for an extremely long time, possibly since the first modern humans appeared more than 200,000 years ago.

The developmental process has guided the course of civilization and history, and it will continue to do so. The process appears to have its own motive and direction, suggesting a greater design that we are only beginning to realize as we move away from our images of a Great Father or Great Mother God. This suggests purpose in life and gives us every reason to have faith; this world and every person in it are not accidents.

Thus far, after completing four stages and contemplating a fifth, the only sure thing that can be said is that development makes each person more of an individual. Jung thought that the purpose of human mental development was "to widen out, to increase, to intensify consciousness."[274] We began as highly intelligent hominids, gathering and hunting for a living on the savannas of Africa. We were probably a contented lot, more or less peacefully living an absolutely instinctual life in a timeless present, getting by: an eternal cycle of birth, copulation, death. At some point fairly early on, the idea of a deity began to creep into our minds, and human development began. It would lead to thousands of years of war and hate, incredible maltreatment of other human beings—especially women— tremendous knowledge and power in the world, transformation of the instincts, and development of individuality. It has been an expensive and painful process, and we are its latest, but not last, product. We could still be blithefully gathering and hunting, but the image of the deity, the Self, led us on the path of development. We now know that the pain along the way has not been in vain; it has been the push behind consciousness development. Consciousness development requires pain to motivate change, otherwise, we humans continue to carry on as we always have.

Suffering in the present time always seems horrible and unbearable but a look back one or two hundred thousand years makes it clear that it is suffering that has brought us to where we are now. As the reason for the pain of poor wretches in our past—slaughtered millions, burned witches, tortured heretics—was not known to them, similarly, the reason for the pain of our present lives is not known to us. But we know that their pain led to the consciousness development that we have now, and so we always have the hope that our pain, while we may not know its reason, is leading toward even greater consciousness for the future.

It is clear that during the last five centuries, Western people have developed strong, well-defined egos in the stage four process. Perhaps that experience has been the greatest purpose of their lives, almost unseen in daily living, as opposed to supposedly earth-shaking events as elections to office, conquests, or discoveries. We now look forward to centuries of stage five, developing psychological awareness and relating to others with increasing shadow integration, slowly dissolving the prejudices that dominated previous centuries. Maybe one's greatest purpose in life is the gradual development we each make as we live out our time, day by day and interaction by interaction in each stage of development, as opposed to the lives of the great figures of history.

Consciousness is no accident. It is not a fluke of nature or a byproduct of evolution. It is a developing process whose ends we cannot even vaguely comprehend. It brings us back to the religious issue: what is the source of consciousness and the developmental sequence, a process possibly in place from our very beginnings? Consciousness and consciousness development may not be proof of, but certainly are evidence of, something in the system greater than the sum of the material parts.

The development that the Western world has undergone in the past 5,000 years has occurred much too rapidly to be the product of evolution. The mechanism which drives the developmental process, the archetype of development, had to be in place before later development occurred. That is, the archetypal pattern which would lead to the founding of the city-states of the ancient world, to the monasteries and convents of the medieval world, and to the nation-states of the modern world, was already present in prehistoric humans, just as the flower is present in the seed. The potential for developing the internal child, the superego, and the ego is already in place when a child is born because it is an innate archetypal sequence. There is every reason to believe the same sequence was present in our prehistoric ancestors. Evolution only involves a natural selection of processes which have already appeared, as smaller animals winning out over larger ones during times of famine. Evolution cannot explain the creation of potential future development, development which had not occurred during the time of the evolving. There is something greater than evolution involved in this process.

Animals have features once considered to be strictly human, as tool use, basic consciousness, self-awareness, language, mourning, the ability to plan ahead, and the ability to work in groups. These are all considered support for straightforward human evolution out of the animal world; animals have all of our characteristics to a limited degree and we have evolved them further. But no animal has consciousness that develops, not even rudimentary development. We have no idea how humans achieved this ability. If it evolved, there should be some hints of it in the animal world, yet there are none. Neanderthals probably existed for over 250,000 years, possibly longer than we have, but there is no evidence that their culture ever developed. Modern humans alone have consciousness that develops. Furthermore, this process has always been involved with religion, the only other thing which humans do not share with animals.

While the conscious mind developed and expanded throughout this great process, the instincts were also transformed. Sexuality has been differentiated to produce romantic love as well as the sexual drive, and appreciation of beauty has developed out of sexual attraction. Aggression has fostered assertion and competition. The basic instinct of eating has developed into the socialization of shared meals. These are changes of development, not evolution.

The future of Christianity

I have said that these changes will lead to the end of Christianity as we have known it, but that does not necessarily mean the end of Christianity for the West; that may or may not happen. What is sure is that the myth of the heroic conquering Son of God is ending. Medieval Christianity was based on the myth of the Great Father God, and when that myth ran its course, Protestantism arose and reinterpreted the same Bible to fit the new myth centered on the Son of God. With that reinterpretation, Christianity endured but it was no longer the medieval religion it had been. It had undergone a metamorphosis into a completely different religion, claiming to have only undergone a reformation of its medieval roots. It is possible that Christianity could undergo another such change—maybe.

Christianity could have a second reformation as our psychology changes. It would call for shadow acceptance, equality of the sexes, and a realization of the Self. That is not an impossible scenario. A twelfth-century theologian, Joachim of Fiore (or Flora), proposed three great ages of humanity, ages of the Father, the Son, and the Holy Ghost. From a symbolic standpoint, it is easy to see that the medieval era was the age of the Great Father God, and the modern West has been the age of the Son of God. That suggests the possibility that the age we are entering could be the age of the Holy Ghost.

The Holy Ghost, or Holy Spirit, has been the overlooked and neglected third part of the Christian trinity. It has remained in the wings of Christianity, mostly ignored for 2,000 years. Pictures of God from the medieval era show both Christ and the Holy Ghost as present but not individually active. Christ became the center of attention with the Protestant Reformation but the Holy Ghost still remained in the background. It is possible that it is now becoming time for the Holy Ghost to be the active figure, and it could serve as an image of the Self in the coming age. It has parallels with Jung's concept of the Self. It can, like the Self, be considered as "God within us." It indicates, like the Self, an absolutely personal relationship with God as the Holy Spirit residing inside.

The traditional symbol of the Holy Ghost is the dove, also a traditional symbol of Aphrodite, the ancient Greek goddesses of love. The motif of Aphrodite in a modern person's dream would probably be associated with relatedness and relating, not necessarily in a sexual sense. The symbol of the dove gives a feminine quality and an emphasis on relating to the lore of the Holy Ghost and thus the Self, qualities which are gradually becoming more emphasized with the other changes occurring in our time. It is in keeping with the feminine nature of the coming era as well as its emphasis on relating. While it is a group symbol, it comes to the individual. However, there are no reports of widespread appearances or activities as with the flying saucer phenomenon, suggesting the required mythic foundation is not present.

If the Holy Ghost does become the dominant image in Western religion, it would not be through any organization as the church has been thought of in the past. There would be no church hierarchy, probably no churches, no preachers, and no group dogma, except for the basic belief itself. It would be a predominantly personal and internal experience, in contrast with the external church of the past two millenniums. It would represent a change in Christianity greater than that which occurred with the Reformation. It is a possibility, although it would be so all-encompassing and non-denominational that it would only be vaguely Christian in any traditional sense.

On the other hand, it may be that Christianity is only prominent in the West for two periods, the medieval world and the West, and no more. Jung noted that Christianity has been the dominant philosophy of the astrological Piscean age for the West; it may be that medieval Catholic Christianity and Protestant Christianity are manifestations of the two fish which make up the zodiacal symbol of Pisces.[275] The constellation of Pisces is formed by two joined fish; there is no third fish, suggesting no third age of Christianity. Jung associated this with leaving the Age of Pisces and entering Aquarius.[276,277]

Max Zeller, an early Jungian analyst, reported in *The Dream - The Vision of the Night* that Jung said that a new religion was being built, "all over the world" and it would be complete in about six hundred years.[278] We'll see what happens, or at least our descendants will. Personally, I have few disagreements with Jung, and if that was his intuition, that's where I'll bet my money. In all likelihood, the great Christian Age is ending and a new age is beginning.

Whatever happens in the West, some form of the Self will come to be considered as the next appearance of the deity. It will be much more low-key than any church establishment in the past, yet it will be much more powerful than any church in the past. Society will coalesce around the myth that each person has a personal relationship with his or her Self. Despite being a widely held group belief, it will be experienced individually.

An experience of the Self is always a possibility in psychotherapy, particularly psychotherapy as Jung conceived it, as the ideal is to bring the individual ego into harmony with the Self. This is the core of the new myth, and hence the core of the new religion. The old approach of becoming as "little children" and accepting exhausted ideals is no more. It is being replaced by a belief in an individual relationship to a personal Self, an adult idea palatable to adults. Psychotherapists have already taken up many of the duties of the clergy; an emotional problem can no longer be met with only prayer as in the past. In time, the therapist will eventually inherit much, if not all, of the role once assigned to the clergy, as it is primarily through exploration of the mind that the Self, one's "God within," might be reached.

This may come about through a change of Christianity into a religion of the Holy Ghost, but it would more likely come from a different direction. The story could arise that some people were taken aboard a flying saucer where they learned that all people are equal in God's eyes, that relating to one another as equals is our role on earth, and that a part of God lives in each of us and it is our purpose to relate to that. Or maybe it is just a matter of Jung's psychology gradually spreading further and further. Or maybe some other scenario, who knows?

As we move into the future, I suggest that you remember the basic principles of the new psychology and keep an open mind, and maybe you will see the new religion forming. Always remember that no Roman would have ever entertained the idea that a cult based on an executed criminal would do as well as it did. We are now in the place of the Romans. Great changes are occurring; pay close attention if developments fit with the new psychology.

CHAPTER XXIV

The West and the Future

Looking back at the West

Our time in history is between two ages, the evening of level four West and the morning of a level five future. This time of transition allows the view of both worlds. We are aware of both the old hierarchy of privilege, with the richer, more powerful, and more white having had more rights, compared with the new call for equal justice and equality before the law. Developmental level four and ego psychology placed a great deal of emphasis on the inequality of people; it is based on an extended social hierarchy with certain people considered to be intrinsically superior to others. Level five psychology reverses that, with a great emphasis on the equality of all people. The level four process was the development of ego strength by controlling the shadow, that is, people lower in the hierarchy. The level five process is the integration of the shadow, that is, seeing others as equal and withdrawing projections of superiority or inferiority from them.

We are leaving a myth of hierarchy and superiority and entering into a myth of equality. In reality, neither is absolutely true or false, but the next age belongs to equality.

After this transition has taken place the West will become a relic of history, much like the medieval world, now mostly forgotten. But the West played a key role in producing the future. Western culture developed, and gave the world, stage four psychology, including rational thought, science, romantic love, and the beginnings of personal individuality. The psychology supporting this was not present before it was developed in Europe and spread to the world. Most of the non-Western world was functioning below stage four prior to the World Wars of the twentieth century; now stage four rational thought is found throughout most of the world to some varying degree. The modern world is very much the product of the European Enlightenment. Not only did Western culture develop this thinking but it also developed the idea that would lead to the end of the dominance of that psychology, the idea of the equality of all people. This consciousness developed solely in the West; it was not present to any significant degree in any earlier culture. Any other culture or civilization may be romanticized to seem like an equal of the modern world (as democracy in the ancient world was actually only for males with rank), but in the final analysis, no other group has achieved the development that the West has.

The future will also see the shadow side of the West. The countries of the West have behaved like adolescents, like narcissistic high school teenagers. They have fought over childish ideas of honor, intimidated their fellow students and stole their lunch money, and demanded that their peers join their gang or suffer their wrath. They have had no moral scruples with stealing as much as possible, including slaves, oil, and land. They have constantly angled to get one up on their peers, willing to fight if things did not go their way. It has been five centuries of astounding greed and arrogance thinly veiled by a cloak of exceptionalism and specialness, of feeling superior to the rest of the world. It has been a mentality of adolescence, and that is probably how the future will describe the psychology of the West and the ego: the internal adolescent.

The enormous success of the West has made it easy for it to overlook the huge amount of luck in its favor and pretend that its success was due to innate superiority. In *Guns, Germs, and Steel*, Jared Diamond makes it clear that the reason the West rose to a leading position is a series of lucky geographical breaks, including the shape of continents, the availability of animals and plants capable of domestication, and the presence of harbors.[279] If, for example, Eurasia was a north-south landmass, and Africa was an east-west one in a temperate zone, the dominant racial and ethnic groups in our time would be far different. The West just got the luck of the draw, nothing more, and it is not special. Consciousness would have arisen pretty much along the same lines, just with different cultures. Genetics are irrelevant; consciousness develops through culture. The West only achieved its position with luck.

Waves of change

We are fortunate, or unfortunate, enough to live in this time of tremendous change, change in the psychology we are founded on, change in the symbols underlying our world, change in the myth of our existence. It is fortunate in that it allows us to see the past and the future in great contrast, as the old myth fades and the new myth enters. It is unfortunate in that each of us is torn between what was and what will be. We have lived through (hopefully most of) an Apocalypse; the twentieth century was the West's bloodiest century, a century of horrors and change which would have been unimaginable to anyone in the past, except perhaps for Saint John, the visionary traditionally held to be the author of the book of Revelation. Jung referred to the middle of the twentieth century as "a time of God's death and disappearance."[280]

I recall Edward Edinger saying, at some point in the early 1980s, that the twentieth century was like the Saturday between the death of Christ on Good Friday and his rebirth on Easter Sunday.

As we continue to live this change, my sincere hope is that we are through the worst of it. Many deny the new psychology and identify with the old way, continuing to project their shadow. Some feel the changes and embrace them with some shadow acceptance but still projecting the doubting and resisting elements of their shadow to others. There is some accepting and some rejecting in each of us and the only way out is to accept that both are in each of us, that is, by accepting one's own shadow. I recall someone, perhaps Jung, writing that the collective consciousness, that is, the group's thinking, was like a great army strung out over miles, with scouts going ahead and laggards behind. The scouts are reaching new territory, and the vanguard of the army is almost there, but many lag behind. We are all a part of that army, and there is some of the scout and the laggard in each of us.

The West's transition into level five psychology has been fostered by three great waves of change which swept over our civilization. The first was that of the 1700s and could be termed Jeffersonian. It was a social movement toward independence and equality, and away from hierarchical dependence. Underlying this was the beginnings of shadow reconciliation psychology. If all people are equal, then the hierarchical foundations of society, as master-slave, king-pauper, and noble-commoner, fall apart. In that one cannot project one's shadow on someone who is truly equal, a gradual movement toward shadow reconciliation began. Reactions included the constructive change of the American Revolution versus the destructive revolt of the French Revolution.

The second wave swept over the West in the late 1800s and could be termed Freudian, reflecting the discovery of the unconscious and the impact of that discovery on modern life. From a psychological perspective, awareness of the shadow was brought into consciousness. Reactions included the desire to explore the unconscious versus a need to repress the shadow. This era saw the beginnings of modern science fiction and its exploration of new worlds, which were echoes of the unconscious. It also included the beginnings of crime detection novels in which a dangerous shadow is brought under control and repressed.

The third wave began after the old myth and the old elite ended in the destruction of World War I. The old elite had guided the West for hundreds of years, as kings, kaisers, and emperors had served as the earthly embodiment of the Self symbol for society. A new myth, the myth of the individual Self, entered consciousness; hence the era could be termed Jungian. The options were to align the ego with the Self or to identify with the Self. With the end of the old ethic, ordinary men assumed positions of power and leadership, and many have been unable to resist the temptation to identify with the dark side of the Self and become inflated, with an inevitable descent into evil. The third wave brought Self symbols into our lives, including atomic energy (the atom as a mandala of power), flying saucers, flying saucers hovering over nuclear missile installations, the threat of nuclear annihilation, and inflated egos identified with the Self; all

314

are part of the same archetypal package, and their appearance in our time is not a coincidence.

The way of what is to come

Although the West is much more psychologically aware than it was a century ago, it is still easy to fall back into ego psychology and think that the other person is the "bad guy." It is easy to feel bias based on the sex or ethnicity of the other person, or based on one's rank in the social hierarchy. It is easy to feel special and better than one's peers if life gives the ego a reason to do so, or less than one's peers after a run of bad luck. It is easy for the ego to identify with the fate the Self has provided and become inflated.

The ego likes a hierarchy, so there is still a strong need for leaders to project one's personal power to; it is easy to look to leaders to solve problems when the solution really is inside. The stage four person wants to either lead or be led, to control or be controlled. It seems so rational to trust people who want to be leaders, who say they know so much more about how the world should be run, and yet they so frequently disappoint. There is often a childlike, naive trust of leaders: someone more successful, someone older, a younger person with more drive, someone with a claim to some sort of class or old family background, someone who can beat up their opponent—even if only in speechifying. Competency and past performance are frequently not issues; too often the critical issue is how well the leader is identified with the myth of the conquering hero. Stage four mythology takes over and reality is forgotten.

But the process of change in the West will proceed. The emphasis will continue to shift toward relating rather than controlling, to equality rather than hierarchy, and to personal identity rather than group identity. The feminine will continue to grow in strength and will be as dominant in the next age as the masculine was in the past. Prejudices will continue to be worn away. Human equality, racial, sexual and otherwise, will become second nature; fairness will be emphasized. There will be less separateness and secrecy with more of a sense of belonging to the group yet with greater independence and individuality.[281] There will be less emphasis on materialism and more on spirituality. There will be much less armed conflict in the West as the drive to exert our will over other people will be greatly diminished. The nation-state, which developed with the Western ego, will not last in its present form; I expect it to have much less power and scope, probably administrative in nature rather than ruling. I would imagine that there will be a world government of some sort in the sense of a centralized governing body but not government as level four control of citizens. There will be no more investments of great degrees of personal power in collective systems, including huge and powerful governments, militaries, or corporations, as we develop from nation-states into a society of individuals. Sex role identification will continue to blur and become more of a spectrum. Psychological self-awareness and shadow integration psychology will gradually become second nature in the next few centuries. The West will become as psychological as the Medieval world was religious, but conducted by relating in amity rather than by rigor and asceticism; it also will be more inwardly focused as was the Medieval world. Some people may have more wealth than others but without massive accumulations of wealth. The age of leaders and followers in a hierarchical sense is ending. Racial, ethnic, and religious splits will heal. It is the beginning of the age of individuals, with greater emphasis on meaning and purpose of each person's life than ever before. There will be increasing emphasis on each person's unconscious and dreams as input to conscious thinking along their path of individuation. The need for work and a job will become a need to create or serve. Knowledge will continue to advance but with consideration of synchronous events, possible continuation of life after death, and other issues that lie outside of the realm of the scientific method and the double-blind experiment. It will be a higher level of civilization with a different set of problems and challenges.

This description may seem like pie in the sky, a list of impossible ideals. But the reason that they are ideals is the lure of the next developmental stage drawing us on. Modern people crave equality and liberty only because it is part of the psychology they are moving into, not because it is some eternal truth. Medieval people did not see people as equal and did not dispute the rights of the royals; they resented the abuse of those rights but they basically upheld them. People of 600 years ago would never have dreamed of considering women equal to men. The idea of universal rights is only universal for our time, as we leave stage four. Society 600 years from now will have its problems, just as we do, but they will be different problems.

Describing the promises of how the West would develop to Luther, Galileo, da Vinci, Copernicus, or Henry VIII, would have excited a similar allure; it is what pulls people further along in the painful process of development. Henry would have loved the idea of a strong, centralized nation-state, and Galileo would have admired the march of science; we now know the difficulties that have come with their dreams, including nation-states on the brink of nuclear warfare. However, it is positive to see that each of the great ages has been more conscious than its predecessors, and the next age promises that people just might be a little more decent to one another than they have in the past. We'll see, or at least our descendants will. They will have their problems too; it's just that we can't see those problems from our time; in fact, we can't even imagine them.

There is a great struggle in the Western soul as it faces one of the greatest changes in humanity's history, moving forward into the future in change while trying to resist change and stay in the past. It is a transition in consciousness so great that the results will not be clear for at least a century if not three. As this great page of history turns, chaos and conflict impact our lives. We have the fate of living in the midst of this, pulled back by the psychology of the past and pulled forward by the psychology of the future.

CHAPTER XXV

Postscript: The Dream of the Twentieth Century

For one last time, I want to return to Jung. I believe that C.G. Jung was an extremely important individual for the West and its development. I have pointed out that our psychology is gradually becoming the individuation which Jung described years ago. I feel it is the general direction the West is headed, and it just may also be true of the world as a whole.

Always with Jung, the critical elements are the integration of the shadow and the anima or animus, and realization of the Self. Of those, typically the first encountered is the shadow. Shadow awareness, shadow acceptance, and shadow integration are, and will be for centuries, main themes of the West. That brings us back to shadow psychology and the people who have born the West's projected shadow, the aboriginal people of the world.

When I first considered this section, I thought of reviewing the history of the Western white male's treatment of aboriginal people since 1492. Such a review is out of the question here, as it would take a volume if not volumes, and because it is so grim one needs to repeatedly take breaks from its horrors. It began with the brutal treatment Columbus administered to American aboriginal people, and continued through innumerable horrors, including such high points as the Atlantic slave trade, the devastation of Native Americans, the brutality of the Raj in India, the Belgian Congo, and later Vietnam, Iraq, and on and on. It has been a holocaust of holocausts.

The horrors the West perpetrated on other racial groups is gradually entering Western consciousness. There is a call for renaming Columbus

Day as Indigenous Peoples' Day, and it seems to be gaining momentum. The reality of *Twelve Years A Slave*[282] is gradually eclipsing the fantasy of *Gone With the Wind*;[283] in the latter, Margaret Mitchell made slavery seem like summer camp for Africans. The reality of slavery has dawned on more and more Americans, even to the point that the Confederate flag has somewhat lost favor in the American South. Acknowledgment of the shadow precedes integration of the shadow, and that is happening; today's politically correct becomes tomorrow's correct. Inch by inch, almost imperceptibly, inner and outer development continues.

Studs Terkel interviewed Admiral Gene LaRocque about his experiences in World War II. LaRocque was at Pearl Harbor on December 7, 1941, when the Japanese attacked. He said that initially he thought the U.S. Army Air Corps was conducting the bombing by accident; he couldn't imagine that the Japanese were capable of such an attack. LaRocque said that the thinking of the time was that the Japanese had poor vision, poor equipment, and only imitated Westerners. "We'd thought they were little brown men and we were the great big white men. They were of a lesser species."[284]

The feats of the Japanese "little brown men" in World War II awakened other "little brown men" to the reality that white men could be beaten. World War II was followed by the independence of India that Gandhi had worked for, and then a host of former European colonies became independent. The United States thought that Europe should give up her colonies, but couldn't resist the urge to semi-colonize them afterward. Fidel Castro and Ho Chi Minh demonstrated that colonialism was passé, but Americans have kept trying, most recently in Iraq and Afghanistan, with less than complete success. European powers have similarly continued to meddle in their former colonies, with equal lackluster success. One wonders when they will finally get the message. My discussion on the matter has gone on for a number of previous chapters in this book. It should be clear that repressing or controlling the projected shadow is the psychology of the past for the West, as is its external manifestation, repressing and controlling "little brown men." We're just having a little difficulty leaving the past.

And that brings me back to Jung and a dream he had on December 18, 1913, as is recorded in detail in *Memories, Dreams and Reflections*[285] and discussed in a 1925 seminar[286]. Jung dreamed that he was with an "unknown, brown skinned man, a savage," described as "small," in a remote landscape. Just before dawn, Jung heard the approach of Siegfried, riding a chariot made of bones of dead people. Jung and the aboriginal man were armed with rifles; they fired and killed Siegfried.

Jung interpreted Siegfried as a symbol of the will, the drive to achieve. He noted that attitude in himself, and felt that the dream meant that he had to sacrifice his own attitude and recognize "higher things than the ego's will." Jung associated the killing of the hero with killing his superior function, that is, letting his inferior functions have energy for expression. A thinking person might set aside a thought-based response and answer from their feelings, for example.

Before further consideration of the dream, there is one other point to cover, and that is the difference between big dreams and little dreams. Most dreams are about the routine of one's personal life. They are personal in nature and stem from one's personal psychology, and could be considered to be "little" dreams. The other type, "big" dreams, contain archetypal material and come from the deeper layers of the mind.[287] Jung said that aboriginal people consider "big" dreams to be of importance to the tribe, not just the dreamer.[288] That is because the material from the collective unconscious may indicate forces that could impact the entire group. "Big" dreams would be reported to the medicine man, who would interpret them as possibly having meaning for the whole tribe.

Jung hadn't made the differentiation between "big" and "little" dreams in 1913. At the time he interpreted his dream from a personal perspective, a commentary on his own personality. I have noted that Jung changed greatly in his life, especially after a heart attack in 1944. It appears to me that it was not until after the heart attack that his ego definitely took second place to his Self. It is easy to see him as being willful and ego-inflated before the heart attack. The dream defined a definite problem that he had, and he interpreted it as such, a problem of his alone.

But while "big" dreams may be interpreted on a personal level, they probably should also be considered on a group level, as to what they may say about the tribe.

Historians have realized the problems the West is facing, and their view is often a less-than-optimistic one; I have referred to some of them in these pages. For example, Oswald Spengler's history is *The Decline of the West*[289] and Jacques Barzun's outstanding history of Western culture is *From Dawn to Decadence;*[290] the titles sum up authors' opinions on the fate of the West quite well. Ideas of correcting the situation usually run along the lines of revitalizing the old myth, perhaps by increasing the sway of traditional religion, or by the self-appointed few increasing social control over the many. A century ago Jung realized the underlying problem was the death of the old myth that had held the West together, and he began work to find a new one. From that we have Self psychology, which I have discussed in this book.

I think Jung found the direction our civilization will go in the future. If we think of him as a medicine man for the Western "tribe," perhaps the greatest medicine man of our time, then his "big" dreams may just be important for us all. I think that is most certainly true of the dream I have summarized above. To me, it is the dream of the twentieth century.

The dream opens with Jung realizing that he is alone with a small, unknown brown-skinned man whom he described as a "savage." This unknown man is a symbol for Jung's own shadow side, his less developed side, which was projected onto an aboriginal man. I don't think that Jung had done much shadow integration by 1913 at age 38; he was just entering midlife. This dream paints a picture of what was going to happen, the direction his life would follow.

Jung and his aboriginal companion are equals in the dream; they are both armed and both carry out the ambush. This was not true in the world of the early twentieth century. There was almost no widespread sense of racial equality or integration at that time. Supposed scientific theories of the day held that non-white people were intellectually inferior; white superiority was virtually an unquestionable fact.

The archetypal nature of the dream elements indicates that this was a "big" dream. The only personal detail was Jung himself. Siegfried is the archetypal Western hero. Jung's companion is an archetypal aboriginal man. Siegfried's chariot was made of the bones of the dead. This was not the material of everyday life. There is almost nothing personal about it. Virtually all of the dream is archetypal. It is a "big" dream.

A "big" dream will probably fit somewhat with the dreamer's personal psychology, even if it is mostly about tribal matters. There is a reason why the dream appeared to one person and not to another member of the tribe. But the abundance of archetypal material in this dream indicates that it should be considered for the group as well as the individual. Now, more than 100 years later, we can see that this "big" dream also pointed to changes which would unfold for the West as a whole, not just for Jung.

For the internal world, the dream indicates a movement toward expressing the inferior functions for the West in general as well as Jung in particular. But it is in the external world that the dream has its most striking interpretation.

It is notable that the ambush occurred at dawn. For the group, this ambush would not simply mark the dawn of a new day, but of a new age. It would be an age with a new hero, not the traditional hero of the West.

The initial hero of the dream is Siegfried, the superstar hero of Wagner's opera by the same name. Jung associated Siegfried with Germany and the idea of "where there's a will there's a way." His association with Germany suggests that he thought of world events at the time. There had been a massive arms race by the great European powers, and World War I would begin just over seven months later. However, he took this no further and did not interpret the dream as meaningful to the West as a whole. Rather, Jung applied the dream interpretation only to his own psychology.

Siegfried is, above all, a symbol of the West's heroic ego, conquering and controlling its shadow in the inner world, and conquering and controlling people carrying the West's projected shadow in the outer world. Siegfried is emblematic of the thinking that would lead to millions and millions of deaths in two World Wars. With the first world war, the old myth guiding the West began its closing act. Just over 30 years after the dream, World War II would be over and European colonization would begin to end.

Jung and his companion, the "brown-skinned" man, killed the traditional Western hero, Siegfried. Jung wrote that he felt "disgust and remorse" afterward, because he had killed "something so great and beautiful." These strong feelings, both of remorse for the deed and admiration for Siegfried, suggest that Jung was only able to carry out the ambush because his shadow companion was present. The companion symbolized Jung's own "primitive" side, his shadow. Jung, allied with his shadow, became the hero of the dream, replacing Siegfried. Jung's role in the dream foreshadowed Bilbo Baggins and Luke Skywalker, the new Western heroes who required the help of their shadow to reach their goal.

Jung's remorse for his deed and his admiration for Siegfried correspond to his attachment to his own ego domination. As I noted, it may well be that this was not resolved until much later in his life, so that the dream was a road map for his future as opposed to a picture of his mind in 1913.

It is especially notable that Siegfried was riding a chariot made of the bones of dead people. I have emphasized the suffering and deaths caused by the West in their treatment of non-Western people, but one can also add in the pain and suffering caused by the West to its own people. It is a butcher's bill of incredible proportion.

The Siegfrieds of this world still want to drive their chariots of death over their fellow human beings, and there is still some Siegfried in all of us in the West. But the "little brown men," both in the world and inside each of us, resist. We know how the drama will play out; the dream of December 18, 1913 made that clear. A new age is dawning and its watchword is equality.

About the Author

John A. Cahman, Ph.D., is a psychologist living in Los Angeles.

Endnotes

[1] Hunter, J. (1991). *Culture wars: The struggle to define America.* New York: BasicBooks.

[2] Ryota, K., Feilden, T., Firth, C., & Rees. G. (2011). Political Orientations Are Correlated with Brain Structure in Young Adults. *Current Biology, 21*, Issue 8, 677–680.

[3] Matthew 18:3 (King James Version)

[4] Harper, K. (2013). *From shame to sin: The Christian transformation of sexual morality in late antiquity* (pp. 27-28). Cambridge, MA: Harvard University Press.

[5] Brown, P. (1988). *The body and society: Men, women, and sexual renunciation in early Christianity* (p. 383). New York: Columbia University Press.

[6] Ellenberger, H. F. (1970). *The discovery of the unconscious: The history and evolution of dynamic psychiatry.* New York: Basic Books.

[7] Jung, C. G. (1975). *Two essays on analytical psychology* (2nd ed.). Collected Works vol. 7, par. 227. R. F. C. Hull (Trans.). NJ: Princeton University Press.

[8] Jung, C. G. (1976). *The symbolic life.* Collected Works, vol. 18, par. 837. R. F. C. Hull (Trans.). NJ: Princeton University Press.

[9] Jung, C. G. (1974). *Symbols of transformation* (2nd ed.). Collected Works, vol. 5, par. 26. R. F. C. Hull (Trans.). NJ: Princeton University Press.

[10] Ibid (par. 32).

[11] Jung, C. G. (1984). *Dream Analysis: Notes of the seminar given in 1928-1930 by C.G. Jung.* (p. 45). W. McGuire (Ed.). NJ: Princeton University Press.

[12] Ibid (p. 46).

[13] Lévy-Bruhl, L. (1985). *How natives think.* NJ: Princeton University Press.

[14] Littleton, C. S. (1985). Introduction. *How natives think.* (pp. xvi-xxi). NJ: Princeton University Press.

[15] Kennedy, P. M. (1989). *The rise and fall of the great powers: Economic change and military conflict from 1500 to 2000* (pp. 3-4). New York: Vintage Books.

[16] Pinker, S. (2011). *The better angels of our nature: Why violence has declined.* New York: Viking.

[17] Jung, C.G. (1975). *Aion: researches into the phenomenology of the Self* (2nd ed.). Collected Works vol. 9ii, par. 13-19. R. F. C. Hull (Trans.). NJ: Princeton University Press.

[18] Bair, Deirdre. (2003). *Jung: A biography* (pp. 469-470). Boston: Little, Brown and Co.

[19] Campbell, W. J. (2010). *Getting it wrong: Ten of the greatest misreported stories in American journalism* (pp. 163-183). Berkeley: University of California Press.

[20] Germond, J. W., & Witcover, J. (1989). *Whose broad stripes and bright stars? The trivial pursuit of the presidency, 1988.* New York: Warner Books.

21 Messing, S., Jabon, M., & Plaut, E. (2016). Bias in the flesh: Skin complexion and stereotype consistency in political campaigns. *Public Opinion Quarterly, 80, Issue 1, Spring*, 44-65.

22 Kramer, S. (Producer), & Zinnemann, F. (Director). (1952). *High Noon* [Motion picture]. U.S.: United Artists.

23 Jung, C.G. (1968). *The archetypes and the collective unconscious* (2nd ed.). Collected Works, vol. 9,i, par. 469. R. F. C. Hull (Trans.). NJ: Princeton University Press.

24 Thomas, E., Roven, C., & Nolan, C. (Producers), & Nolan, C. (Director). (2008). *The dark knight* [Motion picture]. U.S.: Warner Brothers Pictures.

25 Jones, R. P. (2016). *The end of white Christian America*. New York: Simon and Schuster.

26 Dreher, R. (2017). *The Benedict option: A strategy for Christians in a post-Christian nation*. New York: Sentinel.

27 1 Corinthians 7:1-2 (King James Version)

28 Harper, K. (2013). *From shame to sin: The Christian transformation of sexual morality in late antiquity.* (p. 103).

29 2 Corinthians 11:19 (King James Version)

30 2 Corinthians 12:7 (King James Version)

31 Nietzsche, F. W. (2008). *Beyond good and evil: Prelude to a philosophy of the future.* M. Faber (Trans.). New York: Oxford University Press.

32 Smith, J. (1976). *The Book of Mormon* (p. 61). Salt Lake City, UT: Church of Jesus Christ of Latter-day Saints.

33 Ibid (p. 403).

34 Jung, C.G. (1975). *Aion: researches into the phenomenology of the Self* (2nd ed.). Collected Works vol. 9ii, par. 142.

35 Jung, C.G. (1984). *Dream analysis: Notes of the seminar given in 1928-1930 by C.G. Jung.* (p. 242).

36 1 Thessalonians 4:17 (King James Version)

37 Jones, R. P. (2016).

38 Joshua 10:13 (King James Version)

39 Psalms 96:10 (King James Version)

40 Dacey, J. S., & Travers, J. F. (2004). *Human development: Across the lifespan* (5rd ed.) (pp. 32-34). New York: McGraw Hill.

41 Hawkes, J. (1973). *The first great civilizations: Life in Mesopotamia, the Indus Valley, and Egypt* (p. 193). New York: Knopf; distributed by Random House.

42 White, J. M. (1970). *Ancient Egypt: Its culture and history* (p. 42). New York: Dover Publications.

43 Fustel de Coulanges, N. D. (1979). *The ancient city: A study on the religion, laws, and institutions of Greece and Rome* (p. 152). Gloucester, MA: Peter Smith.

44 Flannery, K., & Marcus, J. (2012). *The creation of inequality: How our prehistoric ancestors set the stage for monarchy, slavery, and empire.* (p. 538) Cambridge, MA: Harvard University Press.

45 Exodus 20:4 (King James Version)

46 Watterson, B. (1988). *The essential Calvin and Hobbes: A Calvin and Hobbes treasury* (p. 42). Kansas City, MO: Andrews and McMeel.

47 Landels, J.G. (1978). *Engineering in the ancient world.* Berkeley: University of California Press.

48 Jung, C.G. (1997). *Visions: Notes of the seminar given in 1930-1934 by C.G. Jung.* (pp. 664-665). C. Douglas (Ed.). NJ: Princeton University Press.

49 Barzun, J. (2000). *From dawn to decadence: 500 years of western cultural life: 1500 to the present.* New York: HarperCollins.

50 Kohlberg, L. (1981). *Essays on moral development: the philosophy of moral development.* San Francisco: Harper & Row.

51 Kohlberg, L. (1984). *Essays on moral development: the psychology of moral development.* San Francisco: Harper & Row.

52 Harrison, J. E. (1908). *Prolegomena to the study of Greek religion* (p. 3). Cambridge, MA: The University Press.

53 2 Samuel 11-12 (King James Version)

54 Matthew 27:5 (King James Version)

55 Matthew 26:75 (King James Version)

56 Mark 14:72 (King James Version)

57 Watterson, B. (1992). *The indispensable Calvin and Hobbes: A Calvin and Hobbes treasury* (p. 17). Kansas City, MO: Andrews and McMeel.

58 Eusebius. (1984). *The history of the church from Christ to Constantine* (p. 247). G. A. Williamson (Trans.). New York: Dorset Press.

59 Matthew 19:12 (King James Version)

60 Harper, K. (2013). *From shame to sin: The Christian transformation of sexual morality in late antiquity* (p. 49).

61 Galen. (1963). *Galen on the passions and errors of the soul.* P. W. Harkins (Trans.). Columbus: Ohio State University Press.

62 2 Corinthians 12:7 (King James Version)

63 Matthew 5:29 (King James Version)

64 Matthew 5:30 (King James Version)

65 Pomeroy, S. B. (1975). *Goddesses, whores, wives, and slaves: Women in classical antiquity* (pp. 220-221). New York: Schocken Books.

66 Loevinger, J., & Blasi, A. (1976). *Ego development: conceptions and theories.* San Francisco: Jossey-Bass Publishers.

[67] Dodds, E. R. (1951). *The Greeks and the irrational* (p. 13). Berkeley: University of California Press.

[68] Dodds, E. R. (1951) (page 214).

[69] Mark 16:9 (King James Version)

[70] Jung, C.G. (1997). *Visions: notes of the seminar given in 1930-1934 by C.G. Jung.* (p. 566).

[71] Jung, C.G. (1968). *The archetypes and the collective unconscious* (2nd ed.). Collected Works, vol. 9,i, par. 262.

[72] Jung, C.G. (1966). *Two essays on analytical psychology* (2nd ed.). Collected Works, vol. 7, par. 103. R. F. C. Hull (Trans.). NJ: Princeton University Press.

[73] Flannery, K., & Marcus, J. (2012). (chs. 1 & 24).

[74] Knight, C. (2008). Early human kinship was matrilineal. In N. J. Allen, H. Callan, R. Dunbar & W. James (Eds.), *Early Human Kinship*. Oxford: Blackwell, 61-82.

[75] Gimbutas, M. (1982). *The goddesses and gods of old Europe: Myths and cult images*. London: Thames And Hudson.

[76] Gimbutas, M. (1989). *The language of the goddess: unearthing the hidden symbols of Western civilization*. San Francisco: Harper & Row.

[77] Gimbutas, M. (1991). *The civilization of the goddess*. San Francisco: Harper-SanFrancisco.

[78] Gimbutas, M. (1999). *The living goddesses*. M. R. Dexter (Ed.). Berkeley: University of California Press.

[79] Goodison, L., & Morris, C. (Eds.). (1998). *Ancient goddesses: The myths and the evidence*. Madison: University of Wisconsin Press.

[80] Graves, R. (1960). *The Greek myths* (pp. 13-20). (Vol. 1, Rev. ed.). Harmondsworth, Middlesex, England: Penguin Books.

[81] Fustel de Coulanges, N. D. (1979). *The ancient city: a study on the religion, laws, and institutions of Greece and Rome* (p. 151).

[82] Stokstad, M. (1995). *Art history (Vol. 1).* (pp. 38-40). Upper Saddle River, N.J: Prentice Hall.

[83] Leclerc-Madlala, S. On the virgin cleansing myth: Gendered bodies, AIDS and ethnomedicine. *African Journal of Aids Research, Vol. 1*, 87-95.

[84] George, A. R. (2000). *The epic of Gilgamesh: The Babylonian epic poem and other texts in Akkadian and Sumerian*. London: Penguin.

[85] Dever, W. G. (2005). *Did God have a wife? Archaeology and folk religion in ancient Israel*. Grand Rapids, MI.: W.B. Eerdmans Publishing.

[86] Teubal, S. J. (1984). *Sarah the priestess: the first matriarch of Genesis*. Athens, OH: Swallow Press.

[87] Fry, D. P. (Ed.). (2013). *War, peace, and human nature: the convergence of evolutionary and cultural views*. New York: Oxford University Press.

[88] Suzman, J. (2017). *Affluence without abundance: The disappearing world of the Bushmen*. New York: Bloomsbury USA.

[89] Knight, C. (2008). *Early human kinship was matrilineal*.

[90] Anthony, D. (2007). *The horse, the wheel, and language: How Bronze-Age riders from the Eurasian Steppes shaped the modern world*. NJ: Princeton University Press.

[91] Childe, V. G. (1926). *The Aryans; a study of Indo-European origins*. London: Kegan Paul, Trench, Trubner & Co.

[92] Anthony, D. (2007) (p. 10).

[93] Anthony, D. (2007) (p. 214).

[94] Zeng, T. C., Aw, A. J., Feldman, M. W. (2018). Cultural hitchhiking and competition between patrilineal kin groups explain the post-Neolithic Y-chromosome bottleneck. *Nature Communications, 9*, Article 2077.

[95] Fry, D. P., (Ed.). (2013). (pp. 176-177).

[96] Paglia, C. (2006). Erich Neumann: Theorist of the great mother. *Arion, 13(3)*, 1-14. Boston University.

[97] Spretnak, C. Anatomy of a backlash: Concerning the work of Marija Gimbutas. *Journal of Archaeomythology, 7*.

[98] Jung, C.G. (1997). *Visions: notes of the seminar given in 1930-1934 by C.G. Jung*. (p. 210).

[99] Flannery, K., & Marcus, J. (2012).

[100] Mark 14:7; also Matthew 26:11 & John 12:8

[101] Keeley, L. H. (1996). *War before civilization*. Oxford: Oxford University Press.

[102] Patai, R. (1990). *The Hebrew Goddess* (pp. 50-52). 3rd enl. ed. Detroit, MI: Wayne State University Press.

[103] Onians, R. B. (1991). *The origins of European thought about the body, the mind, the soul, the world, time, and fate: New interpretations of Greek, Roman and kindred evidence also of some basic Jewish and Christian beliefs*. (p. 303). Cambridge: Cambridge University Press.

[104] Deuteronomy 13:15 (King James Version)

[105] 1 Samuel 15 (King James Version)

[106] Genesis 27 (King James Version)

[107] Dodds, E.R. (1951). *The Greeks and the irrational* (p. 17). Berkeley: University of California Press.

[108] Deuteronomy 5:17 (King James Version)

[109] Deuteronomy 7:2 (King James Version)

[110] Dover, K.J. (1980). *Greek homosexuality* (p. 50). New York: Vintage Books.

[111] Onians, R.B. (1991). (p. 5).

[112] Nietzsche, F.W. (1976). *The portable Nietzsche* (pp. 32-33). W. Kaufmann (Ed. & Trans.). New York: Penguin Books.

[113] Hamilton, E. (1973). *The Roman way*. New York: Avon Books.

[114] Dover, K.J. (1980).

[115] Harper, K. (2013). *From shame to sin: The Christian transformation of sexual morality in late antiquity.*

[116] Harper, K. (2013). *From shame to sin: The Christian transformation of sexual morality in late antiquity.* (pp. 19-79).

[117] Finley, M.I. (1979). *The world of Odysseus* (2nd ed.). (p.54). New York: Penguin.

[118] Harper, K. (2013). *From shame to sin: The Christian transformation of sexual morality in late antiquity* (pp. 31 – 37).

[119] Nietzsche, F.W. (1967). *The birth of tragedy and the case of Wagner* (p. 39). W. Kaufmann (Trans.). New York: Vintage Books.

[120] Bentwich, N. (1914). *Josephus*. Philadelphia: The Jewish Publication Society of America.

[121] Fustel de Coulanges, N.D. (1979). *The ancient city: A study on the religion, laws, and institutions of Greece and Rome.*

[122] Harding, M.E. (1947). *Psychic energy: Its source and goal.* (p. 23). New York: Pantheon Books.

[123] Brown, P. (1997). *The rise of Western Christendom: Triumph and diversity 200-1000 AD* (pp. 131 – 132). Oxford: Blackwell.

[124] Harper, K. (2013). *From shame to sin: The Christian transformation of sexual morality in late antiquity.*

[125] Job 1:6 (King James Version)

[126] Harper, K. (2013). *From shame to sin: The Christian transformation of sexual morality in late antiquity* (p. 172).

[127] Acts 9 (King James Version)

[128] Brown, P. (1988). *The body and society: Men, women, and sexual renunciation in early Christianity* (p. 237).

[129] Jung, C.G. (1968). *The archetypes and the collective unconscious* (2nd ed.). Collected Works, vol. 9,i, par. 2, note 2.

[130] Jung, C.G. (1966). *Two essays on analytical psychology* (2nd ed.). Collected Works, vol. 7, par. 504-505.

[131] Psalms 6:5 (King James Version)

[132] 1 Samuel 28 (King James Version)

[133] Colish, M. L. (1998). *Medieval foundations of the Western intellectual tradition, 400-1400.* New Haven: Yale University Press.

[134] Campbell, J. (1969). *The flight of the wild gander: explorations in the mythological dimension* (pp. 217-218). New York: Viking Press.

[135] Radding, C. (1978). Evolution of medieval mentalities: A cognitive-structural approach. *The American Historical Review* 83(3): 577-597.

[136] Radding, C. (1985). *A world made by men: Cognition and society, 400-1200*. Chapel Hill: University of North Carolina Press.

[137] Morris, C. (1972). *The discovery of the individual, 1050-1200*. New York: Harper & Row.

[138] Bynum, C. (1982). Did the twelfth century discover the individual? In *Jesus as mother: Studies in the spirituality of the High Middle Ages* (pp. 82-109). Berkeley: University of California Press.

[139] Bynum, C. (2011). *Christian materiality: An essay on religion in late medieval Europe*. New York: Zone Books.

[140] Bynum, C. (2001). *Metamorphosis and identity*. New York: Zone Books.

[141] Campbell, J. (1969). (pp. 209-211).

[142] Jung, C.G. (1971). *Psychological types*. Collected Works vol. 6, par. 808-811. R. F. C. Hull (Trans.). NJ: Princeton University Press.

[143] Durant, W., & Durant, A. (1961). *The story of civilization: The Age of Reason begins, 1558-1648*. (p. 626). New York: Simon and Schuster.

[144] Fustel de Coulanges, N.D. (1979). *The ancient city: a study on the religion, laws, and institutions of Greece and Rome* (p. 219).

[145] Barzun, J. (2000). *From dawn to decadence: 500 years of western cultural life: 1500 to the present* (pp. 239-241).

[146] Kennedy, P.M. (1989). *The rise and fall of the great powers: Economic change and military conflict from 1500 to 2000* (pp. 70-73).

[147] Roberts, J. M. (1983). *The pelican history of the world* (p. 519). Harmondsworth, Middlesex, England: Penguin Books.

[148] LePan, D. (1989). *The cognitive revolution in Western culture*. Basingstoke: Macmillan.

[149] Shakespeare, W. (circa 1599). *Julius Caesar* (act I, scene ii, lines 140-141).

[150] Naipaul, V.S. (1981). *Among the believers: an Islamic journey* (p. 151). New York: Knopf.

[151] Mortimer, I. (2016). *Millennium: From religion to revolution: How civilization has changed over a thousand years* (pp. 23-26). New York: Pegasus Books.

[152] Snowden, F.M. (1983). *Before color prejudice: The ancient view of Blacks* (p. 58-59). Cambridge, MA: Harvard University Press.

[153] Ibid (p. 99-108).

[154] Ibid (p. 69-70).

[155] Lepore, J. (2018). *These truths: A history of the United States* (p. 56-57). New York: W. W. Norton & Company.

[156] Ibid (p. 120).

[157] Weber, M. (1930). *The Protestant ethic and the spirit of capitalism*. T. Parsons (Trans.). New York: Charles Scribner's Sons.

[158] 2 Timothy 2:3 (King James Version)

[159] The Apostles' Creed

[160] Jung, C.G. (1977). *C.G. Jung speaking: interviews and encounters* (p. 89). W. McGuire & R.F.C. Hull (Trans.). NJ: Princeton University Press.

[161] Zaentz, S. (Producer) & Forman, M. (Director). (1984). *Amadeus* [Motion picture]. U.S.: Orion Pictures.

[162] Rivera, J. (Producer) & Docter, P. (Director). (2009). *Up* [Motion picture]. U.S.: Walt Disney Studios.

[163] King, G., Headington, T., Scorsese, M. & Depp, J. (Producers) & Scorsese, M. (Director). (2011). *Hugo* [Motion picture]. U.S.: Paramount Pictures.

[164] Jefferson, T. (1776). *United States Declaration of Independence*.

[165] Nollenberger, N., Rodríguez-Planas, N., & Sevilla, A.. (2016). The math gender gap: The role of culture. *American Economic Review*, 106(5): 257-61.

[166] Shaw, I., & Nicholson, P. (2003). *The dictionary of ancient Egypt* (p. 200). New York: Harry N. Abrams.

[167] Edinger, E.F. (1992). *Transformation of the God-image: An elucidation of Jung's answer to Job*. Toronto: Inner City Books.

[168] Edinger, E.F. (1996). *The new God-image: a study of Jung's key letters concerning the evolution of the Western God-image*. D. Cordic & C. Yates (Eds.). Wilmette, Ill.: Chiron Publications.

[169] Jung, C.G. (1976). *The symbolic life*. Collected Works vol. 18, par. 18. R. F. C. Hull (Trans.). NJ: Princeton University Press.

[170] Fustel de Coulanges, N. D. (1979). *The ancient city: a study on the religion, laws, and institutions of Greece and Rome*.

[171] Jung, C.G. (1971). *Psychological types*. Collected Works vol. 6, par. 757-762.

[172] Jung, C.G. (1971). *Psychological types*. Collected Works vol. 6, par. 789-791.

[173] Jung, C.G. (1975). *The practice of psychotherapy: Essays on the psychology of the transference and other subjects* (2nd ed.) Para. 442. R. F. C. Hull (Trans.). NJ: Princeton University Press.

[174] Jung, C.G. (1997). *Visions: Notes of the seminar given in 1930-1934 by C.G. Jung* (pp. 1367-1368).

[175] Jung, C.G. (1975). *Letters*, vol. 2: 1951-1961 (p. 377). G. Adler (Trans.). NJ: Princeton University Press.

[176] Jung, C.G. (1970). *Mysterium coniunctionis* (2nd ed.). Collected Works, vol. 14, par. 778. R.F.C. Hull (Trans.). NJ: Princeton University Press.

[177] Jung, C.G. (1969). *Psychology and religion: West and East* (2nd ed.). Collected Works vol. 11, par. 758. R. F. C. Hull (Trans.). NJ: Princeton University Press.

[178] Woodroffe, J.G. (1974). *The serpent power*. New York: Dover Publications.

[179] Shakespeare, W. (circa 1599). *As you like it* (Act II, scene vii, lines 139-166).

[180] Jung, C.G. (1970). *Mysterium coniunctionis* (2nd ed.). Collected Works, vol. 14.

181 1 Peter 5:9 (King James Version)

182 Stowe, H.B. (2003). *Uncle Tom's cabin*. New York: Bantam Dell.

183 Howe, J.W. (1862). *The battle hymn of the republic*.

184 Quart, A. (2018). *Squeezed: why our families can't afford America* (ch. 1). New York: Ecco.

185 Darwin, C. (1859). *The origin of species*. London: John Murray.

186 Genesis 1:27 (King James Version)

187 Genesis 2:7 (King James Version)

188 Jones, R.P. (2016). (pp. 21 – 31).

189 Hofstadter, R. (1963). *Anti-intellectualism in American life*. New York: Vintage Books.

190 Rosin, H. (2013). *The end of men: And the rise of women*. New York: Riverhead Books.

191 Smith, P., Fischer, R., Vignoles, V., & Bond, M. (2013). *Understanding social psychology across cultures: Engaging with others in a changing world* (2nd ed.). (p.139). Thousand Oaks, CA: Sage Publications.

192 Spengler, O. (1926). *The decline of the West - Vol. I & II*. C.F. Atkinson (Trans.). New York: A. A. Knopf.

193 Ibid (p. 21).

194 Ibid (p. 16).

195 Campbell, J. (1973). *The hero with a thousand faces* (2nd ed.). NJ: Princeton University Press.

196 Jung, C.G. (1970). Flying saucers: a modern myth of things seen in the skies, in *Civilization in transition* (2nd ed.). Collected Works vol. 10. R.F.C. Hull (Trans.). NJ: Princeton University Press.

197 Acts 9:4 (King James Version)

198 Fuller, J.G. (1966). *The interrupted journey: two lost hours aboard a flying saucer*. New York: The Dial Press

199 Friedman, S., & Marden, K. (2007). *Captured!: The Betty and Barney Hill UFO experience*. Franklin Lakes, NJ: New Page Books.

200 Mack, J.E. (1994). *Abduction: human encounters with aliens*. New York: Charles Scribner's Sons.

201 Blaustein, J. (Producer) & Wise, R. (Director). (1951). *The Day the Earth Stood Still* [Motion picture]. U.S.: 20th Century Fox.

202 Devlin, D. (Producer) & Emmerich, Roland (Director). (1996). *Independence Day* [Motion picture]. U.S.: 20th Century Fox.

203 Wells, H.G. (1978). The War of the Worlds. In *The collector's book of science fiction by H.G. Wells*. A. Russell (Ed.). Secaucus, N.J.: Castle Books.

204 Jung, C.G. (1975). *Aion: researches into the phenomenology of the Self* (2nd ed.). Collected Works vol. 9,ii, par. 257.

205 Kennedy, K. & Spielberg, S. (Producers) & Spielberg, S. (Director). (1982). *E.T. the Extra-Terrestrial* [Motion picture]. U.S.: Universal Pictures

206 Franco, L.J. & Douglas, M. (Producers) & Carpenter, J. (Director). (1984). *Starman* [Motion picture]. U.S.: Columbia Pictures.

207 Pasulka, D.W. (2019). *American cosmic: UFOs, religion, technology*. New York, NY: Oxford University Press.

208 Jung, C.G. (1973). *Memories, dreams, reflections* (Rev. ed.). (p. 335). A. Jaffé (Ed.) & R. & C. Winston (Translators). New York: Vintage Books.

209 Jung, C.G., & Kirsch, J.. (2011). *The Jung-Kirsch letters: The correspondence of C.G. Jung and James Kirsch*. (pp. 217, 218 & 230). A.L. Conrad (Ed.) & U. Egli & A.L. Conrad (Translators). London: Routledge.

210 Jung, C.G. (1970). Flying saucers: a modern myth of things seen in the skies, in *Civilization in transition* (2nd ed.). Collected Works vol. 10, par. 613.

211 Kean, L. (2010). *UFOs: generals, pilots, and government officials go on the record*. New York: Harmony Books.

212 Hastings, R.L. (2017). *UFOs & nukes: extraordinary encounters at nuclear weapons sites* (2nd ed.). (City not given): Robert Hastings.

213 Kurtz, G. (Producer) & Lucas, G. (Director). (1997). *Star wars* [Motion picture]. U.S.: 20th Century Fox.

214 Kennedy, K., Abrams, J.J. & Burk, B. (Producers) & Abrams, J.J. (Director). (2015). *Star wars: The force awakens* [Motion picture]. U.S.: Walt Disney Studios Motion Pictures.

215 Kennedy, K. & Bergman, R. (Producers) & Johnson, R.C. (Director). (2017). *Star wars: The last jedi* [Motion picture]. U.S.: Walt Disney Studios Motion Pictures.

216 Kurtz, G. (Producer) & Kershner, I. (Director). (1980). *The empire strikes back* [Motion picture]. U.S.: 20th Century Fox.

217 Kazanjian, H. (Producer) & Marquand, R. (Director). (1983). *Return of the jedi* [Motion picture]. U.S.: 20th Century Fox.

218 Tolkien, J.R.R. (1975). *The fellowship of the ring: Being the first part of the lord of the rings*. New York: Ballantine Books.

219 Osborne, B. M., Jackson, P., Walsh, F. & Sanders, T. (Producers) & Jackson, P. (Director). (2001). *The lord of the rings: The fellowship of the ring* [Motion picture]. U.S.: New Line Cinema, New Zealand: WingNut Films.

220 Tolkien, J.R.R. (1975). *The two towers: Being the second part of the lord of the rings*. New York: Ballantine Books.

221 Osborne, B.M., Jackson, P. & Walsh, F. (Producers) & Jackson, P. (Director). (2002). *The Lord of the rings: The two towers* [Motion picture]. U.S.: New Line Cinema, New Zealand: WingNut Films.

222 Tolkien, J. R. R. (1975). *The return of the king: Being the third part of the lord of the rings*. New York: Ballantine Books.

[223] Osborne, B.M., Jackson, P. & Walsh, F. (Producers) & Jackson, P. (Director). (2003). *The lord of the rings: The return of the king* [Motion picture]. U.S.: New Line Cinema, New Zealand: WingNut Films.

[224] Tolkien, J. R. R. (1975). *The hobbit, or, There and back again*. New York: Ballantine Books.

[225] Cunningham, C., Weiner, Z., Walsh, F. & Jackson, P. (Producers) & Jackson, P. (Director). (2012). *The Hobbit: an unexpected journey* [Motion picture]. U.S.: New Line Cinema, Metro-Goldwyn-Mayer, New Zealand: WingNut Films.

[226] Cunningham, C., Weiner, Z., Walsh, F. & Jackson, P. (Producers) & Jackson, P. (Director). (2013). *The Hobbit: the desolation of Smaug* [Motion picture]. U.S.: New Line Cinema, Metro-Goldwyn-Mayer, New Zealand: WingNut Films.

[227] Cunningham, C., Weiner, Z., Walsh, F. & Jackson, P. (Producers) & Jackson, P. (Director). (2014). *The Hobbit: the battle of the five armies* [Motion picture]. U.S.: New Line Cinema, Metro-Goldwyn-Mayer, New Zealand: WingNut Films.

[228] Cameron, J. & Landau, J. (Producers) & Cameron, J. (Director). (2009). *Avatar* [Motion picture]. U.S.: Lightstorm Entertainment & Dune Entertainment, UK: Ingenious Film Partners.

[229] Jung, C.G. (1975). The stages of life, in *The structure and dynamics of the psyche* (2nd ed.). Collected Works vol. 8, par. 749-795. R. F. C. Hull (Trans.). NJ: Princeton University Press.

[230] John 18:36 (King James Version)

[231] Jung, C.G. (1975). *Aion: researches into the phenomenology of the Self* (2nd ed.). Collected Works vol. 9,ii, par. 76.

[232] Jung, C.G. (1975). *Aion: researches into the phenomenology of the Self* (2nd ed.). Collected Works vol. 9,ii, par. 79.

[233] Jung, C.G. (1969). Answer to Job, in *Psychology and religion: West and East* (2nd ed.). Collected Works vol. 11, par. 533-758.

[234] Jung, C.G. (1988). *Nietzsche's Zarathustra: notes of the seminar given in 1934-1939 by C.G. Jung.* (pp. 702-703). J. L. Jarrett (Ed.). NJ: Princeton University Press.

[235] Rowling, J. K. (1998). *Harry Potter and the sorcerer's stone*. New York: Scholastic Press.

[236] Heyman, D. (Producer) & Columbus, C. (Director). (2001). *Harry Potter and the philosopher's stone* [Motion picture]. U.S.: Warner Brothers Pictures, 1492 Pictures, UK: Heyday Films.

[237] Rowling, J.K. (1999). *Harry Potter and the Chamber of Secrets*. New York: Scholastic Press.

[238] Heyman, D. (Producer) & Columbus, C. (Director). (2002). *Harry Potter and the chamber of secrets* [Motion picture]. U.S.: Warner Brothers Pictures, 1492 Pictures, UK: Heyday Films.

[239] Rowling, J.K. (1999). *Harry Potter and the prisoner of Azkaban*. New York: Scholastic Press.

240 Heyman, D., Columbus, C. & Radcliffe, M. (Producers) & Cuarón, A. (Director). (2004). *Harry Potter and the prisoner of Azkaban* [Motion picture]. U.S.: Warner Brothers Pictures, 1492 Pictures, UK: Heyday Films.

241 Rowling, J.K. (2000). *Harry Potter and the goblet of fire*. Scholastic Press.

242 Heyman, D. (Producer) & Newell, M. (Director). (2005). *Harry Potter and the goblet of fire* [Motion picture]. U.S.: Warner Brothers Pictures, UK: Heyday Films.

243 Rowling, J.K. (2003). *Harry Potter and the order of the phoenix*. New York: Scholastic Press.

244 Heyman, D. & Barron, D. (Producers) & Yates, D. (Director). (2007). *Harry Potter and the order of the phoenix* [Motion picture]. U.S.: Warner Brothers Pictures, UK: Heyday Films.

245 Rowling, J.K. (2005). *Harry Potter and the half-blood prince*. New York: Scholastic Press.

246 Heyman, D. & Barron, D. (Producers) & Yates, D. (Director). (2009). *Harry Potter and the half-blood prince* [Motion picture]. U.S.: Warner Brothers Pictures, UK: Heyday Films.

247 Rowling, J.K. (2007). *Harry Potter and the deathly hallows*. New York: Scholastic Press.

248 Heyman, D., Barron, D. & Rowling, J.K. (Producers) & Yates, D. (Director). (2010). *Harry Potter and the deathly hallows - Part 1* [Motion picture]. U.S.: Warner Brothers Pictures, UK: Heyday Films.

249 Heyman, D., Barron, D. & Rowling, J.K. (Producers) & Yates, D. (Director). (2011). *Harry Potter and the deathly hallows - Part 2* [Motion picture]. Warner Brothers Pictures, UK: Heyday Films.

250 Matthew 2:16 (King James Version)

251 Jung, C.G. (1971). *Psychological types*. Collected Works vol. 6, par. 835-836.

252 Jung, C.G. (1988). *Nietzsche's Zarathustra: notes of the seminar given in 1934-1939 by C.G. Jung*. (p. 1442).

253 Jung, C.G. (1984). *Dream analysis: Notes of the seminar given in 1928-1930 by C.G. Jung*. (p. 584).

254 Ibid (p. 604).

255 Rowling, J.K. (2003) (pp. 204-207).

256 Strauss, W., & Howe, N. (1991). *Generations: The history of America's future 1584 to 2069*. New York: William Morrow & Company.

257 Strauss, W., & Howe, N. (1997). *The fourth turning: an American prophecy*. New York: Broadway Books.

258 Edinger, E.F. (1972). *Ego and archetype: Individuation and the religious function of the psyche* (pp. 37-61). New York: G.P. Putnam's Sons.

259 Jung, C.G. (2019). *History of modern psychology: lectures delivered at the ETH Zurich, Volume I, 1933-1934* (p. 29). E. Falzeder (Ed.) & M. Kyburz, J. Peck, & E. Falzeder (Translators). NJ: Princeton University Press.

260 Tocqueville, A. de, Bradley, P., Reeve, H., & Bowen, F. (1963). *Democracy in America* (pp. 375-378). New York: A. A. Knopf.

261 Piketty, T. (2014). *Capital in the twenty-first century* (pp. 293-297). A. Goldhammer (Trans.). Cambridge, MA: Belknap Press.

262 Stiglitz, J.E. (2012). *The price of inequality: how today's divided society endangers our future*. New York: W.W. Norton & Co.

263 Jung, C.G. (1968). *Psychology and alchemy* (2nd ed.). Collected Works vol. 12. par. 563. R.F.C. Hull (Trans.). NJ: Princeton University Press.

264 Taibbi, M. (2014). *The divide: American injustice in the age of the wealth gap*. New York: Spiegel & Grau.

265 Piketty, T. (2014). *Capital in the twenty-first century*.

266 Del Toro, G., Navarro, B., Cuaron, A., Torresblanco, F., & Augustin, A. (Producers) & Del Toro, G. (Director). (2006). *Pan's labyrinth* [Motion picture]. U.S.: Picturehouse.

267 Ortega y Gasset, J. (1957). *The revolt of the masses* (25th anniversary ed.). New York: W. W. Norton & Co.

268 Freehling, W. W. (1994). *Slavery, the Civil War, and the reintegration of American history*. New York: Oxford University Press.

269 Jung, C.G. (1973). *Memories, dreams, reflections* (Rev. ed.). (p. 171).

270 Jung, C.G. (1969). *Psychology and religion: West and East* (2nd ed.). Collected Works vol. 11, par. 292.

271 Jung, C.G. (2009). *The red book: liber novus*. S. Shamdasani (Ed.). New York: W.W. Norton.

272 Jung, C.G. (1988). *Nietzsche's Zarathustra: Notes of the seminar given in 1934-1939 by C.G. Jung*. (p. 707).

273 Kennedy, B. (Producer) & Miller, G. (Director). (1979) *Mad Max* [Motion picture]. Australia: Kennedy Miller Productions.

274 Jung, C.G. (1997). *Visions: Notes of the seminar given in 1930-1934 by C.G. Jung*. (p. 1360-1361).

275 Jung, C.G. (1975). *Aion: Researches into the phenomenology of the Self* (2nd ed.). Collected Works vol. 9, ii, par. 127-149.

276 Jung, C.G. (1975). *Letters*, vol. 2: 1951-1961. (pp. 225-6, 229-30).

277 Greene, L. (2018). *Jung's studies in astrology: Prophecy, magic, and the qualities of time* (ch. 6). Abingdon, Oxfordshire, UK: Routledge.

278 Zeller, M. (1975). *The dream - the vision of the night*. (p. 2). A. Jaffé (Ed.). Los Angeles: The Analytical Psychology Club of Los Angeles.

279 Diamond, J. (2005). *Guns, germs, and steel: the fates of human societies*. New York: W. W. Norton and Co.

[280] Jung, C.G. (1969). *Psychology and religion: West and East* (2nd ed.). Collected Works vol. 11, par. 149.

[281] Jung, C.G. (1984). *Dream Analysis: Notes of the seminar given in 1928-1930 by C.G. Jung*. (p. 23).

[282] Northup, S. (1968). *Twelve years a slave*. Baton Rouge: Louisiana State University Press.

[283] Mitchell, M. (1964). *Gone with the wind*. New York: Scribner.

[284] Terkel, S. (1984). *The good war: An oral history of World War Two* (p. 190). New York: Pantheon Books.

[285] Jung, C.G. (1973). *Memories, dreams, reflections* (Rev. ed.). (pp. 179-181).

[286] Jung, C.G. (1989). (pp. 48, 56, 57, 61). *Analytical psychology: Notes of the seminar given in 1925*. W. McGuire (Ed.). NJ: Princeton University Press.

[287] Jung, C.G. (1975). *The structure and dynamics of the psyche* (2nd ed.). Collected Works vol. 8, par. 555.

[288] Jung, C.G. (1976). *The psychogenesis of mental disease*. Collected Works vol. 3, par. 524 – 525. R. F. C. Hull (Trans.). NJ: Princeton University Press.

[289] Spengler, O. (1926). *The Decline of the West*.

[290] Barzun, J. (2000). *From dawn to decadence: 500 years of western cultural life: 1500 to the present*.